Visual Basic .NET
Class Design Handbook

Andy Olsen
Damon Allison
James Speer of Charteris plc

Wrox Press Ltd. ®

Visual Basic .NET Class Design Handbook

First published May 2002

Published by Wrox Press Ltd,
Arden House, 1102 Warwick Road, Acocks Green,
Birmingham, B27 6BH
United Kingdom
Printed in the United States
ISBN 1-86100-708-6

Trademark Acknowledgments

Wrox has endeavored to provide trademark information about all the companies and products mentioned in this book by the appropriate use of capitals. However, Wrox cannot guarantee the accuracy of this information.

Credits

Authors
Andy Olsen
Damon Allison
James Speer
    of Charteris plc

Additional Material
Steven Sartain

Technical Reviewers
Richard Bonneau .
Damien Foggon
Mark Horner
Anthony Naylor
Phil Powers-DeGeorge
David Schultz
Erick Sgarbi
Imar Spaanjaars

Technical Editors
Benjamin Hickman
Andrew Polshaw

Commissioning Editor
James Hart

Managing Editor
Jan Kolasinski

Project Manager
Beckie Stones

Production & Layout
Sarah Hall
Natalie O'Donnell

Index
Adrian Axinte
Andrew Criddle

Proof Reader
Chris Smith

Cover
Chris Morris

About the Authors

Andy Olsen

Andy is a freelance consultant engaged in training, consultancy, and development work in Microsoft .NET and related technologies. Andy studied Physics at Southampton University in England, and began his professional life as a C developer. As the 1990s came and went, Andy migrated into C++, Visual Basic, Java, and OO Analysis and Design using UML. Andy has been using Microsoft development tools and technologies since 1987, and has fond memories and many tall stories to tell of times gone by.

Andy now lives by the sea in Swansea, with his wife Jayne, and their children Emily and Thomas. Andy is a keen football and rugby supporter, and enjoys running and skiing (badly). You can reach Andy at andyo@olsensoft.com.

Damon Allison

Damon is an IT consultant in Minneapolis, MN focusing on implementing Microsoft technologies. Arguably, Damon has a life outside of programming. He enjoys playing golf and has high hopes someday he'll be good at it.

Dad, I miss you, pal.

James Speer of Charteris plc

James Speer has worked in software development since 1987. Beginning his career with BCPL and C++, James has more recently specialized in distributed middle-tier development using Visual Basic, XML, MSMQ, and SQL Server. James is currently employed by Charteris plc (www.charteris.com) as a Senior Developer providing prescriptive guidance, mentoring, and development expertise for Charteris clients.

Thanks to Lucy for the smiles, Kate for the coffee and to the beautiful game of Football for giving me a life outside of work.

Steven Sartain

Steven Sartain is a database applications developer. He has worked on a number of large .NET applications over the past fourteen months concentrating his efforts in controls development. He is currently working on a product called Visual Genie; designed to integrate tightly into the .NET IDE, Visual Genie will remove the coding burden of developing n-tiered applications. When not spending long hours lonely with his computer, he's spending time with his kids, or enjoying racing around country roads in his car.

I would like to thank my two daughters Nikita and Jade for understanding their fatherless periods whilst working on the text; my wife, Donna, for throwing food in at me to keep me alive; and finally my friend Paul Nichols, for putting up with me.

VB.NET

Class Design

Handbook

Table of Contents

Table of Contents

VB.NET

Class Design

Handbook

Introduction

Introduction

Ask anybody who's heard a bit about Visual Basic .NET what the biggest change over Visual Basic 6 is, and chances are they'll say 'object orientation'. But what does this mean? Visual Basic has been, to some extent, object-oriented since VB5, so what's so groundbreaking about the .NET incarnation? Well, most people emphasize inheritance, stressing that now you can take advantage of the code reuse and polymorphism of class hierarchies. That is indeed one of the most visible ways that object orientation can be used in our code, but there's a crucial, fundamental shift that VB.NET programmers have to get used to, which is not so widely emphasized: in VB.NET, all the code we ever write ends up belonging to a class.

So, every time you sit down and fire up Visual Studio .NET, or notepad, and begin to write VB.NET code, what you are actually doing is designing a class. When you code a Sub you're writing a method; when you declared an Event you're creating fields, methods, and other classes. Understanding this, learning what we can put into a class, and what it all really means to the .NET runtime, is fundamental to being able to take full advantage of Visual Basic .NET. Explaining how to use the language to get the most out of the .NET platform is the goal of this series; explaining how to use it to get the most out of .NET's type system is the goal of this book.

Who Is This Book For?

This book is for VB.NET developers who want to explore the full capabilities of the .NET platform. While it is possible to program VB.NET by just dragging and dropping in Visual Studio, then double-clicking a component and adding code to event handlers, this book is for developers who are interested in coding outside these constraints. If you want to define your own data types, build your own class hierarchies, and build classes with robust interfaces, then you need a deep understanding of the mechanisms VB.NET provides for defining classes. That is the subject of this book.

This book assumes you're already coding with VB.NET, you're already familiar with the basic syntax, and you're regularly writing code that works. You should be familiar with your chosen development tools and know how to compile and run VB.NET code.

You should be aware of .NET's basic object-orientation mechanisms – for example, that objects are instances of classes, how objects are instantiated, and how methods and properties on an object are accessed. We'll recap on the meaning and syntax of most keywords as we discuss them, however.

What Does This Book Cover?

Every time we write code in VB.NET, we're coding a class – it's unavoidable. This book addresses the decisions we make as programmers in this environment, by placing them in the context of what they really are: decisions about class design. So, when we write a Sub and choose whether to make it Shared, whether it is to be Public or Private, what parameters it should take, and so on, this book helps us look at those decisions in the context of how they impact on the design of a class.

This book takes a step back from the code we write every day and asks, "What is it really doing?" It asks you not to consider each VB.NET keyword just in terms of its effect, but to consider how it accomplishes that effect. In the course of this book, we'll see how all our code is compiled into .NET types; how we define type members; how type members are inherited; how types are aggregated into assemblies; how we can control the creation of instances of types; and many more aspects of effective class coding.

What Doesn't It Cover?

This isn't a book about object-oriented analysis and design, UML modeling, or design patterns. It doesn't address the question of how to take a business problem, and decide which classes you should code to solve it. Instead, it focuses on the questions of implementation: how you can code a class that provides a particular kind of behavior.

It also isn't a fundamental introduction to object-orientation, although any VB programmer should already be familiar with the idea of having an instance of an object, and calling methods on it and accessing properties, even if not with the process of defining your own types. If you're comfortable using objects, then this book will not assume more than you know.

What Will You Learn?

The book takes a top-down look at what exactly makes up a class in .NET. We begin by describing what a type is, and how classes relate to the .NET type framework. Then we examine what makes up types: type members. We devote the majority of the book to looking at the different mechanisms VB.NET provides for defining type members (methods, constructors, properties, and events), and finally examine how types go together to make up assemblies.

Chapter by chapter, here's what to expect:

❑   *Chapter 1 – Defining Types*

   This chapter explains what exactly a type is, what role types play in .NET, and what kinds of types exist. We also examine the different types we can declare in VB.NET and how they map to .NET types.

❏ *Chapter 2 – Type Members*

In the second chapter, we examine type members: what they are, how we can define them, and how we can modify them using VB.NET keywords. We also examine the type members inherited by every type from the .NET root class, `System.Object`.

❏ *Chapter 3 – Methods*

Methods are the workhorse of .NET applications; they contain all our program logic. This chapter examines the behavior common to all methods, and how simple methods are defined in VB.NET.

❏ *Chapter 4 – Constructors and the Object Lifecycle*

Constructors are special methods that are called to initialize new instances of a type. In this chapter, we see how these special methods are coded, and how we can use them to control what code can create instances of a type.

❏ *Chapter 5 – Properties*

Properties (both scalar and indexed) are a mechanism allowing us to create specialized methods for accessing data belonging to our type. This chapter examines how properties are implemented, how indexed properties work, and the role of default properties in VB.NET.

❏ *Chapter 6 – Events and Delegates*

The most complex type member in VB.NET is the `Event`. This chapter explains how delegates work, and then how .NET provides its event infrastructure through delegate fields and specialized methods.

❏ *Chapter 7 – Inheritance and Polymorphism*

A type is more than the sum of its members; it also has all the members it inherits from its superclass as well. This chapter explains how .NET type inheritance works, when members are and aren't inherited, and how we can control and exploit it using VB.NET.

❏ *Chapter 8 – Code Organization and Metadata*

When we code a class in VB.NET, we have to make some decisions about where exactly to put it, both logically within a namespace structure, and physically, within a source file, and ultimately, within a .NET assembly. This chapter discusses these issues. We can also add data to our class that may be of use to other programmers who make use of it, using .NET metadata.

What Do You Need?

To make use of this book, you need to be able to compile and execute code written in Visual Basic .NET. This means you will require either:

❏ The .NET Framework SDK obtainable from Microsoft's MSDN site (http://msdn.microsoft.com), in the Software Development Kits category. The download page at time of publication could be reached via the following URL:

http://msdn.microsoft.com/downloads/sample.asp?
url=/msdn-files/027/000/976/msdncompositedoc.xml

❑   A version of Visual Studio .NET that incorporates Visual Basic .NET. The 2002 edition of the Visual Basic .NET IDE is included with the following Microsoft products:

- Microsoft Visual Basic .NET Standard

- Microsoft Visual Studio .NET Enterprise Architect

- Microsoft Visual Studio .NET Enterprise Developer

- Microsoft Visual Studio .NET Professional

The product homepage is at http://msdn.microsoft.com/vstudio/.

There are several .NET implementations for other platforms underway, but at the time of publication, none supported VB.NET compilation.

VB.NET

Class Design

Handbook

1

1

Defining Types

Visual Basic .NET is usually described as an object-oriented programming language. This encourages us to think about our programming in terms of objects. During object-oriented analysis and design, then, we identify the most important objects in our system, and consider how they relate to each other. But during object-oriented programming, we don't write 'objects'; we define classes to represent the behavior and attributes of objects. In fact, in Visual Basic .NET, classes are but one of a whole range of mechanisms we can use to define the behavior of the objects that will exist in our program at run time. When we code in Visual Basic .NET, what we write are in fact *types*. Types represent a combination of behavior and data storage requirements. When our program runs, it creates instances of types (which allocates the data storage required), and makes the behavior of the types available to us.

Choosing what types we need, and what behavior and data storage to give them, is what programming in .NET is all about.

This book aims to help Visual Basic .NET developers gain a deeper and more confident understanding of how they should break down programming problems into separate units of behavior – classes, modules, subroutines, functions, structures, delegates, and so on. In coding a Visual Basic .NET application, we need to decide which types to code, what kind of types they should be, what members they should have, and which code belongs where. This book will give you an awareness of the consequences of those decisions, decisions you make every time you sit down to code part of a Visual Basic .NET application.

We'll begin this book by looking at exactly what a type is. In this chapter, we'll examine .NET's type system, and the kinds of type available to us as developers.

Types

In programming, we use the term *type* to describe a particular kind of value. For example, Visual Basic 6 programmers will be familiar with types such as `Integer`, `Date`, and `String`. For each type, the compiler knows the following information:

- How much memory to allocate when we create a value of this type
- What operations we are allowed to perform using the value

The concept of types is fundamental in "strongly typed" programming languages, which includes all .NET languages. In a strongly typed language, the type of value stored in each variable is known at compile time, so the compiler can predict how we intend to use each of our variables, and can therefore tell us if we get it wrong.

A type is a contract. A variable of a particular type guarantees, contractually, that it will contain all the data you would expect a value of the given type to have, and that we can process it in all the ways we would expect to process a value of that type.

In thinking about types, it's worth remembering that, to a computer, all data is just strings of ones and zeroes. When we have a variable in our program, ultimately that variable is simply holding a binary number of some kind. So, when we ask the computer to display that variable to the screen, perform a calculation on it, or retrieve one if the variable's properties, the computer needs to know what type the variable contains in order to know how to interpret its value, and respond to our request. For example, an integer can be stored in four bytes of binary data. Similarly, a single-precision floating point number is stored in four bytes. Take the following four bytes:

```
00110110 11011011 10001010 01110100
```

If the value were interpreted as an integer, it would represent the number 920357492. Interpreted as a single-precision floating-point value, it has the approximate value of 6.5428267E-6. So, if a variable contains this binary number, and we ask .NET to add one to it, the result is going to depend not only on what value is in the variable, but on the variable's type as well.

A type gives semantic meaning to a string of ones and zeroes in memory. It also associates particular behavior with the data – so that, for example, we can compare values and see if one is greater than another, retrieve a string representing the value, or modify the value in a particular way.

Realizing that all of the logic that makes up our program is encapsulated in the behavior of types, and that all of the state of our program at any given time is represented by instances of these types, is a fundamental step in learning how to take full advantage of .NET.

The .NET Type System

The .NET Framework defines the common language specification (CLS) to facilitate seamless language interoperability. We could therefore choose any .NET Framework language we like to implement our object-oriented design. We're Visual Basic .NET developers, obviously, but it is important to understand the significance of .NET's language independence.

The CLS makes it extremely easy to use several different programming languages in the same application. It defines a set of language constructs that all CLS-compliant languages are required to support. When we compile source code written in a CLS-compliant language, it is compiled into a standard .NET Framework byte code format called Microsoft Intermediate Language (MSIL). This means we can quite happily mix-and-match Visual Basic .NET, Visual C#, Managed Extensions for C++, Visual J#, or JScript .NET within the same application. There are also a host of CLS-compliant languages from third-party vendors, such as COBOL (Fujitsu), Perl and Python (ActiveState), Smalltalk (Quasar Knowledge Systems), and many more besides. Microsoft considers the choice of language a 'lifestyle choice', like whether you prefer coffee or a nice cup of tea.

The fundamental system that enables all of these languages to interoperate smoothly is the **Common Type System**. This system specifies how to declare new types, how to create instances of these types, and how the common language runtime manages the lifetimes of these instances. The common type system is the essential backbone of the .NET Framework, because it enables language interoperability across .NET Framework languages.

Figure 1 shows how the common type system is organized:

Figure 1

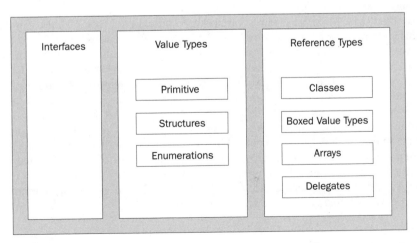

As this diagram shows, the common type system makes a clear distinction between *value types* and *reference types*. It also allows us to define pure interfaces; an interface is a simple definition of a contract, which is then implemented by another type (or types) – it separates out the definition of a contract from the implementation of that contract. All of the other types combine these two things.

Value Types and Reference Types

Value types represent entities that are essentially numerical in nature, such as the date and time, colors, screen coordinates, and so on. Such entities can be represented by a simple binary number of a fixed length – the only complication is in interpreting the meaning of the number. For example, an eight byte long integer can be used to represent a very large range of dates and times; the number can simply be interpreted as an offset of a number of time intervals from a fixed point in time. .NET has a 64 bit DateTime type that represents the number of ticks (units of 100 nanoseconds, or tenths of microseconds) since 00:00:00 on the first of January, 1 C.E. (Common Era, another name for A.D.) according to the Gregorian Calendar. So, a DateTime value type can easily be stored as an eight-byte number. The type then just needs to provide functionality allowing us to extract the year, the month, the day, the hour, minute, second, and so on, from the simple binary value, in a form that we can make use of.

Since a value type like this actually consists of very little data, it is easy for us to pass DateTime information around in our program. If we create a variable a to hold a DateTime, it will need eight bytes of storage, exactly. If we create another variable b to hold a DateTime, it too can take eight bytes of storage. If we now write b = a, the eight bytes of data in a can be quickly copied and placed into b as well. Value types, with their fixed data size, can be quickly copied, and stored right in the variable's allocated memory, making them fast to process.

The same is not true of a more complex type, such as an array. An array is not of a limited, fixed size. When we create a variable c to hold an array of integers, it is not clear how many bytes of storage it will need – it's going to depend on the size of the array we put into it. But, when we create a variable, .NET needs to know how much space to allocate for it. So, .NET resolves this issue using a fixed-size piece of data called a *reference*. The reference value is always the same number of bytes, and refers to a location in the part of the system memory called the managed heap. If we create an array of eight integers (which will require 32 bytes of space), it is created by allocating 32 bytes of the managed heap. When we place that array into the variable c, the location of the array on the managed heap (a reference to the array) is placed into the variable itself. If we then create another variable d to hold an array of integers, and then write d = c, the value of that reference is copied into d so that d points to exactly the same array of integers that c did. An array, because its size is variable, cannot be a value type. Arrays, like classes, are reference types.

We say, then, that value types exhibit ***copy-by-value*** semantics; when we copy one value-type object to another, the compiler performs a byte-by-byte copy of our object. Value types are useful when we don't care how many copies of an object we create; all we care about is its value. When we pass a value-type object into a method, the compiler creates a local copy of the object. When the method returns, the memory that the value-type object was using is automatically reclaimed. This means there are some important limitations to the kinds of uses we can put value types to.

Reference types represent entities that have a unique identity – they exist in one place on the managed heap, and are referenced from variables. For example, imagine we define a `BankAccount` class, and create an object of this class in our application. The .NET Framework common language runtime allocates memory for the object and returns us a reference to this new object.

When we copy a `BankAccount` object into another variable, the variable refers to the same `BankAccount` object. We still only have a single `BankAccount` object, but there are now two variables referring to it. We say that reference types exhibit ***copy-by-reference*** semantics. Likewise, when we pass a `BankAccount` object into a method, the method receives a copy of the reference to our object, not a copy of its value.

The common language runtime keeps track of the memory allocated to all objects on the managed heap. These objects are often known as ***managed objects***. When a managed object is no longer referenced in our application, the object becomes available for automatic garbage-collection. The garbage-collection process runs periodically, reclaiming the resources used by unreferenced managed objects. We'll look at this process in more detail in Chapter 4.

You'll often see, in VB.NET literature, the statement 'value types are stored on the stack'. This is misleading. If we have an array of several value-type entities, these values are stored within the array, but the array is stored on the managed heap. In that sense, the value types are being stored on the heap too. But when we retrieve one of these values from the array, we don't get a reference to the location of the value on the heap, we get a copy of the value from the heap, available for local use. The relevant distinction between value and reference types is that reference types are stored in a unique location on the managed heap; value types are stored wherever they are used.

When a variable of any type is created, it takes on a default, zero value. In the case of value types, this value has the particular meaning assigned to it by the type's semantics; it may represent the number zero, the Boolean state of `False`, the time of 00:00:00 on the 1st of January, 1 C.E., etc. In the case of a reference type, it is a reference that doesn't point to a valid object on the managed heap. Such a reference is called a ***null reference***, and it is represented in VB.NET by the keyword `Nothing`. You can assign the value `Nothing` to a variable containing a reference to an object, and the valid reference will be replaced by a null reference. This is useful, since once an object on the managed heap is no longer accessible through a reference stored anywhere else, it can be disposed of by the .NET garbage collector.

There are three main sorts of .NET value types. We'll discuss each in more depth in the rest of the chapter:

❏ **_Primitive types_**
All programming languages define primitive types such as integers, floating-point numbers, and so on. In .NET, such types are value types. In a moment, we'll discuss the primitive types in Visual Basic .NET, and see how these types map to Microsoft Intermediate Language (MSIL) data types.

❏ **_User-defined value types_**
We can define our own value types to represent small pieces of data in our application. In Visual Basic .NET, structures are user-defined value types – defined using the `Structure` keyword. The .NET framework makes use of custom value types defined in a similar manner, such as `System.DateTime` and `System.Drawing.Point`.

❏ **_Enumerations_**
An enumeration is a special kind of user-defined value type, which represents a type that has a small list of allowable values. An enumeration might allow the values `Yes`, `No`, and `Maybe` for example. Underneath, each of these values is represented by an integer, but defining an enumeration type allows us to assign meaning to a specific set of integer values. In this way, enumerations help us to avoid 'magic numbers' appearing in our code, which will make our code much easier to read and write – it will also make it easier for maintenance programmers to understand what we've written! For example, we can have an enumeration representing error conditions, and use those values to report why an operation failed, rather than relying on error codes with obscure meanings.

Enumerations also help us group related sets of constants into a single place; this helps us understand what the constants mean, and prevents name clashes between constants defined in different enumerations. For example, we might have a `HairColor` enumeration that allows `Blonde`, `Red`, `Brown`, and `Black`, and an `EyeColor` enumeration that can be `Blue`, `Green`, or `Brown`. This allows us to ensure that we can't accidentally give someone blue hair and red eyes, while still allowing us to use brown for either.

These are the reference types that exist in the common type system. We'll elaborate on these later in the chapter:

❏ **_Class types_**
Most of the types we define in a typical application are class types. Classes specify the data and methods for the important entities in our application.

❏ **_Delegates_**
Delegates represent pointers to methods in our application. We can use delegates to specify callback methods, and to register handler methods for graphical user interface (GUI) events such as button clicks.

❑ **Arrays**

Arrays are allocated on the managed heap and accessed by reference. Arrays can be single dimensional, or multi-dimensional. You can also have arrays of arrays, which permit jagged array structures.

❑ **Boxed value types**

Under certain circumstances, it may become necessary to treat a value type as if it were a reference type. We might want to use such a value in a place where only a reference is valid. .NET can take value types and box them, placing a copy of the value on the managed heap, and returning a reference to this 'boxed' value.

Let's begin our journey through the common type system by looking at primitive types in Visual Basic .NET.

Primitive Types

Visual Basic .NET defines ten primitive types, to represent integral numbers, floating-point numbers, Boolean values, dates and times, and characters. These primitive types are defined in such a way as to be interoperable with any other CLS-compliant programming language. Consequently, each of these primitive types is actually just a synonym for a standard `Structure` type in the .NET Framework's `System` namespace. In behavioral terms, there is no effective difference between a value type we define ourselves, and one of these special primitive types. However, these types do benefit from some special support in the VB.NET language:

❑ **Literal syntax**: primitive values can be created using a literal syntax. For example, when we write `3.142` we are using a literal to specify a floating-point value.

❑ **Operator support**: primitive types can be combined using special operators. So, we can use an addition operator (+) to add to numerical values, or the `And` or `Or` operators to combine booleans. In some other .NET languages, it is possible to define types that can be used with operators, but in Visual Basic .NET we can't do this, and operators can only be used on primitive types.

The following table shows the mapping between Visual Basic .NET primitive types and the equivalent structures in the `System` namespace. The table also shows how the Visual Basic .NET compiler translates these types into Microsoft Intermediate Language (MSIL) data types during compilation. We'll discuss MSIL data types shortly:

13

Primitive Type	Equivalent .NET Structure	Equivalent MSIL Data Type	Description
Boolean	System.Boolean	bool	True/False value
Byte	System.Byte	int8	8-bit integer
Char	System.Char	char	Unicode 16-bit character
Date	System.DateTime	System.DateTime	64-bit representation of a date, time, or both
Decimal	System.Decimal	System.Decimal	128-bit decimal value
Double	System.Double	float64	IEEE 64-bit float
Integer	System.Int32	int32	32-bit integer
Long	System.Int64	int64	64-bit integer
Short	System.Int16	int16	16-bit integer
Single	System.Single	float32	IEEE 32-bit float

The following example shows a simple console application to illustrate the use of primitive types in Visual Basic .NET:

```
' primitive_types.vb
Imports System               ' For Console class
Imports Microsoft.VisualBasic ' For vbCrLf
```

We import the System namespace, which contains the Console class. We also import the Microsoft.VisualBasic namespace, which contains a definition for the vbCrLf constant.

```
Module MyModule

  Sub Main()

    ' Use a primitive Visual Basic .NET type
    Dim i As Integer = 100

    ' Use the equivalent .NET Framework type
    Dim j As Int32 = i
```

We can use primitive Visual Basic .NET data types (such as Integer) interchangeably with the equivalent .NET Framework types (such as System.Int32). For the sake of simplicity and familiarity, you should choose and stick to one set of declarations in your code.

Microsoft is keenly advocating mixed-language programming using any combination of .NET Framework languages. If you are developing a multi-language solution, you might prefer to use the .NET Framework structure types explicitly, to emphasize the commonality across these languages. For example, Short *in Visual Basic .NET is the same as* short *in Visual C# and Managed Extensions for C++; the equivalent .NET Framework type is* System.Int16 *in all languages.*

```
Console.WriteLine("Integer: {0}", GetType(Integer).FullName)
Console.WriteLine("Int32:   {0}", GetType(Int32).FullName)
```

We use the `GetType` operator to obtain information about data types at run time and write this information to the command line.

```
' Ask user for numerator and denominator
Console.Write(vbCrLf & "Enter a double: ")

Dim input As String = Console.ReadLine()
    Dim num As Double = Double.Parse(input)

Console.Write("Enter another double: ")
input = Console.ReadLine()
    Dim denom As Double = Double.Parse(input)

' Calculate quotient and display it
Dim res As Double = num / denom

If (Double.IsNaN(res)) Then
   Console.WriteLine("Not a Number.")
ElseIf (Double.IsPositiveInfinity(res)) Then
   Console.WriteLine("Positive infinity.")
ElseIf (Double.IsNegativeInfinity(res)) Then
        Console.WriteLine("Negative infinity.")
Else
   Console.WriteLine("Result is {0}.", res)
   End If
 End Sub
End Module
```

We use various methods defined in the `Double` class, to read and process `Double` values in our application. The `Parse()` method extracts a `Double` value from a `String`; `IsNaN()` tests for "is not a number"; `IsPositiveInfinity()` tests for positive infinity (for example, dividing 100 by 0); and `IsNegativeInfinity()` tests for negative infinity (for example, dividing -100 by 0).

When the application runs, it displays the types for `Integer` and `Int32` as `System.Int32`; this confirms that the `Integer` type in Visual Basic .NET is just another name for `System.Int32`. The application also asks us to enter two floating-point numbers; if we enter 100 and 0, we see the following output on the console window:

```
C:\Class Design\ch01> primitive_types
Integer: System.Int32
Int32:   System.Int32

Enter a double: 432.33
Enter another double: 4576.33
Result is 0.0944708969851387.
```

Viewing the Output from the Compiler

The .NET Framework SDK includes several useful tools for examining files generated when we build a project. One of the most important tools is the MSIL Disassembler, ildasm.exe. This tool enables us to see how the compiler has translated our Visual Basic .NET source code into MSIL byte code. It also enables us to view detailed metadata for our types, which can help us understand how the common language runtime works. This in turn can help us use Visual Basic .NET more effectively. We'll take a detailed look at metadata in Chapter 8.

Some developers dismiss the MSIL Disassembler as being irrelevant and over-hyped. If you find yourself thinking along these lines, we urge you to reconsider. We'll be using the MSIL Disassembler extensively in this book, to investigate how the Visual Basic .NET compiler has compiled our code.

To run the MSIL Disassembler tool, open a command prompt (if you are using Visual Studio make sure you start a Visual Studio .NET command prompt) then move to the folder that contains the executable file, and run ildasm as follows:

```
> ildasm assembly-filename
```

The name and location of the executable file depend on how we built the application:

❑   If we built the application using Visual Studio .NET, the executable file will have the same name as the project and will be located in the bin sub-folder. Also, Visual Studio .NET adds a namespace, which is the same as the project name.

❑   If we built the application using the command-line Visual Basic .NET compiler, the executable file will have the same name as the source file and will be located in the same folder as the source file.

For example, if we built the primitive_types application using the command-line compiler, the application will appear as follows in the MSIL Disassembler window:

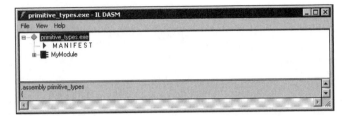

When you expand the **MyModule** icon, the MSIL Disassembler window displays the following information:

Double-click the **Main** icon, to open a read-only view of the MSIL code for the `Main()` method:

```
MyModule::Main : void()
.method public static void  Main() cil managed
{
    .entrypoint
    .custom instance void [mscorlib]System.STAThreadAttribute::.ctor()
    // Code size       189 (0xbd)
    .maxstack  2
    .locals init (float64 V_0,
             int32 V_1,
             string V_2,
             int32 V_3,
             float64 V_4,
             float64 V_5)
    IL_0000:  ldc.i4.s   100
    IL_0002:  stloc.1
    IL_0003:  ldloc.1
    IL_0004:  stloc.3
    IL_0005:  ldstr      "Integer: {0}"
    IL_000a:  ldtoken    [mscorlib]System.Int32
    IL_000f:  call       class [mscorlib]System.Type [mscorlib]System.T
    IL_0014:  callvirt   instance string [mscorlib]System.Type::get_Ful
    IL_0019:  call       void [mscorlib]System.Console::WriteLine(strin
                                                                  objec
    IL_001e:  ldstr      "Int32:  {0}"
```

Note the following points in the MSIL code:

The `Main()` method is marked with the MSIL `managed` keyword. This indicates code that runs in the managed environment provided by the .NET Framework common language runtime. All code we write in Visual Basic .NET will be managed code. A variety of local variables can be found described with MSIL data types such as `float64`, `int32`, and `string`.

Near the end of the MSIL code for Main() (but not visible in the screenshot above), there are instructions to 'box' the result variable. Let's take a look at the IL code:

```
ldstr     "The result is {0}."
ldloc.s   V_5
box       [mscorlib]System.Double
call      void [mscorlib]System.Console::WriteLine(
                              string, object)
```

Each line of IL code consists of a command, followed by any data the command needs to operate on. Data that the program is working with is stored on the stack, which is an efficient (but limited memory) area for storing local variables. Items are loaded onto the stack using IL commands that begin ld for load. Each variable on the stack takes up a fixed amount of memory defined by its type. For reference type objects, the stack contains a reference to the location on the managed heap where the actual object is stored. The managed heap is flexible memory, which can store objects that have variable memory requirements.

The first line loads a string onto the stack (since strings are a reference type, this means it loads a reference to a string onto the stack). The next loads the contents of the variable V_5 (which contains the result of the division operation) onto the stack. When an item is placed onto the stack, it goes on top of any previous stack items. When items are taken off the stack, the top item is removed first. We'll ignore the box command for a moment, and look instead at the call command. This call tells .NET to call a method, called WriteLine, belonging to a class called System.Console, found in the mscorlib.dll assembly, which takes as arguments a string and an object. .NET looks up this method, then takes the two items from the top of the stack and passes them to the method being called. The top item on the stack, though, is our floating point value, the result of the division we performed. This is not an object, it's a value type.

Well, this is where that mysterious call to box comes in. This takes the item on the top of the stack, copies it to the managed heap, and replaces it on the top of the stack with a reference to the boxed value. This allows us to treat the value as an object and pass it in to this method call.

So, when the call to the method comes, the items on the top of the stack are a boxed value, and then a string, and it is these two values that are passed to the Console.WriteLine() method.

Close the MSIL Disassembler windows when you have finished. If you forget to close the MSIL Disassembler windows, the EXE file will remain locked by the MSIL Disassembler. If you try to recompile the application with these windows open, you'll get a compiler error because the EXE file cannot be overwritten.

User-Defined Value Types (Structures)

Applications often require types to encapsulate essentially numeric quantities such as currencies, screen coordinates, and temperatures, not represented by the available primitive types. Using classes in these scenarios would be like using a hammer to crush a nut; the run-time overhead for garbage-collecting these simple objects would be unnecessarily high.

The .NET Framework provides user-definable *value types* as a solution to this problem. In Visual Basic .NET, a value type is written as a Structure. Structure instances are stored wherever they are used – not in their own location on the heap where they would be accessed via reference.

Value types are, then, messy: they leave copies of themselves everywhere. However, they are very easy to clean up. .NET doesn't need to keep track of each copy of the value – if we need the value elsewhere, we'll just send a copy there. So, if a value type is no longer reachable, the memory it was taking up is immediately available for use. As we'll see, the same is not true of reference types.

Because of how value instances are passed around, though, value types should be small. If we define large value types, inefficiencies start to creep in when we pass the value instances between methods in our application, because of the amount of data that has to be copied into and out of the method.

In this section, we'll see how to define and use value types effectively in Visual Basic .NET. Then we'll discuss how to use inheritance with value types. Finally, we'll take a look at boxing and unboxing, which allow value instances to be copied onto the managed heap as required.

Defining and Using Value Types

The rules for defining value types are essentially the same as for defining a class. For example, a value type can have fields, properties, constants, events, methods, constructors, and finalization code. However, there are some important differences:

❑   Structures must have at least one field or event declaration.

❑   Structures always have a default parameter-less constructor. This performs default initialization for variables. Numerical variables are initialized to zero, Boolean flags are initialized to False, and object references are set to Nothing.

❑   We cannot define our own parameter-less constructor, but we can (and should) provide parameterized constructors. Feel free to provide several parameterized constructors if appropriate, so that users of your value type can initialize their objects in a variety of useful ways.

❑ We cannot provide initializers for variables in a structure; we must perform initialization in the constructor (this is different from a `Class`, where we can initialize variables at the point of declaration). However, we are allowed to provide initializers for `Const` variables; that is, we can initialize `Const` variables at the point of definition. When we look at `Const`s in the next chapter, the reason for this will become clear.

❑ Structure objects have a much simpler deallocation mechanism than class objects. Class objects are disposed of by the garbage collector, and the garbage collector calls the object's `Finalize()` method just before the object disappears. Structure objects are deallocated when they go out of scope, rather than being garbage-collected. A `Finalize()` method will not be called because the object has not been deallocated by the garbage collector.

❑ Many examples show structures with `Public` fields. This seems to contradict a basic rule of object-oriented development: "don't declare data public". The tradeoff is one of speed versus encapsulation; `Public` data is (marginally) faster to access because it avoids the overhead of method calls to get at the data, but it clearly breaks the encapsulation of the structure. If in doubt, err on the side of caution and declare your variables as `Private`.

❑ The .NET Framework does not allow us to inherit from a structure. Therefore, the methods defined in a structure cannot be overridden by methods in a subclass. Given this knowledge, the compiler can predict with certainty which methods will be invoked when we use structure objects in our code. This insight enables the compiler to optimize the method invocation for efficiency; for example, the compiler can choose to expand the method body inline rather than executing a traditional method call. The net result is that method calls on structure objects can be less expensive than method calls on class objects.

The following example illustrates these rules:

```vb
'value_types.vb
Structure Money

    ' Private instance variable
    Private centsAmount As Integer

    ' Private class variable
    Private Const currencySymbol As String = "$"

    ' Public constructor
    Public Sub New(ByVal dollars As Integer, _
                   ByVal cents As Integer)
        Me.centsAmount = (dollars * 100) + cents
    End Sub

    ' Another public constructor
    Public Sub New(ByVal amount As Double)
```

```
            Me.centsAmount = CInt(amount * 100)
        End Sub

    End Structure

    Module MyModule

        ' Entry point for the console application
        Sub Main()
            Dim freebie As Money
            Dim salary As Money = New Money(20000, 0)
            Dim carPrice As Money = New Money(34999.95)
        End Sub

    End Module
```

Note the following in this example:

❑   The fields in the structure are declared as `Private`, to maximize encapsulation.

❑   The `currencySymbol` variable is initialized at the point of declaration. This is allowable because `currencySymbol` is a `Const` variable.

❑   There are two constructors in the structure, to initialize structures in two different ways. There is also an implicit parameterless constructor, provided by the compiler.

❑   The `Main()` subroutine in the separate module `MyModule` creates three structure objects, to show how to call the available constructors (including the parameterless constructor).

At the moment, this program doesn't provide any evidence that it's working. We'll add some more functionality to it in a moment, so we can show that it is.

Using Inheritance with Value Types

When we define a structure in Visual Basic .NET, we cannot explicitly specify a base class. All value types implicitly inherit from `System.ValueType`, which is a standard type in the .NET Framework library. `System.ValueType` inherits from `System.Object`, and overrides some of the methods from `System.Object` (`System.ValueType` does not introduce any additional methods).

We can override some of the methods inherited from `System.ValueType` or `System.Object`. One of the most commonly overridden methods is `ToString()`, which returns a string representation of the object. For more information about `System.Object`, see Chapter 2.

Although structures cannot explicitly inherit from an arbitrary class, they can implement interfaces. For example, it is quite common to implement standard .NET Framework interfaces such as IComparable. IComparable allows us to specify how objects should be compared so they can be sorted in a list, and value types will often need to implement it to enable them to interoperate well with other classes in the .NET Framework.

Structures cannot be used as a base class for other classes to inherit; they are not extensible through inheritance. Structures can be very sophisticated types but they are not classes. This language restriction enables the compiler to minimize the amount of administrative code it has to generate to support the structure.

The following example illustrates these inheritance rules:

```vb
' value_type_inheritance.vb

Imports System
Imports Microsoft.VisualBasic


    Structure Money
        Implements IComparable

        ' Private variables
        Private centsAmount As Integer
        Private Const currencySymbol As String = "$"

        ' Public constructors
        Public Sub New(ByVal dollars As Integer, _
                    ByVal cents As Integer)
          Me.centsAmount = (dollars * 100) + cents
        End Sub

        Public Sub New(ByVal amount As Double)
          Me.centsAmount = CInt(amount * 100)
        End Sub

        ' Compare with another Money
        Public Function CompareTo( _
          ByVal other As Object) As Integer _
          Implements IComparable.CompareTo
          Dim m2 As Money = CType(other, Money)
          If Me.centsAmount < m2.centsAmount Then
            Return -1
          ElseIf Me.centsAmount = m2.centsAmount Then
            Return 0
          Else
            Return +1
          End If
        End Function

        ' Return value as a string
        Public Overrides Function ToString() As String
```

```
      Return currencySymbol & _
         CStr(Me.centsAmount / 100)
      End Function

   End Structure
```

The Money structure now implements the IComparable interface. The CompareTo() method, as specified by the IComparable interface, compares the value of this Money instance against another Money instance, and returns an integer to indicate the result of the comparison.

Money overrides the ToString() method, which is defined in the base class System.Object. ToString() returns a string representation of this Money instance. It is always useful to provide a ToString() method in every class or structure.

```
Module MyModule
   ' Entry point for the console application
   Sub Main()

      ' Create an array of 5 items (0..4)
      Dim salaries(4) As Money
      salaries(0) = New Money(9.5)
      salaries(1) = New Money(4.8)
      salaries(2) = New Money(8.7)
      salaries(3) = salaries(2)
      salaries(4) = New Money(6.3)

      ' Display unsorted array
      Console.WriteLine("Unsorted array:")
      Dim salary As Money
      For Each salary In salaries
         Console.WriteLine("{0}", salary)
      Next

      ' Sort the array
      Array.Sort(salaries)

      ' Display sorted array
      Console.WriteLine(vbCrLf & "Sorted array:")
      For Each salary In salaries
         Console.WriteLine("{0}", salary)
      Next

   End Sub

End Module
```

The `Main()` subroutine creates an array of `Money` instances. Element 3 is assigned the value of element 2, which means it contains a copy of its value. Each `Money` instance in the array is displayed by using `Console.WriteLine()`. The `ToString()` method is implicitly called on the `Money` instances, to obtain a string representation of these instances. The `Array.Sort()` method sorts the array. For this to work, the array elements must implement the `IComparable` interface. `Array.Sort()` calls the `CompareTo()` method repeatedly on the array elements, to sort them in the specified order. Finally, the sorted array is displayed on the console.

The application displays the following output on the console:

```
C:\Class Design\Ch01> valuetype_inheritance
Unsorted array:
$9.5
$4.8
$8.7
$8.7
$6.3

Sorted array:
$4.8
$6.3
$8.7
$8.7
$9.5
```

Boxing and Unboxing Value Instances

Value instances are located on the stack. The common language runtime has no knowledge of these instances. However, there are occasions where we want to use a value instance where a reference type is expected. For example, when we insert a value instance into a .NET Framework collection. Consider the following code sample:

```
' Create an ArrayList object
Dim payroll As New System.Collections.ArrayList()

' Add some Money objects
payroll.Add(new Money(30500))
payroll.Add(new Money(54000))
payroll.Add(new Money(27900))
```

`ArrayList` is a standard .NET Framework collection class. Like all the other collection classes, `ArrayList` holds a collection of references to objects. These objects must be reference types, and they must be located on the managed heap.

If we try to add a value-type object (such as a `Money` object) to the `ArrayList`, the common language runtime creates a copy of the `Money` object on the managed heap. This process is known as boxing, and it happens automatically in Visual Basic .NET.

The boxed object holds a copy of the data from the value object; if the boxed object is modified, it won't affect the original value object. Likewise, if the original value object is modified, it won't affect the boxed object.

The following code retrieves an element from the `ArrayList`:

```
Dim myCash As Money = payroll.Item(0)
```

The `Item()` method returns a reference to an object on the managed heap. When we try to assign this to a `Money` instance, the common language runtime extracts the value from the managed object and copies it into our `Money` instance. This process is known as unboxing, and it happens automatically in Visual Basic .NET.

So is it all good news here? Well, yes and no. Visual Basic .NET performs boxing and unboxing implicitly; we don't need to write any special code to make it happen. This is a mixed blessing, because boxing and unboxing imposes an overhead at run time. The best advice we can offer is to be aware of these issues, and limit the amount of boxing and unboxing if possible. If you find yourself doing a great deal of boxing and unboxing, it may more efficient to define your data type as a `Class` rather than as a `Structure`.

Visual C# and Managed Extensions for C++ make you work harder to achieve boxing and unboxing. In Visual C#, boxing occurs implicitly but you must use a cast operation to perform unboxing. In Managed Extensions for C++, you must explicitly box and unbox value instances. The code is a little harder to write but at least you know when boxing and unboxing is taking place, and that can certainly have its advantages.

Enumerations

Enumerations represent integral types that have a limited set of allowed values. To declare an enumeration, we use the `Enum` keyword and specify names to represent the allowable values. We can also specify an underlying integer data type for the enumeration (`Byte`, `Short`, `Integer`, or `Long`).

The following example declares a simple enumeration to represent medals in a competition.

```
' enumerations.vb
Imports System

Module MyModule

   Enum Medal As Short
      Gold
      Silver
      Bronze
   End Enum
```

We can use enumerations in our code as follows:

```
Sub Main()
    Dim myMedal As Medal = Medal.Bronze
    Console.WriteLine("My medal: " & myMedal.ToString)
End Sub

End Module
```

Here, we have created an enumeration instance named `myMedal` and assigned it the value `Medal.Bronze`. Notice we have qualified the enumeration member (`Bronze`) with its enumeration name (`Medal`). This is because the scope of enumeration members is limited to the enumeration declaration body.

Here are two good reasons for using enumerations in your code:

❑ Enumerations use meaningful names to represent the allowable values. These names make it easier for other developers to understand the purpose of these values.

❑ Enumerations are strongly typed. We cannot assign integer values to an enumeration instance; instead, we must use one of the enumeration member names. This helps avoid programming errors that might arise if we used raw integer variables.

In the .NET Framework, enumerations are treated as a special kind of value type. This is appropriate, because enumerations map to integer-based data types internally.

Class Types

In general, in object-oriented terminology, a class defines the methods and data for a specific type of object in the system. Many developers in the object-oriented community use the phrase **abstract data type** when they talk about classes. We need to be careful in .NET, because a class is only one kind of abstract data type – the term can equally be applied to structures. Whatever terminology you use, we can all agree that an object is an instance of a class.

In the .NET Framework, a class is a **reference type**; objects are allocated on the common language runtime's managed heap, and the lifetime of these objects is controlled by the runtime.

In this section, we'll focus on defining classes; during these discussions, remember that classes are reference types in the .NET Framework.

Defining Classes in Visual Basic .NET

We use the `Class` keyword to define a class. A class can contain data and functionality. The following table describes the kinds of data members we can define in a class:

Kind of data member	Description
Variable	A variable is a piece of data that is stored in objects of this class. We can also use the `Shared` keyword, to define data that is shared by all objects of the class.
Property	A property is similar to a variable, except that its value must be retrieved and modified through 'get' and 'set' methods in the class.
Constant	A constant is a read-only value that is shared by all objects of the class.
Event	An event is a message that an object can send to interested listener objects. In the .NET Framework, we use the terminology **event source** to denote an object that can raise events, and **event receiver** to denote an object that can receive events.

The following table describes the kinds of member functions we can define in a class:

Kind of member function	Description
Method	A method is a function or subroutine that provides some aspect of functionality for objects of this class. We can also use the `Shared` keyword to define methods that apply to the class itself, rather than to a particular object.
Constructor	A constructor is an initialization method. Every time we create an object of a particular class, a constructor is called to initialize the state of the object.
Finalization method	A class can have a single finalization method named `Finalize()`. The common language runtime calls this method just before an object is destroyed by the garbage-collection process. This is a good place to perform tidying-up operations before the object disappears from the scene.

The following class definition illustrates these kinds of members. It's unlikely we'd define all these in the same class, but we've listed them all here for illustrative purposes. We'll consider the design heuristics for each kind of member in later chapters.

```
'class_members.vb
Class AClass

    ' Variable (usually private, for encapsulation)
    Private AVariable As Integer

    ' Property (usually public, for ease of use)
    Public Property AProperty() As Integer
        Get
            Return AVariable
        End Get
        Set(ByVal number As Integer)
            AVariable = number
        End Set
    End Property

    ' Constant (class-wide read-only value)
    Public Const AConstant As Integer = 42

    ' Event (to alert event receiver objects)
    Public Event AnEvent()

    ' Method
    Public Sub AMethod()
        ' Method implementation code
    End Sub

    ' Constructor (to initialize new objects)
    Public Sub New()
        ' Constructor implementation code
    End Sub

    ' Finalization method (to tidy-up objects)
    Protected Overrides Sub Finalize()
        ' Finalization code
    End Sub

    ' Nested class definition
    Private Class ANestedClass
        ' Class definition
    End Class

End Class
```

Modules

Visual Basic .NET also allows us to define modules, using the `Module` statement. Modules are similar to classes but have some important differences:

- ❑ They cannot be instantiated

- ❑ They are not inheritable

- ❑ They are implicitly shared

- ❑ Their members are accessible without providing the `Module` name

- ❑ A module with a `Main()` method can be compiled into an EXE without needing to provide any extra information to specify the application's entry point

When developing console application examples it is very convenient to put any classes or other types declared inside a `Module` then invoke whatever we are demonstrating inside the module's `Main()` method. This approach is used extensively throughout this book. We'll discuss modules further in Chapter 2.

Confusingly the word module is used to describe .NET Framework modules – single DLL or EXE Windows PE (Portable Executable) files that form the basis of building blocks of assemblies.

Defining Visibility for Classes

When we define a class (or any type, for that matter), we can specify its visibility. We can make the type private to its declaration context or visible to other code in the same assembly, or visible to code in any assembly.

***Assemblies** are a key concept in the .NET Framework. In the simplest case, an assembly is a single module (. exe file or . dll) file. When we write an application, we can decide whether we want to define all our classes (and other types) in the same assembly, or spread the classes across different assemblies for deployment purposes. For more information about assemblies, including a discussion on how to organize class definitions in assemblies, see Chapter 8.*

Defining the visibility for types is an important consideration in large systems, where the number of types can easily run into the hundreds. The aim is to limit visibility as much as possible, but no more. By hiding types from other parts of the system, the system becomes more decoupled and easier to maintain. We can change a type more easily if there are no dependencies on it elsewhere in the system.

The following example shows how to specify class visibility:

```
'class_visibility.vb
Module MyModule
```

MyClass1 is *implicitly* public to all assemblies, which means it can be accessed in any other code in any assembly:

```
Class MyClass1
    ' Members ...
End Class
```

MyClass2 is *explicitly* public to all assemblies.

```
Public Class MyClass2
    ' Members ...
End Class
```

MyClass3 is visible in this assembly, but cannot be seen outside this assembly.

```
Friend Class MyClass3
    ' Members ...
End Class
```

MyClass4 is private to this declaration scope. Private classes are useful for implementing logic within a class, without exposing this logic to other parts of the application.

```
Private Class MyClass4
    ' Members ...
End Class

Sub Main()
    ' Program code ...
End Sub

End Module
```

We can compile this example and view the MSIL code in the MSIL Disassembler:

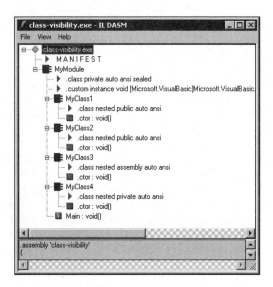

In this screenshot, notice the following:

❏   MyClass1 and MyClass2 are qualified with the MSIL keyword public

❏   MyClass3 is qualified with the MSIL keyword assembly

❏   MyClass4 is qualified with the MSIL keyword private

A further visibility qualifier, Protected, means that a member is only visible in the defining class and classes that inherit from it, see Chapter 7 *Inheritance and Polymorphism* for further details. Protected and Friend can be used together but all other qualifiers are mutually exclusive.

Nested Classes

All the things declared in a class are effectively nested within it. There is nothing to stop you nesting any type within a class, including other classes. For instance, you may want to declare a data structure that is only useful inside a particular class (that cannot be created using a structure) and the simplest way to do this is use a nested class.

All types can be nested and while it is hard to envisage how to usefully nest an interface, it is possible. Note that the visibility of a nested type is limited by its containing type.

Creating and Disposing of Class Objects

We can write constructors in our class, to initialize objects when they are created. If we don't define any constructors in our class, the compiler will generate a no-argument constructor on our behalf. This will allow the client code to create objects without specifying any parameters to the constructor.

> *The CLS also enables us to write shared constructors, to initialize the*
> *shared (class-wide) variables in our class. We'll discuss shared*
> *constructors in Chapter 4.*

The common language runtime tracks objects on the managed heap, and deallocates them when they are no longer required in our application. The garbage-collection mechanism prevents memory leaks, and makes it easier for us to manage complex object relationships in our applications.

We can write a `Finalize()` method, to tidy up the object just before it is deallocated. The `Finalize()` method is similar to a class terminate method in Visual Basic 6.0, or a destructor in C++. However, finalizers can cause a significant run-time overhead because of the way the garbage-collection process executes finalization code. The garbage-collection process has to maintain a list of all defunct objects that require finalization, and ensure these objects are finalized at the appropriate time. Given the non-deterministic nature of object deallocation, we can never be sure when the finalization code will run.

For these reasons, the .NET Framework provides an alternative approach to object disposal. The class library contains an interface named `IDisposable`, which has a single method named `Dispose`. We can implement the `IDisposable` interface in our class, and write a `Dispose()` method to tidy up our object. Consumers of our class can call the `Dispose()` method when they decide our object's time is up. The `Dispose()` method should call `GC.SuppressFinalize()`; this is a standard .NET Framework method, to suppress finalization on objects that have already been disposed.

It would be great if we could guarantee consumers only call `Dispose()` once per object. Unfortunately, we can make no such assumptions. We need to handle the possibility that `Dispose()` might be called more than once, and ensure that `Dispose()` doesn't do anything on subsequent calls. We also need to make sure our object doesn't do anything if any of its methods are called after the object has been disposed.

There is one further potential fly in the ointment. If the consumer doesn't call `Dispose()` at all, the object's disposal code will never be executed. Instead, the object will simply be garbage-collected when it is no longer in use. Why does it matter whether the object is disposed or garbage-collected? The answer is simple, timing:

❑　Object disposal is deterministic; it happens as soon as the client code calls the `Dispose()` method.

❑　Garbage collection is non-deterministic; it happens whenever the garbage-collection process happens to run next. This may be in 2 seconds or 2 hours.

The solution is to write a `Finalize()` method that calls `Dispose`; this way, we can guarantee the object's disposal code will be executed once (and only once) during the object's lifetime.

The following example shows how to implement this mechanism for a simple class. You can reuse this model in any class that requires explicit disposal.

```vb
' object_lifetime.vb

Imports System
Imports Microsoft.VisualBasic

Module MyModule

  Class MyClass1
    Implements IDisposable

    ' Some data, and a flag to indicate if disposed
    Private name As String
    Private disposed As Boolean

    ' Constructor
    Public Sub New(ByVal n As String)
      name = n
      disposed = False
      Console.WriteLine("Constructor for {0}", name)
    End Sub

    Public Sub CheckDisposal()
      If Not disposed
         Console.WriteLine("{0} still in use", name)
      End If
    End Sub

    Public Sub Dispose() Implements IDisposable.Dispose
      If Not disposed Then
         ' Tidy up object...
         Console.WriteLine("Dispose for {0}" & vbCrLf, name)
         ' Prevent multiple disposals
         disposed = True
         ' Suppress finalization for this object
         GC.SuppressFinalize(Me)
      End If
    End Sub

    Protected Overrides Sub Finalize()
      Console.WriteLine("Destructor for {0}", name)
      Dispose()
    End Sub
  End Class
End Class
```

This class supports explicit and implicit disposal using the Dispose() method and the overridden Finalize() method respectively. We have also created a CheckDisposal() method to make sure that an object is still in use before we try to dispose of it.

```
Sub Main()

    ' Create an object, then dispose it immediately
    Dim object1 As New MyClass1(1)
    object1. CheckDisposal ()
    object1.Dispose()

    ' Call method on disposed object (does nothing)
    object1.CheckDisposal()

    ' Try to dispose object again (no need really...)
    object1.Dispose()

    ' Create another object, but don't dispose it
    Dim object2 As New MyClass1(2)
    Console.WriteLine("The end is nigh")

End Sub
End Module
```

When we run the application, it displays the following messages on the console. These messages confirm that the objects have been initialized and disposed of correctly in our application; object1 is disposed of manually in our code, and object2 is garbage-collected by the common language runtime:

```
C:\Class Design\Ch01> object_lifetime
Constructor for 1
1 still in use
Dispose for 1

Constructor for 2
The end is nigh
Destructor for 2
Dispose for 2
```

Delegates

Delegates are an important part of the common type system in the .NET Framework. A delegate is like a type-safe pointer to a method in a class. We define a delegate to specify the signature of methods we would like to call through the delegate (the delegate itself has no implementation). We can then create a delegate object and bind it to any method whose signature matches that of the delegate.

Delegates are useful in the following scenarios:

❑   When registering a method as a callback method with another object. When something important happens to that object, it can invoke our callback method. An example of this usage is defining callback methods for events on graphical user interface (GUI) controls such as buttons and text fields.

❑ When choosing one of a series of methods (with the same signature) for use in an algorithm. For example, we might have methods to calculate the sine, cosine, and tangent of an angle. We can use a delegate to specify which of these methods to use in the algorithm.

There are three required steps when defining and using delegates:

❑ Declare the delegate

❑ Create a delegate object, and bind it to a particular method

❑ Invoke the method by using the delegate object

Chapter 6 examines delegates in detail. We'll present a simple example for now, to illustrate the syntax and clarify the concepts. The application allows users to calculate the sine, cosine, or tangent of an angle. Each of these tasks is the same, except that we need to call a different math function in each case to calculate the result. Delegates fit the bill perfectly here.

Declaring Delegates

To declare a delegate, use the Delegate keyword as shown in the following example:

```
'delegates.vb
Imports System

Module MyModule

    Public Class Trigonometry
        Delegate Function TrigOp(ByVal radians As Double) _
        As Double
```

This delegate can be bound to any function that takes a Double argument and returns a Double result. For example, we can bind TrigOp() to any of the following methods defined in the standard System.Math class:

❑ Public Shared Function Sin(ByVal As Double) As Double

❑ Public Shared Function Cos(ByVal As Double) As Double

❑ Public Shared Function Tan(ByVal As Double) As Double

Invoking a Method Using a Delegate Object

Delegates allow us to separate the selection of a method from its invocation.

The following code shows the PerformOp() subroutine, which receives a delegate object as an argument to indicate which mathematical operation to invoke. To invoke the specified function, we call Invoke() on the delegate object:

```
' Perform the operation indicated by "op"
    Private Sub PerformOp(ByVal op As TrigOp)

        ' Get the angle and convert it from degrees into radians
        Console.Write("Enter an Angle (in degrees): ")
        Dim angle As Double = Console.ReadLine
        Dim radians As Double
        radians = (angle / 360) * 2 * Math.PI

        ' Invoke function specified by the "op" delegate
        Dim result As Double
        result = op.Invoke(radians)

        ' Round result to 4 figures, and display it
        result = Math.Round(result, 4)
        Console.Writeline("Result = " & result.ToString())

    End Sub
```

Notice that everything in this subroutine is the same, regardless of which mathematical operation is involved. The choice of mathematical operation is encapsulated in the delegate object.

Binding Delegates to Methods

In the client code, we need to bind the delegate to the appropriate method and provide a way for the user to select which operation they want to perform.

```
Sub Main()
    Console.WriteLine("Enter Operation to Perform")
    Console.Write("Sin, Cos, or Tan: ")
    Dim operation As String = Console.ReadLine

    Select Case operation
        Case "Sin"
```

The compiler converts a delegate declaration into a class. The class has a constructor that takes a method address as a parameter. When we create a delegate object in our code, we must specify the name of the method that we want to bind to this delegate object.

```
            Trig.PerformOp(New Trigonometry.TrigOp(AddressOf Math.Sin))
```

Here, we create a new TrigOp delegate object and bind it to the Math.Sin function (the AddressOf keyword obtains the address of the Math.Sin function). We pass the new delegate object into a subroutine named PerformOp, to perform the required processing using Math.Sin.

The bindings for Cos and Tan are very similar: we bind the delegate objects to the functions Math.Cos and Math.Tan respectively:

```
        Case "Cos"
            Trig.PerformOp(New Trigonometry.TrigOp(AddressOf Math.Cos))
        Case "Tan"
            Trig.PerformOp(New Trigonometry.TrigOp(AddressOf Math.Tan))
        Case Else
            Console.WriteLine("Not a valid operation")
    End Select
  End Sub
End module
```

This is a great example of delegates. It shows how we can use delegates to simplify our code, and significantly reduce duplication. The application should produce results similar to this:

```
C:\Class Design\Ch01> delegate
Enter Operation to Perform
Sin, Cos, or Tan: Sin
Enter an Angle (in degrees): 90
Result = 1
```

Interfaces

Now that we've seen how classes and structures work in Visual Basic .NET, let's turn our attention to interfaces. An interface is similar to a class, except that none of the methods in an interface have any implementation. An interface just specifies a set of related methods that must be implemented by other classes and structures. You cannot instantiate interfaces, because they contain no implementation.

> *An interface can also contain properties, indexers, and events. For more information about these kinds of members, see Chapter 2.*

Interfaces play an extremely important role in object-oriented design. We can define interfaces to represent contractual obligations, without worrying about how these obligations will be satisfied by classes and structures in the application. Interfaces allow us to separate *what* an object can do, from *how* the object will do it.

By convention, all interfaces in the .NET Framework start with the letter I. This makes it easy to distinguish interfaces from classes and structures. For example, the .NET Framework class library has interfaces such as IDisposable, ICloneable, IComparable, and so on.

In this section, we'll see how to define new interfaces in Visual Basic .NET. We'll also see how to use inheritance to build a hierarchy of interfaces. Then we'll discuss how to implement interfaces in a class. Finally, we'll see how to use interfaces to write generic code in our applications.

Declaring Interfaces

Use the `Interface` keyword to declare an interface and then declare the necessary functions and subroutines. Consider the following example:

```
Interface IConnectable

    Function Connect() As Boolean
    Sub Disconnect()

End Interface
```

The `IConnectable` interface indicates the ability to connect to and disconnect from some resource. The interface doesn't specify the type of resource to connect to, or how to acquire or release the connection.

This is an example of programming by contract. We have specified the ability to connect and disconnect, without restricting ourselves to a particular implementation detail. This has several benefits:

❑   It enables us to defer decisions about how to implement this behavior. We can write the implementing classes and structures later in the development process.

❑   It allows us to provide several alternative implementations for the same interface. For example, we might define a class that implements `IConnectable` by connecting over HTTP, and another class that implements `IConnectable` by connecting over DCOM.

❑   It provides a hook for future extensions to our code. We can come back to our application in six months time and define new implementing classes if necessary, without having to change code that relies on them as the interface stays the same.

Defining a Hierarchy of Interfaces

Interfaces can inherit from other interfaces. This allows us to define a hierarchy of responsibilities in our type system. The following example defines an interface named `ITimedConnectable`, which extends `IConnectable` by introducing the concept of connection timeouts:

```
Interface ITimedConnectable
    Inherits IConnectable

    Sub Timeout(ByVal millisecs As Long)

End Interface
```

Note that the interface does not implement any timeout functionality, nor does it store any data about timeouts. This is an essential characteristic of interfaces – interfaces just define a set of method names that can be implemented by other classes. We'll see how to implement interfaces in the next section.

Implementing Interfaces

A class or structure can implement any number of interfaces; this is often referred to as *multiple inheritance of interface*. However, the CLS only allows us to inherit from a single class; this is often referred to as *single inheritance of implementation*. The CLS does not support multiple inheritance of implementation.

The following example defines a class named MessageQueue, which implements the ITimedConnectable interface and the (standard) IDisposable interface:

```
Class MessageQueue
    Implements ITimedConnectable
    Implements IDisposable

    ' Implement Connect method from ITimedConnectable
    Public Function Connect() As Boolean _
        Implements ITimedConnectable.Connect

        ' Implementation code to connect

    End Function

    ' Implement the Disconnect method
    Public Sub Disconnect() _
        Implements ITimedConnectable.Disconnect

        ' Implementation code to disconnect

    End Sub

    ' Implement the Timeout method
    Public Sub Timeout(ByVal millisecs As Long) _
        Implements ITimedConnectable.Timeout

        ' Implementation code to specify a timeout

    End Sub

    ' Implement the Dispose method from IDisposable
    Public Sub Dispose() _
        Implements IDisposable.Dispose

        ' Implementation code to dispose object

    End Sub
```

```
        ' Additional method needed by MessageQueue
        Public Sub SendMessage(ByVal msg As String)

            Console.WriteLine("Sending message: {0}", msg)

        End Sub

    End Class
```

Note the following in this example:

❑ The MessageQueue class has two Implements clauses, to specify the interfaces implemented by this class. The CLS allows us to implement any number of interfaces.

❑ The MessageQueue class implements all the methods specified by its declared interfaces. Each implementation method is qualified with an Implements clause, to indicate which interface method it implements.

❑ The MessageQueue class can contain additional members to support the implementation of a message queue. All that matters from an interface perspective is that MessageQueue implements at least the methods required by its interfaces.

Using Interfaces

Interfaces enable us to write generic code, where we are more interested in what an object can do than knowing its exact type. Consider the following subroutine:

```
Sub MyGenericRoutine(ByVal tc As ITimedConnectable)

    tc.Timeout(5000)
    tc.Connect()
    tc.Disconnect()

End Sub
```

This subroutine can take any object that implements the ITimedConnectable interface. Nothing in this code limits us to a specific type of object. Any extra functionality the object might provide is irrelevant to this subroutine.

If for some reason we need to know what type of object has been passed in, we might be tempted to use the TypeOf operator as follows:

```
Sub MyGenericRoutine(ByVal tc As ITimedConnectable)

    tc.Timeout(5000)
    tc.Connect()
' Test for specific type (not good practice)
    If TypeOf tc Is MessageQueue Then
        Dim mq As MessageQueue = CType(tc, MessageQueue)
        mq.SendMessage("Hello")
    End If
```

```
    tc.Disconnect()

End Sub
```

In this example, we test the argument `tc` to see if it is a `MessageQueue` object. This might seem like a neat trick, but it goes against the grain of object-oriented programming. Testing for explicit types is often a sign of a poor design, or a lack of understanding of how the application should be structured. Furthermore, testing for particular object types in client code makes the application less resilient to change when new classes are added in the future. We'll come back to this issue in Chapter 7, when we discuss how to use inheritance effectively in Visual Basic .NET.

Summary

In this chapter, we've seen how the .NET Framework defines a common type system that spans all .NET programming languages. We've investigated the use of primitive types, classes, structures, enumerations, interfaces, and delegates in Visual Basic .NET applications.

- ❑ Primitive types map onto predefined value types in the .NET Framework class library. For example, if we declare an `Integer` variable in our Visual Basic .NET code, the compiler maps this to `System.Int32`. This in turn translates into the `int32` type in Microsoft intermediate language (MSIL) code.

- ❑ Classes represent reference types. When we create a class object, it is placed on the common language runtime's managed heap. Class objects exhibit copy-by-reference semantics. When a class object is no longer referenced, the object becomes available for garbage collection.

- ❑ Interfaces specify a contractual agreement that we can implement in other classes and structures. Interfaces enable us to decouple the 'what' from the 'how' in our design.

- ❑ Enumerations are integral data types that have a restricted set of allowable values. In the .NET Framework, enumerations are treated as value types.

- ❑ Structures represent value types. When we create a value instance, it is located on the stack. Value instances exhibit copy-by-value semantics. When a value instance goes out of scope, it is popped off the stack. Value instances are not subjected to garbage collection.

- ❑ Delegates represent pointers to methods. We can create a delegate to specify which method we want to invoke, and then invoke the method when we are ready. Delegates form the basis of the event mechanism in the .NET Framework.

Now that we've seen how to define types in Visual Basic .NET, the remaining chapters investigate how to design and implement these types correctly and effectively.

VB.NET

Class Design

Handbook

2

2

Type Members

Type members are the fundamental programming constructs used to build types within the .NET Framework. Type members in VB.NET include constants, fields (also, confusingly, known as variables), properties, subroutines, functions, constructors, and events. In this chapter, we'll see how these type members are mapped into the .NET Framework, and how they are used in each of VB.NET's programmable types – classes, structures, modules, and so on.

All object-oriented programming languages (C++, Java, C#, VB.NET) offer differing levels of support for type members. For example, the Java programming language does not have explicit support for properties, instead get and set methods are defined on the class. Type member support also vastly differs between the numerous languages targeted for the .NET Framework. C#, for example, supports operators in addition to the type members listed above.

This chapter will first describe the terminology of type members (shared and instance members, access modifiers and visibility, and so on), before looking at each kind of member we can code into our VB.NET types. We'll see how the many kinds of members we write in VB.NET actually map to only a few kinds of .NET type members.

We'll also look at the members that every .NET type has by default, by virtue of the fact that all .NET types extend System.Object. System.Object defines type members that the class designer can override to increase predictability and consistency with classes found in the .NET base class library.

About Type Members

There are, fundamentally, two kinds of member that a type can have – ***data members*** (which are places to store state), and ***function members*** (which are pieces of application logic). In looser OO parlance, we would say that objects have state, and behavior. When we describe a type, we are defining a template for objects, and those objects will need a place to store that state, and a description of their behavior. State goes in the data members, while behavior goes in the function members.

In VB.NET, we can code types with the following members:

- ❑ Constants

- ❑ Fields (also called variables)

- ❑ Properties

- ❑ Functions

- ❑ Subroutines

- ❑ Constructors

- ❑ Events

- ❑ Nested types (which can be classes, structures, interfaces, enumerations, or delegates)

Some of these are state, some of them are behavior. Some, such as events, actually combine state and behavior. Nested types are really separate types, as we saw in Chapter 1, and so shouldn't be confused with the other kinds of type member.

Another way to divide type members into two groups is to split them between ***instance members*** and ***shared members***. Instance data members store the state of a particular instance of the type. If we have several instances of the type, each may contain a separate set of state information, stored in its instance data members. Shared data members store state that is shared by all instances of the type – indeed, they can be accessed even without there being any instances of the type at all.

Shared function members can only access and alter state stored in shared data members. Instance function members can access and modify the state stored in the data members of the instance on which they are called, as well as shared state.

Shared members are sometimes called static members, because they exist at a single, static location within the application.

Modifying Members

When we specify a type member, we can modify what kind of member it will be through the use of type member modifiers. So, for example, when we specify a Sub, we can describe it using modifiers such as Shared, Public, Shadows, and so on.

These modifiers fall into three main categories:

❑   Access Modifiers (Public, Private, Protected, Friend, Protected Friend)

❑   The Shared modifier

❑   Inheritance behavior modifiers (MustOverride, Overridable, NotOverridable, Overrides, Shadows, Overloads)

Access modifiers specify whether the member of the type is visible from code in other types, and if so, which types. The rules are simple: Public members are visible everywhere the type is visible. Private members are visible only from other members of the same type. Protected members are visible wherever Private members are visible, plus from within types that inherit from the type in which the member is specified. Friend members are visible only from types in the same compiled assembly as the type containing them. Protected Friend members are visible anywhere Protected or Friend members are visible.

All members except constants (Consts), which are always Public, can have an access modifier specified. The behavior if none is specified depends on the kind of member, and the type within which it is declared. We'll look at these in a little more detail shortly.

The Shared modifier specifies that a particular type member is a shared member, not an instance member. By default, all members (except constants and nested types) of classes, structures, and interfaces are instance members, and all members of modules are shared. We'll look at these in a moment also.

Inheritance behavior modifiers all affect the way access to members is resolved in a set of types related through inheritance. We'll look at these in detail in Chapter 7, and see how they enable important object-oriented behaviors such as polymorphism.

Here's a quick summary of the different type members we can declare in VB.NET, which kinds of type definition they can be written in, whether they can be shared, and how .NET treats them.

Member Type	Valid In	Instance or Shared	Resulting .NET Construct
Const	Class, Structure, Module	Implicitly shared	Constant
Field (variable)	Class, Structure	Instance	Field (except where declared as WithEvents, when it is compiled as a Property)
Shared field (variable)	Class, Structure, Module	Shared (sharing is implicit in Module)	Shared field (except where declared as WithEvents, when it is compiled as a Shared Property)
Property	Class, Structure, Interface	Instance	Method(s)
Shared Property	Class, Structure, Module	Shared (sharing is implicit in Module)	Shared method(s)
Function	Class, Structure, Interface	Instance	Method
Shared Function	Class, Structure, Module	Shared (sharing is implicit in Module)	Shared method
Sub	Class, Structure, Interface	Instance	Method
Shared Sub	Class, Structure, Module	Shared (sharing is implicit in Module)	Shared method
Sub New (constructor)	Class, Structure	Instance	Special method

Member Type	Valid In	Instance or Shared	Resulting .NET Construct
Shared Sub New (constructor)	Class, Structure, Module	Shared	Special method
Event	Class, Structure, Interface	Instance	A field, two methods, and possibly a nested delegate
Shared Event	Class, Structure, Module	Shared (sharing is implicit in Module)	A shared field, two shared methods, and possibly a nested delegate
Class, Structure, Interface, Enumeration, or Delegate	Class, Structure, Module, Interface	Implicitly shared	A nested type (ultimately, a class, value type, or interface)

As should be clear from this table, ultimately, there aren't that many different kinds of type member that .NET understands, but VB.NET provides us with many ways to declare them. A .NET field will contain our type's data members, and .NET methods our function members. Ultimately, all our logic is represented in MSIL as the contents of methods. All program state (other than transient state within a method) is represented as fields. But VB.NET gives us a great many options for how we declare our code, and it is the goal of this book to help you make decisions about which of these members to use where, when coding your applications.

Type Member Accessibility

When designing a class, we do not want to expose all of our type members to every class and every object. Doing so would lead to difficulty when debugging and maintaining the code. Defining a type member with access modifiers allows us to control the accessibility of our type members to code outside the class. The code that is allowed to access the type member is said to be within that type member's accessibility domain. VB.NET defines four access modifiers and allows two of them to be used in combination:

Access Modifier	Accessibility Domain
Public	Unrestricted access to type member.
Protected	Accessible in current class or classes deriving from current classes.

Table continued on following page

Access Modifier	Accessibility Domain
Friend	Accessible to any code executing in the same assembly as the class.
Private	Accessible within the current class only.
Protected Friend	A union of protected and friend access levels. Accessinle to any code in the same assembly or any class deriving from the class that may or may not be executing in the same assembly.

Public and Private accessibility levels are straightforward and are by far the most common access modifiers. A public instance member can be called by anyone with a reference to the class. Private members are not available outside the class. Private members are a key mechanism for enabling encapsulation and data hiding, two core concepts of object orientation.

Protected members are crucial when designing a class with the intention that others will inherit from it. Protected members can be used to give a derived class access to specific functionality or data that will help it in implementing its functionality. For example, an application might call for a set of classes to be written, each representing a kind of bank account (savings account, checking account, and so on). So, we might design an Account class, and two other classes, SavingsAccount and CheckingAccount, which inherit from it. Now, these two classes will inherit all of the non-private instance members declared in Account, but they won't inherit any of the shared members, or the constructors, and they won't inherit access to any private fields or methods defined on the Account class. Protected access is a great way to allow these classes exclusive access to behavior and state defined in a superclass, without allowing just any code access to it. So, the common logic for setting up an account entry in a database, or for storing certain administrative account details, might be best placed in protected members of the Account class. This makes them accessible only to classes that actually represent accounts, not to other classes.

Friend members are similar to protected members in that they expose limited functionality outside the current class. Any code accessing the class from within the same compiled unit of the application as the class will have access to the Friend member. Any code accessing the class from outside the application will be denied access.

Let's examine the Friend and Protected accessibility members in more detail. In the following example, we have an Account class and a CheckingAccount class that derives from Account. The Account class defines the protected member retrieved, to contain the time that account data was retrieved (potentially useful for enforcing record timeouts, and ensuring transactionality). Since CheckingAccount derives from Account, CheckingAccount has access to retrieved. The Sub Main() procedure cannot access the protected member since the code it resides in is outside the accessibility domain defined by the Protected access modifier.

The Account class also defines an AccountHolder property with Friend accessibility. By definition, any code executing in the same assembly has access to the Friend member. In our case, all code in this application has access to AccountHolder. If Account was compiled into a DLL and thus located in a different assembly, the Friend property would be inaccessible.

```
Imports System

Module Bank
  Sub Main()
    Dim acct As New Account()
    Console.WriteLine(acct.AccountHolder)

    'fails since not accessible
    'Console.WriteLine(acct.retrieved)

    'Since retrieved is protected, CheckingAccount will be able
    'to access it since it derives from Account
    Dim cAcct As New CheckingAccount()
  End Sub
End Module

Public Class CheckingAccount
  Inherits Account
  Sub New()
    MyBase.New
    'Allowed since we derive from Account
    Console.WriteLine(MyBase.retrieved)
    Console.WriteLine(MyBase.AccountHolder)
  End Sub
End Class

Public Class Account
  Protected retrieved As DateTime
  Private acctHolder As String

  Public Sub New()
    retrieved = DateTime.Now()
    acctHolder = "DEFAULT"
    'Normally Retrieve from DB
  End Sub

  Friend Property AccountHolder As String
    Get
      Return acctHolder
    End Get
    Set(ByVal Value As String)
      acctHolder = Value
    End Set
  End Property
End Class
```

Compiling and running this code produces the following output with the system date set to 3/15/2004.

```
C:\ClassDesign\ch02>bank
DEFAULT
3/15/2004 10:44:44 AM
DEFAULT
```

How do we know what accessibility domain to give our type members? In general, we want to provide the least amount of accessibility needed to provide the functionality we are looking for. If we create a helper function within a class to retrieve data from a database and populate the class's state, chances are we do not want anyone outside the class to access this function. We would declare this helper function as private (or possibly protected).

In the following chapters, we will look at specific access strategies we might apply to methods, properties, and constructors, as well as investigating the impact of access modifiers on inheritance.

Shared Type Members

Fields, properties, and methods by default are accessible only with a reference to an object. However, not all functionality is best implemented tied to an instance of a class. .NET allows us to define type members that are callable directly from the class without requiring an instance of the class to be created. Fields, methods, events, and properties can all be declared in this fashion. The VB.NET keyword `Shared` allows us to define such type members. By definition, constants and nested types are implicitly shared and don't require the `Shared` modifier.

Shared type members are useful if a particular function is not tied to an instance of the class, but rather can stand alone. For example, a `Time` class may define a `GetCurrentTime()` method that returns the `Time` object representing the current system clock time. Creating an instance of `Time` just to call `GetCurrentTime()` makes no sense, since we're only interested in the time object that will be returned. Since this method is general to the `Time` class and is specific to each instance, it is best implemented as a `Shared` member. We'll see in Chapter 4 more about how shared methods can be used to assist in the creation of specialized objects.

Modules

Modules are an interesting case. The syntax used to write a module is very similar to that used when writing classes, but the behavior of members is different. Modules cannot be instantiated, and their members are accessed via the module, similarly to the way shared members of a class are accessed.

Modules, when compiled into IL, are actually turned into classes and the type members are declared as shared. From the .NET viewpoint, the module is simply a syntactic shortcut to design a class with shared members. The use of modules should be limited in your VB code and emphasis should be kept on sound OO design, using Shared methods on classes that provide class-level functionality. An excellent alternative to modules would be creating classes with shared type members (because this allows you the flexibility at a later date to add instance capabilities to the class). Behind the scenes, .NET would treat the compiled code the same as it would in modules, plus it would be more intuitive to anyone who reads the code.

Since all members of a module are implicitly shared, a compiler error occurs when trying to use the Shared keyword on a type member within a module. One side effect of this is that if you're looking at some code in the middle of a module, and forget that it's not a class, you might not realize that the members you're looking at are shared.

Nonetheless, modules can be convenient when designing applications because of their simplicity. Numerous modules can be created to group similar functions. But if you're using modules, you should remember you are not taking advantage of object orientation. Modules make a good place to store constants, and to contain global functions that don't have any associated state (for example, mathematical algorithms). A module is also a good place to store the Main() method as used throughout this book. For anything else, you should consider a more object-oriented approach.

Constants

Constants are symbols that have unchanging values and are determined at compile time. When code that uses a constant is compiled from VB.NET into IL, the VB compiler will insert the constant's value in the resulting assembly, just as if it were a literal.

Since the values are inserted straight into IL, constants may only be a type that can be specified as a literal (any other type won't take a value until run time). In VB.NET, we can specify literal numbers, booleans, characters, dates, and strings, so these are the types that can be stored in a constant.

A constant is accessed in other code with the same syntax as if it were a shared field belonging to the class in which it is specified. It can only be read from, not written to. So, a constant BAR specified in a class called Foo could be accessed from anywhere where it was visible using the syntax Foo.BAR.

The following example, coords_constant.vb, illustrates the use of constants. It is good programming practice to group related constants together for simplicity when developing. We have chosen to create a separate class for the constants; however, we could have included them within the MyTest module as well.

```
Imports System

Module MyTest
  Sub Main()
    Console.WriteLine("Please enter a value from " & _
      Counter.MIN_COUNT & " to " & Counter.MAX_COUNT)
    Try
      Dim input As Integer = Console.ReadLine()
      if input < Counter.MIN_COUNT or _
        Input > Counter.MAX_COUNT Then
        Console.WriteLine("Value is out of acceptable range!")
      Else
        Console.WriteLine("The value " & input.ToString() & _
                          " is acceptable!")
      End If
    Catch e As InvalidCastException
      Console.Write("The value you entered was not numeric!")
    End Try
  End Sub
End Module

Public Class Counter
  Public Const MAX_COUNT As Integer = 500
  Public Const MIN_COUNT As Integer = 100
End Class
```

Compiling and running this code produces the following output (which will vary
depending on the input):

```
C:\Class Design\ch02\>coords_constant
Please enter a value from 100 to 500
200
The value 200 is acceptable!
```

Let's take a look at the resulting IL for the Sub Main() procedure by decompiling the
executable, using the .NET Framework's ildasm.exe utility to view the IL and
metadata associated with the executable. The following IL is the beginning portion of
the Main() method, stopping at the beginning of the Try block. Notice that the values
100 and 0x1f4 (500) are inserted directly into the IL, illustrating how .NET embeds
constants into the resulting executable.

```
.method public static void  Main() cil managed
{
  .entrypoint
  .custom instance void [mscorlib]System.STAThreadAttribute::.ctor() =
( 01 00 00 00 )
  // Code size       135 (0x87)
  .maxstack  4
  .locals init (int32 V_0,
          class [mscorlib]System.InvalidCastException V_1)
IL_0000:  ldstr      "Please enter a value from "
  IL_0005:  ldc.i4.s   100
  IL_0007:  call       string
[Microsoft.VisualBasic]Microsoft.VisualBasic.CompilerServices.StringTy
pe::FromInteger(int32)
```

```
    IL_000c:   ldstr     " to "
    IL_0011:   ldc.i4    0x1f4
    IL_0016:   call      string
[Microsoft.VisualBasic]Microsoft.VisualBasic.CompilerServices.StringTy
pe::FromInteger(int32)
    IL_001b:   call      string [mscorlib]System.String::Concat(string,
                                                                string,
                                                                string,
                                                                string)

    IL_0020:   call      void
[mscorlib]System.Console::WriteLine(string)
    .try
//code omitted for brevity
```

.NET's practice of embedding constants into the executable code has a potentially serious downfall. Let's say the constants are defined within another assembly (a DLL for example), and our code was compiled against the DLL. At compilation time, the values of the constants are read from the DLL and placed directly into our code. What happens when the constants within the DLL are changed? Our code is unaware of the changes and needs to be recompiled against the DLL for the changes to be reinserted into the executable. Constants, by design, do not version well within the .NET Framework.

When using constants, it is extremely important to ensure that the value is truly a constant and cannot change for any reason. While such an example sounds trivial, in practice this rule is often not followed.

Assume we are coding a class that uses a connection string to a database. Instead of typing the same string throughout the code, you code the connection string as a constant and use the constant instead. Without thinking, you have locked the code into that particular connection string. If any portion of that connection string changes (database name, IP address, protocol, data provider, etc.), you will be in perhaps a difficult position to recompile and redeploy all of the code that uses it, just to fix the connection string.

If for any reason the constant value could change, avoid constants. An alternative solution would be to implement an application configuration file. Application configuration is extremely flexible within the .NET Framework and proves to be an excellent mechanism for providing application-specific information.

Fields

Fields, often referred to as variables (although only instance variables and class variables are actually fields), are a quick way to expose a piece of data within a class. If not used properly, fields can lend themselves to elusive bugs. Fields directly expose data in a quick and simple fashion, but violate the OO concepts of data hiding and encapsulation. Fields can have Public, Protected, Friend, or Private (default) accessibility.

A field is simply a variable contained in a class. When the .NET runtime creates an instance of the class in memory, memory is allocated to hold the contents of the field. Because the field is created at runtime and has its own memory space, the field is not subject to the versioning problems associated with constants.

Fields can be initialized by including an assignment operation on the same line as the declaration. Instance fields are initialized at the time the instance is created, immediately before a constructor is executed. If no initializer is provided, the field will be initialized with the default value for its type. For reference types, this is Nothing (the .NET value null). For numbers, it is zero, and for booleans, false. Note that strings and arrays are reference types.

The following code (point_publicfield.vb) creates an object called Point that represents a point (X,Y) on a two-dimensional axis. Since the fields X and Y are integers, the compiler will by default initialize them to the integer default of 0.

```
Imports System
Module PointPublic
  Sub Main()
    Dim p as Point = New Point()
    Console.WriteLine("(" & p.X & "," & p.Y & ")")
    p.X = -100
    p.Y = -100
    Console.WriteLine("(" & p.X & "," & p.Y & ")")
  End Sub
End Module

Public Class Point
  Public Y as Integer      'Public Field
  Public X as Integer      'Public Field
End Class
```

Compiling and running this code produces the following output:

```
C:\ClassDesign\ch02>point_publicfield
(0,0)
(-100,-100)
```

Looking at the IL created for the Point class, we notice that the X and Y fields are given their own locations within the IL. The IL simply confirms that each variable is of type int32 with public access and they are called X and Y. Notice that the field will accept any value that is within the int32 range.

```
.field public int32 Y
.field public int32 X
```

Public fields are simple to use, but are very dangerous and not recommended for two reasons:

❏ ***Public fields are unrestricted*** – In this example, Sub Main can change the values of X and Y to any integer value. If the application logic requires that the point's X and Y values must be greater than 0, every piece of code using the Point class must be responsible for enforcing the rule before setting the X and Y public fields.

❏ ***Public fields make the class difficult to version*** – Once deployed, we cannot change the names of X and Y or binary compatibility will be compromised. We also cannot turn the public fields into properties without compromising binary compatibility.

In practice, public fields should almost always be avoided. Any data that is to be exposed on a public interface is more flexible in the form of a property. Constant data is better coded as a constant.

Friend fields are a little more excusable, since they can be accessed only from classes in the same assembly. This means that you can guarantee how the value of the field will be changed, since all code changing it is within the same assembly. But it is always possible to store data in a private field and only allow it to be altered through a method or property, so there is really no reason not to in any code intended for production use. It takes a little more typing, but it will pay back in terms of later flexibility.

Fields can be declared as ReadOnly. Read-only fields cannot be reassigned after they are first assigned when the instance is created, using a field initializer. This means they are effectively constant for the entire duration of the life of the instance. If a read-only field stores a reference to an object, then that reference cannot be reassigned to point to another object, although the state of the object can be altered by accessing its members.

Read-only fields can be made public, if you wish to expose a particular member of the class for other code to use. One example of a situation where this technique may be legitimate is in providing a lock for multithreaded code. If a particular part of an object's functionality should only be accessed by one thread at a time, the object may need to provide an object, on which threads using the object may lock before calling the thread-sensitive code. Such an object might be exposed as a read-only field, preventing the lock from being replaced with another.

On the other hand, the same effect, with additional flexibility, can be achieved using a read-only property, so the technique is not necessary. In order to avoid potential confusion, it may be best to implement it as a property, which users of the class will be more used to.

Properties

Properties are a way to extend the functionality of data elements on types and instances, by being able to restrict the incoming values and provide read-only and write-only data members. To build on the last example, if the business requirement stated the value of the (X,Y) coordinate must be in a grid's top-right quadrant, the rules would be applied when the property is set. If the argument violates the rule, an `ArgumentOutOfRangeException` is thrown. The following code can be found in `point_properties.vb`:

```
Imports System

Module PointProperties
  Sub Main()
    Dim p as Point = New Point()
    Console.WriteLine("(" & p.X & "," & p.Y & ")")
    Try
        p.X = -100
        p.Y = -100
    Catch e as ArgumentOutOfRangeException
        Console.WriteLine(e.Message)
    End Try
    Console.WriteLine("(" & p.X & "," & p.Y & ")")
  End Sub
End Module

Public Class Point
  Private yCoord as Integer
  Private xCoord as Integer
  Public Property X as Integer
    Get
        Return xCoord
    End Get
    Set(ByVal Value as Integer)
      If Value < 0 then
        Throw New ArgumentOutOfRangeException("Value", _
          "X Coordinate must be greater than 0")
      End If
      xCoord = Value
    End Set
  End Property

  Public Property Y as Integer
    Get
        Return(yCoord)
    End Get
    Set(ByVal Value as Integer)
      If Value < 0 then
        Throw new ArgumentOutOfRangeException("Value", _
          "Y Coordinate must be greater than 0")
      End If
      yCoord = Value
    End Set
  End Property
End Class
```

Compiling and running this code produces the following output:

```
C:\ClassDesign\ch02>point_properties
(0,0)
X Coordinate must be greater than 0
Parameter name: Value
(0,0)
```

Properties have greater flexibility and power over fields because they provide data encapsulation. Data encapsulation, also referred to as data hiding, is the mechanism where the implementation details of a class are kept hidden from the user of the class. In our example, the user does not have direct access to xCoord and yCoord. xCoord and yCoord can only be accessed via the X and Y properties. The advantage of using data encapsulation comes when the implementation of the class needs to change. Data encapsulation allows us to control what values the user can assign to a property, giving us power to prevent an invalid state since we can filter and possibly reject incoming values if they would incorrectly disrupt the object's state. In our Point example, if the requirements change so that the X coordinate should return double the value of the xCoord variable, we could change the implementation of the class without changing the interface and breaking binary compatibility; see the changed code in point_property2.vb:

```
Public Property X as Integer
  Get
     Return(xCoord * 2)
  End Get
  Set(ByVal Value as Integer)
     if Value < 0 then
        Throw New ArgumentOutOfRangeException("Value",
          "X Coordinate must be greater than 0")
     End If
     xCoord = Value
  End Set
End Property
```

Properties provide additional advantages over fields by allowing the ability to define read-only and write-only properties. By omitting either the Get or Set part of the property, and using the WriteOnly or ReadOnly keywords, we create a property that can only be written to, or read from.

Write-only properties are rare. An example of a WriteOnly property could be a password, credit card number, or PIN number. Anything we do not want users of the class to read from the object, we would make WriteOnly. Write only properties can't be used on the right hand side of an assignment expression – only on the left.

In a similar fashion, properties are made ReadOnly by including the Get property accessor, omitting the Set accessor, and utilizing the ReadOnly keyword in the property declaration. ReadOnly properties cannot be used from the left hand side of an assignment expression. Examples of ReadOnly properties could be values derived from other properties, or status information about the state of an object.

Within the .NET environment, properties are somewhat different from other type members. Within IL, properties are broken down into get_ and set_ methods. For example, a read/write property with the name X would have get_X() and set_X() accessor methods defined within the class's IL. The compiler will also emit a property definition into the IL to provide the association between the property and the get_ and set_ access modifiers. In this example, we have a read/write property called Z that simply sets and gets a zCoord private field. In the IL, the property is defined with the .property instruction. The property instruction directs the caller to either the Point::get_Z or the Point::set_Z accessors. If this property was defined as ReadOnly, the set_ accessor would be omitted. Likewise, a WriteOnly field does not include a get_ accessor.

```
    Public Property Z As Integer
      Get
         Return zCoord
      End Get
      Set(ByVal Value as Integer)
         zCoord = Value
      End Set
    End Property
```

Here is the IL code for the property itself. Notice how the property simply redirects the caller to the get_Z and set_Z method accessors.

```
.property int32 Z()
{
   .get instance int32 Point::get_Z()
   .set instance void Point::set_Z(int32)
} // end of property Point::Z

//the get_Z and set_Z method accessors

.method public specialname instance int32
        get_Z() cil managed
{
   // Code size       11 (0xb)
   .maxstack  1
   .locals init (int32 V_0)
   IL_0000:  ldarg.0
   IL_0001:  ldfld       int32 Point::zCoord
   IL_0006:  stloc.0
   IL_0007:  br.s        IL_0009
   IL_0009:  ldloc.0
   IL_000a:  ret
} // end of method Point::get_Z

.method public specialname instance void
        set_Z(int32 Value) cil managed
{
   // Code size       8 (0x8)
   .maxstack  8
   IL_0000:  ldarg.0
   IL_0001:  ldarg.1
   IL_0002:  stfld       int32 Point::zCoord
   IL_0007:  ret
} // end of method Point::set_Z
```

You may be asking yourself why we need the .property IL block at all, if its entire purpose is to redirect the caller to another accessor. Indeed, calls to the property will be converted into calls to the methods themselves at compile time. The extra piece of information is required by development tools like Visual Studio .NET, which use the .property IL block to provide more detailed information about the class to the developer. For example, when Visual Studio .NET provides automatic code completion, it can distinguish between a method and a property and gives the property a different icon for display purposes.

Methods

Methods are blocks of executable code within a type that define the behavior of objects belonging to that type. They are typically responsible for performing actions that manipulate the object's state.

All methods have a name, a set of parameters, and a return value. As we will see, it is also possible to define multiple methods with the same name as long as they contain different parameter lists. Defining multiple methods with the same name is called method overloading.

Within the .NET Framework, a method that does not return a value is said to return void. The VB.NET syntax defines void methods as subroutines, and they are declared with the Sub keyword. In fact, if you look at the IL for a subroutine, you will see it is simply a method declared with a void return type.

```
Imports System

Module SubVoid
    Sub Main()
        Console.WriteLine("Hello World!")
    End Sub
End Module
```

Here is the IL. Notice the words public, static, and void are attached to this method. By default, methods in a module are public and static (shared). Because this method is a subroutine, it returns void.

```
.method public static void  Main() cil managed
{
    .entrypoint
    .custom instance void [mscorlib]System.STAThreadAttribute::.ctor() =
( 01 00 00 00 )
    // Code size       11 (0xb)
    .maxstack  8
    IL_0000:  ldstr      "Hello World!"
    IL_0005:  call       void
[mscorlib]System.Console::WriteLine(string)
    IL_000a:  ret
} // end of method SubVoid::Main
```

Methods that return values are functions and are declared with the `Function` keyword.

Method Overloading

The method *signature* includes the method's name, and the number and type of parameters. For example, if two methods with identical names differ only by their number and types of parameters, the .NET Framework considers the methods different. The practice of creating methods with the same names, but different signatures is referred to as method overloading.

If two methods exist with the same signature, the compiler will generate an error message on compilation.

Note that a method's signature does not include a return type. Methods in VB.NET cannot be overloaded based solely on their return type. This is not enforced by the .NET platform, but rather by the VB language. The CLR supports the ability for two methods to only differ by return type; however, the VB language (and many other .NET languages including C#) do not. A compiler error will be generated if two methods in the same class differ only by return type. Each language enforces the restriction, not the .NET runtime. In practice, the issue is seldom a limiting factor in class design. Methods can be defined to return a `System.Object` value or different method names can be given.

A related capability offered by VB.NET is the ability to have optional parameters on methods, and also to have a method take an unlimited number of arguments, in the form of a parameter array. We'll look at these capabilities in Chapter 3.

Properties vs. Methods

Properties and methods are very similar. In fact, as we've seen, properties are syntax shortcuts to defining methods. While both methods and properties can be used to perform activities, properties should be used to represent a piece of data and methods should be used to perform actions. Most often, a property is simply used to change the state of one variable within a class. Methods are often used when needing to perform actions that change an object's overall state. When it comes to querying that state, a method may seem like the obvious choice, but a read-only property would serve just as well. How should you choose?

When designing classes, you will undoubtedly find yourself choosing between using properties and methods. The recommended approach to answering the question is to ask yourself if the purpose of the procedure to set or retrieve a piece of data or perform a more general action. Use properties to set and retrieve a piece of data, use methods to perform actions.

So, for example, imagine we have a class representing a connection to a server. A connection has several pieces of information associated with it – the address of the server, whether the connection is live or not, and the number of bytes of data transferred. It also has a number of actions associated with it – connect, disconnect, and so on. Our challenge as a developer of such a class is to decide which of these things are methods, and which are properties.

Obviously, the actions are methods. It makes no sense having a connection action be triggered by setting (or, worse, getting) a property value. So, we would expect to code `Connect()` and `Disconnect()` methods. What about those attributes? Well, the server address is a classic candidate for a property. It is something we will want to be able to set, and retrieve, and once set, it won't be changed by any other methods. So, we'll have a property called `Server`. Whether the connection is live is going to depend on whether the `Connect()` or `Disconnect()` methods have been called. But it's not something we can set directly. This is probably a candidate for a read-only property, perhaps called `Live`. The last one listed above, the number of bytes transferred, is a little bit more of a challenge. Clearly we can't set this value, but the choice between a read-only property and a method to retrieve the number is a lot less clear cut. Since the value returned at any given time will be different, and is not a part of the object's state that is changed through means under our control, it might be argued that a property is inappropriate. Ultimately, since the resulting code is identical, it is largely a matter of personal preference.

When naming your properties and methods, stick to nouns for properties to signify data and verbs for method names to signify an action. For example, if you are designing a customer class in a banking scenario, Name, Address, and Telephone make ideal property names because they describe a piece of data. Withdraw, Deposit, and Transfer make ideal method names because they describe an action.

For more naming convention guidelines, refer to the specifications set forth in the .NET SDK's Design Guidelines for Class Library Developers.

Constructors

When an object is created, it is given a default initial state. Fields, as we have seen, can be set to an initial value when they are declared, or they accept the default value of their declared type. More often than not, you need more control over the initial state; the creating code would like to perform initialization routines that cannot be done with simple assignment statements. Often, we want to be able to pass in parameters to specify these initial values.

Constructors are type members that are called to initialize an object's state before the reference is returned to the caller. They are compiled as methods, under the special .NET name of `.ctor`, although .NET treats them specially. Constructors are subroutines declared with the `New` keyword in Visual Basic. They are similar to methods in that they can have zero or more arguments. Constructors do not have a return type, and they are executed after the instance fields are assigned their initial values.

Constructors are different from normal methods because they can only be called at the time the object is created. After creation, the constructor cannot be called and is not in the object's declaration space. The constructor is a special member that is only callable during object creation. Once the object is created, the constructor is no longer available to be called.

In the following example, `point_constructor.vb`, we have a `Point` class with two constructors. The constructor declared with no parameters is called the default constructor. The constructor declared with x and y parameters is called a parameterized constructor.

```vb
Imports System
Module Test
  Sub Main()
    Dim p1 as New Point()
    Dim p2 as New Point(100,100)
    Console.WriteLine(p1)
    Console.WriteLine(p2)
  End Sub
End Module

Class Point
  Private xVal as Integer
  Private yVal as Integer

  Sub New()
  End Sub

  Sub New(x as integer, y as Integer)
    Me.xVal = x
    Me.yVal = y
  End Sub

  Public Property X as Integer
    Get
      Return(me.xVal)
    End Get
    Set
      Me.xVal = value
    End Set
  End Property

  Public Property Y
    Get
      Return(me.yVal)
    End Get
    set
      Me.yVal = value
    End Set
  End Property

  Public Overrides Function ToString() as String
    Return("(" & X & "," & Y & ")")
  End function
End Class
```

Compiling and running this code produces the following output:

```
C:\ClassDesign\ch02>point_constructor
(0,0)
(100,100)
```

It is possible to create a class without a constructor, as seen in point_constructor2.vb:

```
Imports System

Module Test
  Sub Main()
    Dim p1 as New Point()
    Dim p2 as New Point()
    p2.Y = 100
    p2.X = 100
    Console.WriteLine(p1)    'Prints: (0,0)
    Console.WriteLine(p2)    'Prints: (100,100)
  End Sub
End Module

Class Point
  Private xVal as Integer
  Private yVal as Integer

  Public Property X as Integer
    Get
      Return(me.xVal)
    End Get
    Set
      Me.xVal = value
    End Set
  End Property

  Public Property Y
    Get
      Return(me.yVal)
    End Get
    set
      Me.yVal = value
    End Set
  End Property

  Public Overrides Function ToString() as String
    Return("(" & X & "," & Y & ")")
  End function
End Class
```

Compiling and running this code produces the following output:

```
C:\ClassDesign\ch02>point_constructor2
(0,0)
(100,100)
```

In the second example, the Point class does not have a constructor. Without a constructor, how are p1 and p2 created? The answer lies in the VB.NET compiler. If an object is without a constructor, vbc.exe will automatically inject a default constructor into the resulting IL. vbc.exe will only inject a default constructor if there are no constructors defined for the class. If you include a parameterized constructor, but omit the default constructor, vbc.exe will not inject a default constructor into the IL. If any code relies on the default constructor and the default constructor is not declared or implicitly inserted, that code will fail since the default constructor will no longer be in the class definition.

Here is a snippet of the Point class's IL code. The .ctor() method confirms the VB code has inserted the default constructor. This IL has been trimmed considerably to illustrate the default constructor is indeed present. Notice that the constructor is simply another method call on the class. The main difference between a constructor and a method is that the constructor is only available at object creation.

```
.class private auto ansi Point
        extends [mscorlib]System.Object
{
  .field private int32 _x
  .field private int32 _y
  .method public specialname rtspecialname
          instance void   .ctor() cil managed
  {
    // Code size       9 (0x9)
    .maxstack  8
    IL_0000:  ldarg.0
    IL_0001:  call         instance void
[mscorlib]System.Object::.ctor()
    IL_0006:  nop
    IL_0007:  nop
    IL_0008:  ret
  } // end of method Point::.ctor
  //OMITTED REST OF POINT IL FOR SPACE
}
```

Notice also that there is a call included in the IL to the .ctor() method (that is, the default constructor) on the System.Object class. This is an automatic call to the constructor of the class's superclass, which is inserted by the compiler. It ensures that if any of the object's state, as defined in its superclass, needs to be initialized specifically by the superclass, that this initialization is performed.

It's also possible for us to specify what is termed a 'shared constructor'. A shared constructor is run when a type is first loaded into the runtime, after the values of any shared fields have been initialized. It allows us to perform any more complex initialization of shared state, but it is somewhat misleading to think of it as a constructor, since it doesn't actually initialize a new object.

Events

An event is a type member that enables an object or class to provide notifications to other classes or code waiting for the event to occur. Events have two parties. First, someone must perform an action that others might be interested in knowing about (the publisher). Second, someone needs to be waiting for the event to occur and be ready to act (the subscriber).

The most familiar usage of events occurs in GUIs. If the user clicks a button, the Click event is triggered. Alternatively, if the user presses a key in a textbox, the textbox raises a Keypress event. However, events are not limited to GUIs. They are useful whenever your class needs to signal state changes that clients of that class may be interested in receiving.

VB.NET makes the creation and consumption of events relatively painless. To create an event, you first create an Event type member on the type that will be firing the event. To fire the event, the RaiseEvent VB keyword is used followed by the name we gave to this event: RaiseEvent(EventName). The event will now be raised to anyone listening.

In order to listen to an event, the subscriber has two choices: either they can use a VB.NET syntactic shortcut, or they can register an event handler manually. To use the syntactic support, the subscribing class creates a field to contain an instance of the publishing class using the WithEvents keyword. Then a method is declared with the keyword Handles, and the name of this field, and the event to which the method responds. If the object in the WithEvents field fires that event, then the Handles method is called.

But, as with so much of VB.NET, this is hiding a lot of functionality behind a friendly syntax.

Let's look first at what the publisher is doing. The publisher, remember, has an event type member, and fires an event by calling RaiseEvent() with the name of this event member. This is actually compiled as a private field, which stores all the registered event handlers, and two methods (one to register an event handler, one to unregister). When RaiseEvent() is called, all of the event handlers are retrieved and called.

When we declare an event member, we can either specify an existing delegate type that defines the signature of methods that can handle the event, or we can specify the signature at the time of declaring the event. If we specify the signature on the event declaration, then a nested delegate type is created to represent the signature.

An event handler, then, is a delegate of the type defined by the event declaration that points to a method that will handle the event. Such handlers are added by calling the appropriate generated method on the publishing type.

So, what does the subscriber do, to receive and handle the event? Well, the field declared WithEvents is actually compiled as a property. When a value is assigned to the field, it is processed by the generated property accessor, which looks through the type for a method that is designated as handling an event on objects in this field. It then creates a delegate instance (of the type appropriate to the event), and registers the method as a handler by calling the appropriate generated method on the publishing type.

So, events are a convenient syntax for creating and using instances of delegates.

Let's reiterate the steps needed to publish and subscribe to an event:

1. A class (publisher) is created with an Event type member. This event will be raised when an interesting action occurs.

2. The subscriber creates a field holding an instance of the publisher using the WithEvents keyword. The WithEvents keyword signifies the subscriber has the ability to listen to events raised.

3. The publisher raises the event with the RaiseEvent keyword.

4. The subscriber dedicates a method that will execute when the event is raised. The method is declared with the Handles keyword to designate which event it will listen to.

It is important to understand that event information is only meaningful if someone is listening. If the event is raised without a listener, the event goes unrecognized. Because of the optional nature of subscribing to events, important information that must be referred to the client should not be implemented as an event. Such information should be passed back via return values or exceptions. Unlike events, clients are forced to receive any data returned via these return values.

At first sight, events are very confusing. Events are perhaps more challenging than other type member because they require two separate pieces of code to interact and their interaction is not guaranteed (if the event is not raised or subscribed to). A more detailed discussion of events can be found in Chapter 6.

The System.Object Contract

All types defined within the .NET Framework ultimately derive from .NET's root class, System.Object. Every accessible member of System.Object is also exposed in our classes. If we do not inherit from another class, the class will implicitly inherit from System.Object. The compiler will enforce this requirement, which means we usually omit the Inherits System.Object declaration on the class. Since every class either inherits from another class, or from System.Object, it should be obvious that ultimately every class is derived from an inheritance hierarchy with System.Object at the top.

Even though we don't always explicitly acknowledge our types' inheritance from this root class, it is important to remember that every type we generate has inherited a contract from System.Object. There are certain methods that must be implemented in a particular way in order to fulfil our obligations under this contract. To allow this, we have the ability to override System.Object's overridable type members. Overriding System.Object's members gives your classes better continuity with those found in the .NET base class library set. The vast majority of the .NET classes provide custom overrides of System.Object's type members to provide functionality tailored to the class. System.Object has the following overridable public methods commonly implemented in classes:

```
Equals(Object) As Boolean
GetHashCode() As Integer
ToString() As String
```

ToString()

ToString() has the job of returning a string representation of the current object. By default, the System.Object.ToString() method will print out the object's type name. Notice that ToString() is called whenever we use objects of our class somewhere where a string is required. If we have a Console.WriteLine(Object) call, it is equivalent to Console.Writeline(Object.ToString()).

The vast majority of the time, the class name is not very useful. The same results are returned for every instance of the class, regardless of the instance state of the class. What we normally need is a descriptive string that is particular to the object instance, not every object of the class. Overriding System.Object.ToString() allows us to customize the string representation for a particular instance, as can be seen in overrides_tostring.vb, below:

```
Imports System

Module Test
    Sub Main()
        Dim f as New ObjectFriend("Visual Basic", 1)
        Dim f2 as New ObjectFriend("Visual C#", 2)
        Console.WriteLine(f)
        Console.WriteLine(f2)
    End Sub
End Module

Public Class ObjectFriend
    Private Name as String
    Private Value as Integer

    Public Sub New(Name as String, Value as Integer)
        Me.Name = Name
        Me.Value = Value
```

```
      End Sub
      Public Overrides Function ToString() as String
         Return(Name & " has the value " & Value)
      End Function
End Class
```

Compiling and running this code produces the following output:

```
C:\ClassDesign\ch02>overrides_tostring
Visual Basic has the value 1
Visual C# has the value 2
```

Equals()

Quite often we need the ability to compare objects for equivalence.
System.Object.Equals() gives us such an ability. .NET defines two forms of
equality: reference equality and value equality. By default,
System.Object.Equals() will test for reference equality. Reference equality occurs
when two references point to the same underlying object. The following example
illustrates this.

```
Imports System
Module Test
   Sub Main()
      Dim f as New ObjectFriend("Visual Basic", 1)
      Dim f2 as New ObjectFriend("Visual Basic", 1)
      Console.WriteLine(f2.Equals(f))     'False!  f2 and f reference
separate object instances.
      f = f2
      Console.WriteLine(f2.Equals(f))     'True!   f2 and f reference same
object instance.

   End Sub
End Module

Public Class ObjectFriend
   Private Name as String
   Private Value as Integer

   Public Sub New(Name as String, Value as Integer)
     Me.Name = Name
     Me.Value = Value
   End Sub
   Public Overrides Function ToString() as String
      Return(Name & " has the value " & Value)
   End Function
End Class
```

Compiling and running this code produces the following output:

```
False
True
```

What does this tell us about the functionality of `System.Object.Equals()` and reference equality? In the first test of `System.Object.Equals()`, the object references f and f2 pointed to separate instances of ObjectFriend, making the test for reference equality return False. By setting f = f2, both object references point to the same underlying object, meaning reference equality is satisfied. An object will always equal itself, for example f2.Equals(f2) will always return True.

Many real-world objects need the ability to test for value equality. Value equality is satisfied if two objects have identical state. Overriding `System.Object.Equals()` allows us to perform a custom value equality test.

```
Imports System
Module Test
   Sub Main()
      Dim f as New ObjectFriend("Visual Basic", 1)
      Dim f2 as New ObjectFriend("Visual Basic", 1)
      Console.WriteLine(f2.Equals(f))    'True!
      f = f2
      Console.WriteLine(f2.Equals(f))

   End Sub
End Module

Public Class ObjectFriend
   Private Name as String
   Private Value as Integer

   Public Sub New(Name as String, Value as Integer)
      Me.Name = Name
      Me.Value = Value
   End Sub
   Public Overrides Function ToString() as String
      Return(Name & " has the value " & Value)
   End Function

   Public Overrides Overloads Function Equals(Obj as Object) as Boolean
      'Value equality test
      If Not IsNothing(Obj)
         If TypeOf Obj is ObjectFriend then
            If CType(Obj, ObjectFriend).Name = Me.Name and CType(Obj,
ObjectFriend).Value = Me.Value then
               Return True
            End If
         End If
      End If
      Return False
   End Function

End Class
```

Compiling and running this code produces the following output:

```
True
True
```

Here, since we are testing for value equality, we examine the state of the two instances in question. We could check for any portion of each object's state. This example tests both the name and value state items for value equality.

It's important, when coding an `equals()` method (and indeed, when coding any method that takes an object argument) to check that the argument passed is a valid object reference, not a null reference. We do this using the `IsNothing()` function. If the argument passed is `null`, our response should always be to return `False`.

GetHashCode()

The .NET Framework includes the `HashTable` as a fundamental collection object available to developers. `HashTables` store key-value pairs, by placing the pairs in 'hash buckets' according to the key object's integer hash code. The `HashTable` class uses the hash code to sort the objects internally and also to provide faster sorting and searching. Storage by hash code allows the `HashTable` to find a particular key with minimal effort. Where does the hash code come from? In order to provide a hash code for your class, you must override `System.Object.GetHashCode()`.

In order to appreciate what we must consider when implementing `GetHashCode()`, it's worth appreciating a little how `HashTable` stores, then retrieves, a key.

When we ask a `HashTable` to store a value under a certain key, it creates an object binding the key to the value, and then places the pair into one of its hash buckets, which it determines by evaluating the key's hash code. When we later ask to retrieve a value, passing in a key, the `HashTable` calculates the key's hash code again, determining which hash bucket it should look in. Then it compares the key to each key in the bucket in turn, until it finds one that matches, according to its `Equals()` method. It uses this to look up the attached value, and returns it.

If a key is placed into a `HashTable` and then subsequently altered, it is quite possible for it to become irretrievably lost – if the key is in the wrong bucket, it won't be found. If our object can't return a consistent hash code, then it might suffer precisely this fate. It's also clear that our `Equals()` and `GetHashCode()` methods must be consistent in informing the `HashTable` about our object's state. If we aren't careful when writing a hash code implementation, we could easily build classes that aren't usable as keys in a `HashTable`.

By default, `System.Object.GetHashCode()` guarantees that a unique hash code will be returned for each class instance. The Common Language Runtime cannot guarantee producing similar hash codes for objects containing similar state. If we want this behavior (separate objects with identical state should be regarded as the same object), overriding `System.Object.GetHashCode()` gives us the opportunity to return a consistent hash code dependent on the object's state.

Within the .NET Framework, many classes implement their own version of `GetHashCode()`. For example, `System.String` returns the same hash code for identical strings. `System.Int32` returns the same hash code for identical integers.

When basing a hash code on the values of an object's members, it is logical to calculate the hash code from the hash codes of the instance's members. For example, for our class ObjectFriend, a good hash code strategy might be to take the hash codes of the Name and Value fields, and combine them. For example, we might write the following hash code mechanism:

```
Public Overrides Function GetHashCode() As Integer
    Return Name.GetHashCode() XOr Value.GetHashCode()
End Function
```

In our example, we use the exclusive or operator XOr. XOr uses a bitwise comparison and returns an integer as the result. By combining the GetHashCode() calls from both our instance variables (Name and Value), we are guaranteed to get a unique hash code when our object state is identical.

Another technique, which is particularly useful in types that have a lot of numeric values making up their state, is to multiply the hash code of each data member by a different prime number, and add up the results.

When determining an algorithm for calculating hash codes, the following guidelines are recommended:

- ❑ Keep the algorithm simple! Lengthy algorithms for GetHashCode() slow down execution.

- ❑ The algorithm should give a random distribution of values. A random distribution gives the hash table the best performance, because it evenly distributes keys among buckets.

- ❑ Use instance fields in the calculation, don't rely on random numbers.

- ❑ Ideally, the instance state used in the calculation will be immutable; meaning the values are initialized on creation and not changed during the object's lifetime. This will prevent the object getting lost in a HashTable.

- ❑ Objects that are equal according to the Equals() method should always return the same hash code. This means that if we override Equals() we should always override GetHashCode().

Regardless of if you use the HashTable class in your application, overriding Equals() and GetHashCode() is good programming practice and makes the class interface more intuitive and predictable for developers using it. Many algorithms that implement sorting and comparison rely on these methods. Implementing GetHashCode() and Equals() allows your classes to participate in many of .NET's pre-built objects (like HashTable) and enables developers writing sorting and searching algorithms to generalize their procedures for objects taking advantage of these members.

Value and Reference Semantics and Mutability

One rule of thumb in object-oriented programming, which serves many developers well, is that all types that have value semantics are immutable, while those that have reference semantics are mutable.

Types that have value semantics are types that represent a description of an entity. For example, I might have a Date class, representing a date in terms of day, month, and year. If I have two date objects referring to the same day, I want to consider them to be equivalent; they both describe the same thing. If I was using a HashTable to store appointments against dates, I'd want to be able to retrieve my appointments for a particular date using any object instance that describes that date. I shouldn't have to have exactly the same instance that was used to store the appointment in the first place.

Such types can be made immutable. Immutability means that once an instance has been created, it cannot be altered at all, ever. If we want an instance representing a different value, we can create another instance. In VB.NET, an immutable type will have a constructor that initializes the object's data members, and may well have read-only properties to allow access to those data members. Immutable types may still have behavior, but it may not change their state at all. Immutable types should also be marked as NotInheritable so that they can't be extended into mutable variants.

You should also ensure that the state of an immutable type is also immutable. If you must store a reference to a mutable type in an immutable class, you should defensively copy it, so that the reference is not shared with other classes. A shared reference to such a member could lead to the object's state being changed by another object, which would defeat the purpose of making the class immutable.

Making a class immutable makes it safer and easier to implement the Equals() and GetHashCode() methods. Instances of such types can be used safely as HashTable keys. They can generally be thrown around in programs as if they were value types, whether they are implemented as structures or classes. You never need to worry if passing an immutable object to a method will lead to the object's state being changed.

Mutable classes, on the other hand, should always be implemented with reference semantics. If a type is mutable, it represents an actual entity, whose state is under the control of the program. Such entities are not equivalent to other entities whose state happens, at the moment, to be the same. So, the only safe test for equality is that provided in System.Object. The same goes for GetHashCode() – the semantics inherited from Systemm.Object are correct, treating an object as only being the same as itself. This allows such objects to be used in HashTables, although you will need to use the same instance to retrieve a value, not a separate instance.

These are merely guidelines that many object-oriented developers follow; rules that you can break whenever you have good reason. But they are a good, strong rule of thumb, and one question worth asking yourself as you sit down to write a class is whether it should be mutable or immutable.

72

Summary

Type members are the programming constructs used to build a class. This chapter discussed the attributes of type members, and briefly touched on each type member and usage guidelines associated with each.

Constants are used to provide readability and act as a single point of change for known values. Constants are shared members by default and are used whenever values are guaranteed not to change.

Fields are variables used to hold state in a class. To provide data encapsulation, fields are commonly created with the `Private` access modifier. `Public` fields lock the class interface and data together, making it difficult to version the code without breaking compatibility.

Properties represent a piece of data exposed by the class, but are really methods. Properties extend the concept of a field by adding a layer of abstraction between a class's internal and external representation. Properties give the designer the ability to change the internal workings of the class while maintaining the same external interface and not sacrificing compatibility. Properties can be designated `ReadOnly` or `WriteOnly` to prevent unwanted usage of the property.

Methods typically perform actions that manipulate an object's state. Multiple methods can have the same name with different signatures to provide multiple implementations. Such a practice is called method overloading.

Events provide a way for classes to notify listeners when actions have occured. VB.NET simplifies raising and consuming events by providing the `RaiseEvent` and `Handles` keywords. Since events are not required to be handled, they should typically be used to send information not critical to the central operation of the class.

Constructors allow you to customize the object creation process. If no constructor is specified the Visual Basic compiler will inject a default constructor into the class's IL.

To make objects more compatible with the .NET Framework, it is common practice to override public members exposed via the root of the .NET object hierarchy: `System.Object`. Overriding `ToString()` allows you to return a customized string representation for the instance of the class. Overriding `Equals()` allows you to determine equality by performing a value comparison between two instances of a given type. Overriding `GetHashCode()` allows the object to take advantage of sorting and searching optimizations found in the `HashTable` class. An object overriding `GetHashCode()` should also override `Equals()`. We also discussed ***mutable*** and ***immutable*** types, and appropriate strategies for their use.

VB.NET

Class Design

Handbook

3

3

Methods

Classes represent real-world entities such as a car. A car has attributes such as its color, make, and model. It also has controls to operate the car such as a steering wheel and gears.

Methods represent the 'controls' of an entity while **properties** (covered in Chapter 5) represent the visible attributes of an entity. Whereas a class represents an aspect of a business model, a method should serve to represent a single discrete task or process.

The controls of a car are both abstract and encapsulate its inner workings. The car can be driven without any knowledge of how the engine works. As a designer of a class, you should provide the same levels of abstraction and encapsulation you take for granted when driving your car or when writing client code that uses someone else's classes.

Hiding the actual implementation of a method from the user, while considered good design, imposes a duty on the programmer: a method must really do what you claim. The description of what a method does and how to use it is a "semantic contract". It is crucial to get this right, if everyone understands it (and sticks to it) there won't be any problems if the actual implementation of the method changes later.

VB.NET Method Syntax

We will start by looking at how to declare a method in VB.NET. The declaration itself is not fixed and, aside from the name of the method, can include keywords controlling scope, inheritance, polymorphism, overloading, and parameters; not to mention method return values. Inheritance and polymorphism are covered in Chapter 7 so here we'll concentrate on the other aspects of methods.

The distinction between a method that returns a value and a method that does not return a value is made by choosing either the Function keyword or the Sub keyword. Functions should return a value, subroutines cannot; this is consistent with all previous versions of Visual Basic. This is really just a language construct and there is essentially no difference between Functions and Subs when they are compiled into the underlying MSIL. This is demonstrated by the fact that most other .NET languages make no distinction between these types of method.

Functions

Below is a basic declaration of a function:

```
Public Function DoubleMyNumber(ByVal yourNumber As Double) As Double
    Return (yourNumber * 2)
End Function
```

The Return statement is by far the easiest way to return values but we'll look at all the options available later.

Subroutines

Below is a basic declaration of a subroutine:

```
Public Sub HalveMyNumber(ByRef yourNumber As Double)
    yourNumber = yourNumber / 2
End Sub
```

Method Scope and Visibility

As with all type members, we can declare method scope and visibility with the familiar keywords Public, Private, and so on:

❑ **Public** – This is the default when no directive is specified. However, declaring methods without any scope keywords is bad practice. By default, these methods will be available to everyone and everything. This breaks our encapsulation rule, exposing business logic and internal data to any client program. Only methods which form part of the public interface of the class should be declared public.

❑ **Private** – Private methods are usable only from within the class itself, providing encapsulation to hide business logic and internal data from client programs.

- **Friend** – Friend methods declared within a class are only accessible if an instance of the class is actually created first. Declaring Friend methods inside standard code modules is better practice as Friend methods then become automatically available from within the entire assembly. They are not available to either derived classes or any client code outside of the defining assembly and make excellent candidates for worker or utility routines that can be utilized by all other classes defined in the assembly.

- **Protected** – These methods are accessible only within the class itself and derived classes. These allow you to provide and accept data from subclasses. It is useful to expose variables in this way so any needed business logic can be imposed by the base class rather than just hope that the sub-class is well designed and will provide us with acceptable values.

- **Protected Friend** – This provides a combination of Protected and Friend access privileges.

Scope Example

If we imagine a hypothetical automated train system that is controlled solely by a computer (there are in fact several systems in the world that could at least in theory operate without human intervention) we might start with a class that defined a train and its various controls.

```
Public Class Train

    Protected Sub StopTrain()
      ApplyBrakes()
      StopEngine()
    End Sub

    Private Sub StartEngine()
    End Sub

    Private Sub StopEngine()
    End Sub

    Private Sub ReleaseBrakes()
    End Sub

    Protected Friend Sub ApplyBrakes()
    End Sub

End Class
```

The Train class is our base class; all of the methods exposed by this class are available only inside the class itself and derived classes. The methods in this class mimic the kind of functionality available to the driver of the train. The reasons you would want to restrict access to methods directly controlling the train should be obvious. Note however that some of the (protected) methods in the class are accessible by derived classes.

One possible type of train is a passenger train so it makes sense to implement this as a class that inherits from `Train`.

```
Public Class PassengerTrain
   Inherits Train

   Friend Sub StopAtStation()
      StopTrain()
      UnlockDoors()
   End Sub

   Private Sub UnlockDoors()
   End Sub

   Public Sub OpenDoors()
   End Sub

   Public Sub PullEmergencyCord()
      Mybase.ApplyBrakes()
   End Sub

End Class
```

When examining this class, it now becomes clear why some methods need to be available to derived classes. If a passenger pulls the emergency cord, you want the train to stop but you wouldn't want to give the passengers direct control of the brakes.

We can also see other types of scope. A controller class in the same assembly could call the `StopAtStation()` method and the way we've implemented the `UnlockDoors()` means that the doors of the train should stay closed until the train has stopped at a station.

Arguments and Parameters

While it is possible to implement useful methods that accept no parameters this is quite limiting. Most methods will operate on data in some way, therefore the data (or a reference to it) must be passed to the method. Parameters passed to methods are usually referred to as **Arguments**. Methods that accept arguments are, slightly confusingly, called **Parameterized** methods.

Passing arguments to methods is normally the preferred design approach for distributed applications where a stateless model is often used in the application middle-tier. Parameterized methods can reduce the number of round trips required to interact with an object. This has performance benefits in a distributed computing environment where the client and server programs reside on different computers.

Parameter Directives – ByRef/ByVal

When an argument is passed to a method, we can pass the actual value (ByVal) or we can pass a reference (ByRef) to the location in memory where the data resides.

Passing data ByVal involves making a physical copy of the data from the client code (the argument) into the method (the parameter). Both the client code and the method then have separate variables holding their own separate copy of the data.

Passing data ByRef involves copying a reference to the data only. Both the client code and the method then hold separate references to the same data or object. The value of a ByRef parameter can be modified by the method but a ByVal cannot. This can cause problems if your method alters a value passed into it by reference, as these changes are visible outside the method context. The changes a method makes that can affect other code are called "side effects".

> *Passing arguments by value –* ByVal *is now the default in VB.NET;* ByRef *was the default in previous versions of Visual Basic. This can be viewed as desirable behavior as it reduces the likelihood that methods will have "side effects".*

The basic declaration of a parameterized method is as follows:

```
Class ByValByRef
    Public Sub MethodByVal(ByVal SomeData As Integer)
        ' A copy of SomeData is passed into Method ByVal
    End Sub

    Public Sub Method(SomeData As Integer)
        ' The default ByVal is assumed
        ' A copy of SomeData is passed into Method ByVal
    End Sub

    Public Sub MethodByRef(ByRef SomeData As Integer)
        ' The SomeData argument is a reference to the data being passed
    End Sub
End Class
```

Notice that a parameter declared without any ByRef or ByVal instruction will default to ByVal; but it is bad programming practice not to include either a ByRef or ByVal keyword; parameters should be declared as explicitly as possible.

> *This can potentially cause bugs in code migrated from previous versions of Visual Basic. A method that previously assumed the default of* ByRef *will now assume the new default –* ByVal

79

Passing Reference Types versus Value Types

Choosing whether to pass arguments ByRef or ByVal not only depends on how you want the method to behave, but also on the type of data that you want to pass. It's at this point that we need to widen our perspective.

As we know all data in .NET is either a value type or a reference type. As discussed in Chapter 1, value types include primitive data types, structures, and enumerations. A simple assignment of a value type to another variable results in two variables containing separate data. In fact, all value type assignments including passing arguments to method parameters (ByVal) result in the copying of data to the new variable. The life span of a value type can be directly controlled by the program. When a value-type variable goes out of scope, the variable and all of its data are removed from the stack, immediately freeing up memory.

Reference types derive from System.Object and can be any object (including arrays and strings); they are heap based. Reference variables point to an object that is located on the heap. Unlike a stack, a heap can store dynamically sized variables so you only need to keep a reference to these potentially large and variable sized types in the stack.

Recall from Chapter 1 that when a value type is converted to a reference type it is boxed, which involves copying the data from the heap to the stack. Obviously, when you create any method that does this a large numbers of times (maybe when processing large arrays) you need to take into account the performance implications involved. Note that, when a value type is passed ByRef it is implicitly boxed. The reverse process converting a reference to a value type is called unboxing and has similar implications.

A reference type can have many references pointing at it. It won't go out of scope on the heap until all these are removed from the stack. The heap is governed by the garbage collector and an object will consume memory until the garbage collector removes it from the heap. We'll look at these issues further in Chapter 4 where we discuss object lifecycle in more detail.

Passing Value Types ByVal

Let's create a simple method to demonstrate what happens when we pass a simple value type (a Double) into a method ByVal. Our method simply calculates the gross price of a product by adding tax to its net price.

Compile the following code, from passing_byval.vb:

```
Imports System

Class MathsClass
    Public Function AddTaxByVal(ByVal ValNetPrice As Double) As Double
        ValGrossPrice = ValNetPrice * 1.175
        Return ValGrossPrice
```

```
      End Function
    End Class

    Module TaxCalculate
      Sub Main()
        Dim NetPrice As Double = 24.99
        Dim Maths As New MathsClass()
        Console.WriteLine("Calculate Tax ByVal")
        Console.WriteLine("The Net price is - {0}", NetPrice)
        Console.WriteLine("The Gross price including tax is - {0}", _
          Maths.AddTaxByVal(NetPrice))
        Console.WriteLine("The Net price is - {0}", NetPrice)
      End Sub
    End Module
```

If you execute the application, you should see:

```
C:\Class Design\ch03\>Passing_ByVal
Calculate Tax ByVal
The Net price is - 24.99
The Gross price including tax is - 29.36325
The Net price is - 24.99
```

Our net price variable NetPrice has remained unchanged after making our AddTaxByVal() method call. This is because a physical copy of NetPrice has been created in the method. The ValNetPrice variable within this method now contains its own separate copy of the data, which it can change without affecting NetPrice in the TaxCalculate Module.

Passing Value Types ByRef

Let's compare the previous example with passing an argument ByRef. The source can be found in passing_byref.vb:

```
Imports System

Class MathsClass
  Public Function AddTaxByRef(ByRef RefNetPrice As Double) As Double
    RefGrossPrice = RefNetPrice * 1.175
    Return RefGrossPrice
  End Function
End Class

Module TaxCalculate
  Sub Main()
    Dim NetPrice As Double = 24.99
    Dim Maths As New MathsClass()

    Console.WriteLine("Calculate Tax ByRef")
    Console.WriteLine("The Net price is - {0}", NetPrice)
    Console.WriteLine("The Gross price including tax is - {0}", _
      Maths.AddTaxByRef(NetPrice))
    Console.WriteLine("The Net price is - {0}", NetPrice)
  End Sub
End Module
```

Running the code, you will see the following:

```
C:\Class Design\ch03\>passing_byref
Calculate Tax ByRef
The Net price is - 24.99
The Gross price including tax is - 29.36325
The Net price is - 29.36325
```

Notice how our original NetPrice variable has changed after calling AddTaxByRef(). When we pass a value ByRef, a reference to the variable is passed to the method, instead of a copy of the variable itself. This means that the AddTaxByRef() method has full access to the data in the NetPrice variable (called RefNetPrice inside the method) and can change the data if it wants to. Any changes made by AddTaxByRef() are visible to the client code in TaxCalculate. In essence NetPrice, and the RefNetPrice parameter of AddTaxByRef() both reference the same data.

One thing to note about this code is that we have used a function for AddTaxByRef(). Functions should be used to return a value back to the client code. This is not necessary in this example because the value is passed ByRef and changes are therefore visible in the client code; returning it as well is, in this case, redundant.

It may occur to you that passing arguments ByRef can be used routinely to return a value from a method. This may seem especially useful as you could use this approach to return more than one value. However, code is far more readable if you use explicit function Return values. Multiple return values can be provided by creating a class or structure that contains the data you want to return, then returning an instance of that type. If the values are just primitive, numerical types they could also be contained in a structure.

Passing Reference Types ByVal

When reference types are passed ByVal, we are asking to pass the value of an object. The value of an object, however, is actually its location in memory. The value of an object is not the value of one of its properties, or a value returned by one of its methods. Therefore, the method parameter actually receives the value of the object's location on the heap. Reference types passed ByVal cannot be permanently reassigned to a different reference. A method may get an instance of another object of the same type as the parameter, and then assign the parameter against this second instance. However, the reassignment will be lost as soon as the method returns to the client code. This could be a good thing in some situations, if you have a requirement to pass an object to a method but prevent the client code from viewing changes made to the object. For instance, pass the object ByVal, reassign the parameter to a different object and any changes made to the new object will not be visible to the client code.

Passing Reference Types ByRef

To pass a reference type to a method, we must pass the variable holding the object reference. If the method parameter is declared as ByRef, the parameter is actually a reference to a reference of the object. We then have a double reference – the method parameter is a reference to the calling argument, which in turn is a reference to our object on the heap.

The difference between passing a reference type ByRef and ByVal is a subtle one, but important nevertheless. Unlike passing reference types ByVal, passing a reference type ByRef allows us to reassign the parameter and the argument to a different object. This can improve the safety of passing objects to methods that change the state of an object. A parameterized method can be declared to receive an object as an argument, the method can then create a new second object of the same type and change its state, and then if conditions apply, the parameter object can be reassigned against the second object.

ByRef and ByVal Best Practice

Let's summarize some best practices, the main differences between ByRef and ByVal, and their usage in Functions and Subs:

❏   ByVal makes a duplicate copy of the value of the argument into the parameter. Use ByVal when you do not want the client code to view any changes made to the parameter by the method.

❏   ByRef passes a reference to the argument. The parameter and argument reference the same data. Use ByRef when you want the client code to view any changes made to the parameter by the method or if you want to reassign an object to a different instance and have the reassignment visible to client code.

❏   ByVal is the default when no keyword is specified but it is better to specify ByRef or ByVal rather than rely on this.

❏   Watch out for Visual Basic code migrated from earlier versions. ByRef was the default in earlier versions of Visual Basic but ByVal is the default in VB.NET

❏   Functions can return a single value only and Subs don't directly return any values. If you need a method to return several values, you could use a Sub and pass all parameters ByRef.

Much better would be to create an interface that defines the set of values you want to return and then return an object implementing that interface. Another option, if you are dealing with a small set of numeric values is to create a structure and return that.

❏   Do not use a Function that does not return a value; this can be confusing and using a Sub will make the purpose of the method clearer.

❏   Do not use a Function that returns a value passed in as a parameter ByRef. Any changes made to the parameter will already be visible to the client code as the argument was passed ByRef.

Passing Objects versus Passing Structures

As already discussed in Chapter 1, classes (objects) are reference types and structures are value types. We know that reference and value types are handled differently when passed as arguments, and we know that a method can handle parameters differently depending on whether the argument is passed ByVal or ByRef.

Here we will demonstrate and compare:

1. Passing an object ByVal

2. Passing a structure ByVal

3. Passing an object ByRef

4. Passing a structure ByRef

To illustrate the differences between passing reference types (an object) and value types (a structure); we will use a Passenger entity, which will be represented as a class (reference type) and a structure (value type). The Passenger entity will have a Name property and a travel Status property. The Passenger name can be any string value and the travel status has been enumerated as either Economy or FirstClass.

The code includes methods to change the Passenger name; four variations are supplied to cover both ByRef and ByVal for the Passenger object and Passenger structure.

The console application code below can be found in class_structure.vb:

```
Imports System
Public Module ClassVsStructure

    Public Enum TravelStatus
        FirstClass = 1
        Economy = 2
    End Enum

    ' Class to define a Passenger as a reference type
    Public Class PassengerClass

        Private m_Name As String
        Private m_Status As TravelStatus

        Public Property Name() As String
            Get
                Return (m_Name)
            End Get
            Set(ByVal Value As String)
                m_Name = Value
            End Set
        End Property
```

```
    Public Property Status() As TravelStatus
      Get
        Return (m_Status)
      End Get
      Set(ByVal Value As TravelStatus)
        m_Status = Value
      End Set
    End Property
End Class


' Structure to define a Passenger as a value type
Public Structure PassengerStruct
    Public Name As String
    Public Status As TravelStatus
End Structure
```

This simple code declares our Passenger entity as both an object and a structure. We are also using an Enum to provide safe limitations on our travel status. Enums were discussed in some detail in Chapter 1.

Now we add code to change the passenger's name. Four versions are required, ByRef and ByVal each for the PassengerClass object and the PassengerStruct structure:

```
' Changes the Name property of the Passenger Class ByVal
Public Sub ChangeName_Obj_ByVal(ByVal details As PassengerClass, _
                                ByVal NewName As String)
    details.Name = NewName
End Sub

' Changes the Name property of the Passenger Class ByRef
Public Sub ChangeName_Obj_ByRef(ByRef details As
                                PassengerClass, _
                                ByVal NewName As String)
    details.Name = NewName
End Sub

' Changes the Name property of the Passenger Structure ByVal
Public Sub ChangeName_Struct_ByVal(ByVal details As
                                PassengerStruct, _
                                ByVal NewName As String)
    details.Name = NewName
End Sub

' Changes the Name property of the Passenger Structure ByRef
Public Sub ChangeName_Struct_ByRef(ByRef details As
                                PassengerStruct, _
                                ByVal NewName As String)
    details.Name = NewName
End Sub
```

To test the methods add the following client code for the Main() Sub:

```
Sub Main()

    Dim passengerObj As PassengerClass = New PassengerClass()
    Dim passengerStr As PassengerStruct = New PassengerStruct()
    passengerObj.Name = "Lucy"
    passengerObj.Status = TravelStatus.Economy
    passengerStr.Name = "Kate"
    passengerStr.Status = TravelStatus.Economy
```

First, the initial values of the passenger's name and travel status are assigned to both the Passenger object and Passenger structure. Then initial values are displayed ('**Before**'):

```
    Console.WriteLine("Before - Object, Name & Status - {0}, {1}", _
                      passengerObj.Name, _
                      passengerObj.Status)
    Console.WriteLine("Before - Structure, Name & Status - {0}, " + _
                      "{1}", passengerStr.Name, _
                      passengerStr.Status)
    Console.WriteLine()
```

Now we call the various methods on both passengerStr and passengerObj.

Test 1 – ChangeName_Obj_ByVal() is called passing the PassengerClass object ByVal.

```
    ChangeName_Obj_ByVal(passengerObj, "Lucy (Changed ByVal)")
```

Test 2 – ChangeName_Struct_ByVal() is called passing the PassengerStruct structure ByVal.

```
    ChangeName_Struct_ByVal(passengerStr, "Kate (Changed ByVal)")

    Console.WriteLine("Test 1 - Object,    Name & Status - {0}, " + _
                      "{1}", passengerObj.Name, _
                      passengerObj.Status)
    Console.WriteLine("Test 2 - Structure, Name & Status - {0}, " + _
                      "{1}", passengerStr.Name, _
                      passengerStr.Status)
    Console.WriteLine()
```

Test 3 – ChangeName_Obj_ByRef() is called passing the PassengerClass object ByRef.

```
    ChangeName_Obj_ByRef(passengerObj, "Lucy (Changed ByRef)")
```

Test 4 – ChangeName_Struct_ByRef() is called passing the PassengerStruct structure ByRef.

```
      ChangeName_Struct_ByRef(passengerStr, "Kate (Changed ByRef)")
      Console.WriteLine("Test 3 - Object,    Name & Status - {0}, " + _
                   "{1}", passengerObj.Name, _
                   passengerObj.Status)
      Console.WriteLine("Test 4 - Structure, Name & Status - {0}, " + _
                   "{1}", passengerStr.Name, _
                   passengerStr.Status)
      Console.WriteLine()
   End Sub
End Module
```

After compiling and executing this, the following output should be produced at the command line:

```
C:\Class Design\ch03\>class_structure
Before - Object, Name & Status - Lucy,Economy
Before - Structure, Name & Status - Kate,Economy

Test 1 - Object,    Name & Status - Lucy (Changed ByVal),Economy
Test 2 - Structure, Name & Status - Kate,Economy

Test 3 - Object,    Name & Status - Lucy (Changed ByRef),Economy
Test 4 - Structure, Name & Status - Kate (Changed ByRef),Economy
```

❑   **Before** – The initial values of the passenger's name and travel status are assigned to both the Passenger object and Passenger structure.

❑   **Tests 1 and 2** – The respective name change methods are called on the object and structure entities, passing the new name ByVal. Displaying the new state of each, we can see that the Name property of the PassengerClass object has changed, but the Name property of the PassengerStruct structure has not.

The Passenger object's ChangeName_Obj_ByVal() method received the object parameter ByVal, but the parameter is a reference type so it actually receives the value (memory location) of the variable holding the reference to the object – a reference to a reference to the object. Changes made to the passenger name inside ChangeName_Obj_ByVal() are therefore visible to the client code.

The Passenger structure's ChangeName_Struct_ByVal() method simply receives its structure as a value and makes its own private member-by-member copy. Changes made to the passenger name inside the ChangeName_Struct_ByVal() method are not visible to the client code.

❏ **Tests 3 and 4** – The respective name change methods are called passing the new name ByRef. Displaying the new state, we can see that the Name property of both the PassengerClass object and the PassengerStruct structure has changed.

Both ChangeName_Obj_ByRef() and ChangeName_Struct_ByRef() receive their Passenger parameters ByRef; regardless of reference type or value type, the respective parameters are pointers to the object and structure. ChangeName_Obj_ByRef() and ChangeName_Struct_ByRef() have direct access to the data and this is reflected in the output results as both values have changed.

Reassigning Reference Types

Here we extend the previous example to demonstrate what happens when you reassign reference types by:

❏ Passing an object ByVal and reassigning the object

❏ Passing an object ByRef and reassigning the object

It is not necessary to demonstrate reassigning the Passenger structure as structures are value types and the rules for reassignment are straightforward.

We'll create two methods to upgrade our PassengerClass object to first class. They upgrade the travel status to FirstClass using object reassignment. Add the two additional methods to the StructureVsClass module (this code will be provided as object_reassign.vb):

```
' Upgrades the Object ByVal
Public Sub UpgradeCustomer_ByVal(ByVal details As PassengerClass)

    Dim newDetails As PassengerClass = New PassengerClass()
    newDetails.Name = details.Name
    newDetails.Status = TravelStatus.FirstClass

    ' Assign ByVal parameter to local object
    details = newDetails

End Sub

' Upgrades the Object ByRef
Public Sub UpgradeCustomer_ByRef(ByRef details As PassengerClass)

    Dim newDetails As PassengerClass = New PassengerClass()
    newDetails.Name = details.Name
    newDetails.Status = TravelStatus.FirstClass

    ' Assign ByRef parameter to local object
    details = newDetails

End Sub
```

Now we replace the Main() method with:

```
Sub Main()
    Dim passengerObj As PassengerClass = New PassengerClass()
    passengerObj.Name = "Lucy"
    passengerObj.Status = TravelStatus.Economy
    Console.WriteLine("Before - Object, Name & Status - {0}, {1}", _
                    passengerObj.Name, _
                    passengerObj.Status)
```

The two versions of the UpgradeCustomer method, UpgradeCustomer_ByRef() and UpgradeCustomer_ByVal() are called:

```
UpgradeCustomer_ByVal(passengerObj)

Console.WriteLine("After ByVal,    Name & Status - _ {0}, {1}", _
    passengerObj.Name, passengerObj.Status)

UpgradeCustomer_ByRef(passengerObj)

Console.WriteLine("After ByRef,    Name & Status - {0}, {1}", _
                passengerObj.Name, _
                passengerObj.Status)
    End Sub
```

If you run the updated example, you should see the following output:

```
C:\Class Design\ch03\> object_reassign
Before - Object, Name & Status - Lucy, Economy
After ByVal,    Name & Status - Lucy, Economy
After ByRef,    Name & Status - Lucy, FirstClass
```

ByVal – UpgradeCustomer_ByVal() receives the object parameter ByVal but does not change the value of the Status property in the client code. Reference type parameters passed ByVal cannot be permanently reassigned to different objects/different memory locations. The object reassignment in the code above is reversed when the method returns.

ByRef – UpgradeCustomer_ByRef() receives the object parameter ByRef and can change the value of the Status property in the client code. Reference types passed ByRef can be permanently reassigned to different object instances/memory locations. The object reassignment in the code above remains permanent after the method returns.

Passing Strings

Although Strings are reference types, they actually derive from the System.String class. This class overrides some of the typical behavior of a reference type, making strings behave in a similar manner to, but not the same as, a value type.

`String`s are immutable – that is, they cannot be changed from their initial value. Simple string operations that seem to update the value of a `String` actually return a different `String` object, rather than a modified version of the original. This is an important consideration as methods that extensively process string parameters can drain system resources. As they are reference types, changing a `String` actually results in two strings being created on the heap, the original, and the modified version. The string variable will reference the new `String` object.

> *Extensive string manipulation should be performed using the `StringBuilder` class found in `System.Text`, which limits the number of objects that have to be created to represent strings.*

Passing Arrays

Arrays are reference types in VB.NET and the rules detailed in *Passing Reference Types ByVal* and *Passing Reference Types ByRef* are observed. This even applies to arrays containing solely value types such as `Integers`. This is demonstrated in the example (`passing_arrays.vb`) below:

```
Imports System
Imports Microsoft.VisualBasic
Module PassingArrays

   Dim counter As Integer

   Public Sub AddOne(ByVal InputArray() As Integer)
      For counter = 0 To UBound(InputArray)
         InputArray(counter) = InputArray(counter) + 1
      Next
   End Sub
End Module
```

Here we declare a method `AddOne()`, which accepts an array of `Integers` passed `ByVal`. The method iterates through an array of `Integers` adding 1 to each member of the array.

```
Sub Main()
   Dim listOfNumbers() As Integer = {2, 4, 6, 8}
   For counter = 0 To UBound(listOfNumbers)
      Console.WriteLine("{0}", listOfNumbers(counter))
   Next
   Console.WriteLine()
   AddOne(listOfNumbers)
   For counter = 0 To UBound(listOfNumbers)
      Console.WriteLine("{0}", listOfNumbers(counter))
```

```
      Next
      Console.ReadLine()
   End Sub
End Module
```

The client code in the Main() sub declares an array (listOfNumbers) then prints out the contents of the array. Then we call the AddOne() method and print out the contents of the array again.

Running the program will produce the following output even though the array contains integer value types and the array was passed ByVal:

```
C:\Class Design\ch03\>passing_arrays
2
4
6
8

3
5
7
9
```

If you need a method to temporarily manipulate an array or change the contents of an array without the changes being visible to client code, use a separate array declaration within the method, then use the Clone() method (or the Copy() method, which may save some overhead) to copy the contents of the array passed as the parameter into the other. This will duplicate the array and prevent changes from being reflected in client code.

Creating a separate array is demonstrated in the following example (passing_arrays2.vb):

```
Module PassingArrays

   Dim counter As Integer

   Public Sub AddOne(ByVal InputArray() As Integer)
      For counter = 0 To UBound(InputArray)
         InputArray(counter) = InputArray(counter) + 1
      Next
   End Sub

   Public Sub AddTwo(ByVal InputArray() As Integer)

      Dim tempArray() As Integer
      tempArray = InputArray.Clone
      For counter = 0 To UBound(tempArray)
         tempArray(counter) = tempArray(counter) + 2
      Next
   End Sub
```

Then change the client code as follows:

```
Sub Main()
    Dim listOfNumbers() As Integer = {6, 8, 7, 6}
    Dim theObject As Class1 = New Class1()

    For counter = 0 To UBound(listOfNumbers)
        Console.WriteLine("{0}", listOfNumbers(counter))
    Next

    Console.WriteLine()
    theObject.AddOne(listOfNumbers)

    For counter = 0 To UBound(listOfNumbers)
        Console.WriteLine("{0}", listOfNumbers(counter))
    Next

    Console.WriteLine()
    theObject.AddTwo(listOfNumbers)
    For counter = 0 To UBound(listOfNumbers)
        Console.WriteLine("{0}", listOfNumbers(counter))
    Next

    Console.ReadLine()
End Sub
```

The additional output generated following the `AddTwo()` method remains the same as that generated following the `AddOne()` method. The `Clone()` method has created a duplicate array into `tempArray`, which is independent, and not a reference to `InputArray`.

Passing Parameter Arrays (ParamArray)

`ParamArrays` are a special type of parameter that allows client code to specify an arbitrary number of arguments. Each of the arguments passed to the method is separated with a comma in the normal way; however, each argument is collected into one special `ParamArray` parameter.

In normal circumstances, there is a one-to-one relationship between each argument and each parameter (with the exception of optional parameters); `ParamArrays` allow an unlimited number of arguments to be passed to a method and can contain values of any type.

`ParamArrays` also support being passed a regular array of values rather than a dynamic number of arguments. However, `ParamArrays` differ from standard arrays in that they can only be passed `ByVal`; the Visual Studio IDE actually inserts the `ByVal` keyword for you.

Because the number of parameters specified within a `ParamArray` will vary, `ParamArrays` must be declared as the last parameter in the method signature. This is to help the CLR distinguish between the `ParamArray` and any other parameters. For the same reasons, there also can only be one `ParamArray`, and the array must be one-dimensional.

Here's a simple code extract, `paramarray_sample.vb`, demonstrating a `ParamArray`:

```
Imports System
Module ParamArraySample

    Public Class Math
        Public Function AddSomeNumbers(ByVal ParamArray NumberList() _
                                As Integer) As Integer
            Dim Count As Integer = 0
            Dim LoopValue As Integer
            For LoopValue = 0 To NumberList.Length - 1
                Count = Count + NumberList(LoopValue)
            Next
            Return Count
        End Function
    End Class

    Sub Main()
        Dim Numbers() As Integer = {27, 8, 9, 1}
        Dim Math As New Math()

        Console.WriteLine("The total is - {0}", _
            Maths.AddSomeNumbers(27, 8, 9, 1))

        Console.WriteLine("The total is - {0}", _
            Maths.AddSomeNumbers(Numbers))
    End Sub

End Module
```

A method that takes a `ParamArray` as a parameter can be invoked in two ways. The first `Console.WriteLine` statement demonstrates the passing of a dynamic number of separate arguments. The second `Console.WriteLine` statement demonstrates passing a simple one-dimensional array. Both have the same effect when received within the method. The output is:

```
C:\Class Design\ch03> paramarray_sample
The total is - 45
The total is - 45
```

Passing Enumerated Values (Enums)

Enumerations provide an excellent way to pass arguments to methods where the argument has limited or fixed boundaries. Enumerations are used to clarify lists of data represented as numerical values such as validation tables and lookup tables. Enumerations can also be considered collections of constants.

This is an example of an Enum of vehicle types:

```
Public Enum VehicleType
   Saloon = 1
   Sports = 2
   Estate = 3
   Hatchback = 4
   MPV = 5
End Enum
```

Component business logic would declare its type as VehicleType rather than Integer in order to evaluate and compare data of type VehicleType.

When it is used as a method parameter, IntelliSense in Visual Studio .NET will display enumerated data as a list of all possible values. Enums make code clearer and more concise because they eliminate the need for 'magic numbers' (hard-coded values) and multiple constant values.

```
Public Function GetListOfVehicles(ByVal VType As VehicleType) _
                                                 As String()
   ' Do some stuff here to get a list of vehicles by type
End Function
```

Calling a method such as the one above makes full use of IntelliSense; the developer can select a valid entry from the VehicleType list, or pass a variable declared as the same type as VehicleType.

Method Overloading

It is a basic OO design principle that a method name should reflect what the method actually does. Often, several methods are required that do similar things, but accept different arguments. In previous versions of Visual Basic, convoluted method names such as PrintForm, PrintReport, and Print methods might be used to cope with this. In VB.NET, we can now call all of these methods Print, because that's what they do.

Overloading is used extensively within the base class libraries and can be identified in the IntelliSense information displayed when coding a method call in Visual Studio. The first version of the method is displayed with "1 of n", followed by the method signature. The spinner controls or the up/down arrow keys can be used to navigate to each version of the method.

Overloading is particularly useful in utility-type classes, where a consistent approach of two (or more) variations on *every* method could be implemented. For example, we may have a class to abstract a data access component. The class supports retrieving customers from the database using a GetCustomer() method. Two versions of this method could be coded to accept a customer ID as a Long value, and the customer ID embedded in an XML node.

The Overloads keyword allows us to specify several variations of the same method all with the same name, and differing only by the method signature. The *signature* (sometimes referred to as prototype) of a method is the combination of both its name and its argument list.

A method DisplayCalculatedCost(), which accepts two arguments, an Order object and a Double:

```
Private Sub DisplayCalculatedCost(ByVal objOrder As Order, _
                              ByVal OrderCost As Double)
End Sub
```

has the following signature:

```
DisplayCalculatedCost (Order, Double)
```

While the function CalculateCost():

```
Public Function CalculateCost(ByVal OrderCost As Double, _
                          ByVal DeliveryFee As Double) As Double
   Return OrderCost + DeliveryFee + HandlingCharge
End Function
```

has the following signature:

```
CalculateCost (Double, Double)
```

As you can see the return type is not considered part of the method's signature. This defines one of the rules of overloading; two or more methods cannot overload each other if they differ only by return types.

Consider the signature resulting from a ParamArray argument type. As discussed earlier, the compiler creates a signature reference for each possible outcome of the function. In the case of a ParamArray, this list is potentially infinite. This is demonstrated by:

```
Public Function CalculateCost(ByRef OrderCost As Double, _
                          ByVal ParamArray DeliveryFee() _
                          As Double) As Double
End Function
```

resulting in the signatures:

```
CalculateCost (ByRef Double)
CalculateCost (ByRef Double, Double())
CalculateCost (ByRef Double, Double)
CalculateCost (ByRef Double, Double, Double)
CalculateCost (ByRef Double, Double, Double, Double)
...and so on
```

When you want to overload a method, a number of rules apply:

- ❏ Each overload must differ by one (or more) of the following:
  - • Parameter count
  - • Parameter data types
  - • Parameter order
- ❏ Each method should use the same method name; otherwise, you are simply creating a totally new method.
- ❏ A Function can overload a Sub as long as they differ by parameter listing.
- ❏ You cannot overload a method with a property of the same name or vice versa.

You might be surprised to see that just changing the order of parameters overloads a method (argument_order.vb):

```
Imports System
Public Module ArgumentOrder

Public Function Add(ByVal Num1 As Integer, ByVal Num2 As Double) _
                                              As Double
    Return Num1 + Num2
End Function

Public Function Add(ByVal Num2 As Double, ByVal Num1 As Integer) _
                                              As Double
    Return Num1 - Num2
End Function

Sub Main()

    Dim Num3 As Double = Add(2, 4.2)
    Dim Num4 As Double = Add(4.2 , 2)

    Console.WriteLine("The first Add Method " & Num3)
    Console.WriteLine("The Second Add Method " & Num4)

End Sub
End Module
```

Here we have defined two methods called Add(), which both take two arguments, an Integer and a Double. The only difference is the order in which the arguments are passed.

```
Add(Integer, Double)
Add(Double, Integer)
```

The first method really does add the numbers but the second subtracts them:

```
C:\Class Design\ch03\> argument_order
The first Add Method: 6.2
The Second Add Method: -2.2
```

Simply by switching the order in which we pass parameters we can call different methods. While you would probably never implement a design quite this bad, it does demonstrate that overloading methods by parameter order alone is usually a bad idea. It will make your code hard to read and people calling your methods will get confused.

Here is an example of overloading a function in a more useful manner:

```
Public Overloads Function CalculateCost(ByVal OrderCost As Double) _
                               As Double
    Return MyClass.CalculateCost(OrderCost, 0, 0)
End Function

Public Overloads Function CalculateCost(ByVal OrderCost As Double _
                               ByVal DeliveryFee As Double) _
                               As Double
    Return MyClass.CalculateCost(OrderCost, DeliveryFee, 0)
End Function

Public Overloads Function CalculateCost(ByVal OrderCost As Double, _
                               ByVal DeliveryFee As Double _
                               ByVal HandlingFee As Double) _
                               As Double
    Return OrderCost + DeliveryFee + HandlingFee
End Function
```

These methods have the following signatures:

```
CalculateCost (Double)
CalculateCost (Double, Double)
CalculateCost (Double, Double, Double)
```

These methods calculate the cost of some goods with an optional delivery fee and handling charge. Notice the use of the MyClass keyword to identify that we are calling the local version of the overloaded method. All the methods call the final implementation passing the appropriate number of zeros.

It could be argued that if two or more overloaded methods accept different arguments and return different data they should be implemented as different methods and not multiple variations of the same method. There are advantages, however, in providing different versions of a method that do return the same data type. .NET allows distributed applications to exist on a global level and there is a genuine likelihood that software components will be consumed by many applications. Exposing different flavors of a method to suit the needs of different consumers can enhance the richness of a component.

Essentially, an overloaded method is simply a different method that happens to share a name with an existing method, and you should always carefully consider whether giving two methods different names will create greater clarity in your class interface than creating two methods that only differ by their parameter list. As a rule, overloaded methods should always share exactly the same semantic meaning. To use the add() example we showed earlier, we could have several versions of this method that all took different types of number as arguments, so long as they all returned the sum of the two (or more) values passed in. But if we were to create a method that concatenated strings, or combined non-numerical values, or, worse, did some mathematical operation on numbers other than adding them, we would be unwise to give it the same name.

Optional Parameters

Optional parameters allow arguments to be passed selectively and are a reasonable alternative to overloading methods. An example of the syntax for an Optional parameter is:

```
Public Function CalculateCost(ByVal OrderCost As Double, _
                    Optional ByVal DeliveryFee As Double = 0, _
                    Optional ByVal HandlingFee As Double = 0) _
                    As Double
End Function
```

A method with optional parameters is considered to have multiple signatures, one for each variation of calling the procedure. The creation of two optional types results in three separate signatures for the function:

```
CalculateCost (Double)
CalculateCost (Double, Double)
CalculateCost (Double, Double, Double)
```

Optional parameters now require a default value to be specified within the method declaration (unlike previous versions of Visual Basic). If an Optional parameter is used, all subsequent parameters also have to be Optional. This is because the CLR has to have a way to match input arguments against parameters. For example, if a method is declared with five input parameters and the third input parameter is declared as optional, then the fourth and fifth parameters must also be optional.

Because a default value must always be specified within the method declaration for optional parameters, the IsMissing function is no longer supported. A method with optional arguments will always receive values for all of its arguments, regardless of whether they are supplied by the caller, or by the defaults.

One thing to reiterate, if the first parameter is Optional, every parameter in the method signature must also be Optional. This could lead to situations where a method is invoked with no arguments. If it is not a valid call, error trapping should be included to deal with situations where all arguments are equal to their default value.

It is possible to implement overloading and optional arguments for the same method, although it is best avoided, as it can create unnecessary confusion. In general, explicit overloading should be preferred to optional parameters.

Shared Methods

Shared methods present a mechanism to make a method available whether or not an instance of a class has been created. In effect, unlike other methods, all functionality and data consumed, processed, and returned by a shared method is global among all instances of the class. Therefore, shared methods are used to perform actions that are not associated with any particular object instance, but *all* instances of a class. For example, they can be used to create global variables or constants and stateless functions for an application. For instance, many of the mathematical functions (Math.Sin(), Math.Cos(), etc.) found in the .NET Framework Class libraries are implemented as shared methods. Another use for shared methods is in instantiating classes that have private constructors; this is covered further in Chapter 4.

In the code extract below (shared_methods.vb) we create a Driver class, which contains a DriverName property and a shared method (SaveDrivers()) to save all Driver objects in the collection passed to the database.

```
Imports System
Imports System.Collections

Module SharedMethods

    Public Class Driver
        Private m_DriverName As String

        Public Shared Function SaveDrivers(ByRef DriverCollection _
                                    As ArrayList) As Integer
            ' Code to save drivers to database should go here
            Console.WriteLine("Saving drivers...")
            Dim objDriver As New Driver()
            For Each objDriver In DriverCollection
                Console.WriteLine("Saving Driver - {0}", objDriver.DriverName)
            Next
            Console.WriteLine()
        End Function

        Public Property DriverName()
            Get
                Return m_DriverName
            End Get
            Set(ByVal Value)
                m_DriverName = Value
            End Set
        End Property
    End Class
End Class
```

```
Sub Main()
  ' This is our holding collection
  Dim DriversCol As New ArrayList()

  ' These are the two separate instances of Driver objects
  Dim objDriver1 As New Driver()
  Dim objDriver2 As New Driver()

  ' Set their respective properties
  objDriver1.DriverName = "Kate"
  objDriver2.DriverName = "Lucy"

  ' Add the drivers to the holding collection
  DriversCol.Add(objDriver1)
  DriversCol.Add(objDriver2)

  ' Calling a shared method from the first Driver object
  objDriver1.SaveDrivers(DriversCol)

  ' Calling a method from the second Driver object
  objDriver2.SaveDrivers(DriversCol)
```

However, because the SaveDrivers() method does not strictly belong to any particular instance of the Driver object, the method should be called from the class itself:

```
  Driver.SaveDrivers(DriversCol)

  Console.ReadLine()
  End Sub
End Module
```

Our client code declares two instances of Driver class type and sets the respective DriverName properties. Then the SaveDrivers() method is invoked three times to demonstrate all possible calls to the shared method. Calling the SaveDrivers() method from any instance of a Driver object is technically possible. However, this leads to confusing code. The point of shared methods is that the method does not belong to any particular instance. We need not create instances to use a shared method and the SaveDrivers() method should be invoked from the Driver class itself.

Public shared methods are often a lot like global procedures. You can write a complete program in such methods, without ever instantiating an object – and in doing so, you'll be writing a completely procedural program. But in a fully object-oriented approach it is frequently important to the functioning of instances of a class for them to be able to communicate with one another. Private and protected shared methods provide an excellent means for objects to do just that. They can be called from within private shared and instance methods, and can store state in shared data members. We'll see some powerful uses for shared methods in object creation in Chapter 4.

Returning Values

VB.NET supports two mechanisms for methods (functions) to return a value. Using the `Return` statement is the preferred technique for returning a value back to the client code and ending a method.

```
Public Function Method1() As String
    Return "Some Data"
End Function
```

By default, you don't need to specify a type (in this case `String`) for the returned value but if you use the `Strict` compile option then you must. It is good practice, however, to avoid methods returning an unexpected type. VB.NET like earlier version of VB supports assigning a return value to a method name:

```
Public Function Method2() As String
    Method2 = "Some Data"
End Function
```

Most people find that the `Return` statement more intuitive and that it makes code more readable and easier to maintain. For instance, if you change the function name, you don't have to hunt through code looking for and reassigning the returns. In theory a `Function` must return a value (that is the only difference from a `Sub`), but the VB compiler will not even warn you if your function doesn't.

Best practices for returning values:

- ❏ Use the `Return` statement rather than other approaches; it makes code easier to read.

- ❏ Recall from the section on passing values `ByRef` that changes performed on data passed in this way are seen by the calling code. While it is perfectly possible to return values from a method in this way, it can make code very difficult to follow and is considered poor design practice.

- ❏ The `Return` statement should be used only once if possible within a method, as it is best to have only one point of termination; implementing methods with multiple exit points can complicate error tracing.

- ❏ It is generally considered good practice to place `Return` statements outside of any `Finally` blocks: if an exception is thrown in the `Try` block, the `Return` statement in the `Finally` block will still be called, potentially masking the exception. Additionally, you should note that if you return from within a `Try` block, any attached `Finally` block will be executed before the method returns.

Invoking Methods

Previous versions of Visual Basic were inconsistent on the use of parentheses when invoking subroutines and functions. Generally, subroutines did not require them (but allowed you to put them in) whereas functions did. VB.NET standardizes the use of parentheses by enforcing their use on all method invocations, subroutine or function, whether returning a value or not.

Design Considerations

To recap this chapter, we can close with some issues to bear in mind when designing methods:

❑ Be careful when consuming String types in methods. Strings derive from System.String, and therefore are reference types. Strings are immutable, so seemingly simple changes to strings will actually return different string objects. This can be expensive in terms of performance. If extensive string manipulation is required, use the StringBuilder class.

❑ If a method does not return a value, define the method as a Sub rather than a Function.

❑ Passing reference types ByRef allows you to reassign the object. The method parameter effectively becomes a double pointer, first, to the client-code variable reference, then to the object itself.

❑ Structures, as value types, are less expensive to use: they do not depend on the garbage collector to tidy up unused memory. Structures now support methods and properties unlike their user-defined type counterparts in previous versions of Visual Basic.

❑ Arrays are reference types but ParamArrays are passed in as value types. If you need to pass a single one-dimensional array as a method argument, and you do not want the method to change the contents of the array, you can pass the array as a ParamArray. Alternatively, use the Clone() method to duplicate the array; this will also prevent the client code form seeing any changes to the array.

❑ All parameters following an Optional parameter must also be Optional. If the first parameter is Optional then all parameters are Optional and you may want to include error-checking code to prevent arguments being invoked with their default values when no arguments are passed in.

❑ Using enumerated lists of values as method arguments aids code clarity and helps prevent bugs. Enumerated lists are displayed in IntelliSense allowing the programmer to accurately select an appropriate value. This will provide some degree of safety when evaluating method parameters within the method itself.

❏ Try to standardize the overloading of methods. Overloaded methods can be confusing when developing client code, as several implementations of the same method are available, each accepting a different set of arguments. This can be compounded when each of these methods also returns a different value type.

Consider that overloaded methods coded in this manner should have been coded as separate methods as they serve different purposes.

If overloaded methods have to be used, consider overloading all methods in the class uniformly, thus exposing the same functionality for each method.

❏ When invoking a shared method, refer to the class name rather than an object instance variable; shared methods belong to the class itself and may be used by other objects of a different class type, without having to instantiate an actual object.

❏ Use the `Return` statement to return control and the return value back to client code. The `Return` statement is more obvious that setting the value of the function equal to the return value. Minimize the number of `Return` statements; ideally, a method should have only one exit point.

Summary

Correctly named and specified methods make an application more understandable and easier to maintain. To use methods effectively it is crucial to understand what types need to be passed in to a method, what happens to them when they are, and what will actually be returned. If you follow the best practices laid out in this chapter you'll create better classes that are easier to use and debug, and shouldn't have any unwanted side effects.

Creating methods is simple in any object-oriented language, including VB.NET. However, as we'll see in Chapter 7, *Inheritance and Polymorphism,* we can elaborate on them to do some clever and unusual things.

In the next chapter, we'll go on to look at the lifecycle of an object, particularly at the special sort of method called the constructor.

VB.NET

Class Design

Handbook

4

4

Constructors and the Object Lifecycle

Before Visual Basic .NET, VB programmers were very limited in how they created objects. Objects could not be passed values at creation, or given an initial state. Visual Basic .NET opens the doors for new and much more useful object creation techniques.

Before we dig deep into the process of object creation, we will briefly examine how objects are created and managed from within the .NET Framework. .NET, or more specifically the CLR, is responsible for all the low-level memory allocation and de-allocation. As .NET developers, we are not required to free our objects from memory when we are finished with them. However, we will briefly discuss some methods with which we can have control of this.

Following this, we will cover the following different ways objects can be created:

- ❑ By defining different constructors, as well as the default – including the use of optional parameters, to control how and if an object can be instantiated

- ❑ By discussing the chaining of constructors – why and how this is done – right back to System.Object

- ❑ By using the ICloneable interface, rather than just using a copy constructor, to create exact copies of another object

- ❑ By making use of serialization and deserialization to save or transmit an object and its values so that it can be used in a different application

- ❑ By creating a *Singleton* object, which means that when different instantiations exist, they point to the same object

- ❑ By creating a *Factory* object, where a method can return a different kind of object depending on the parameters passed to it

The language improvements with Visual Basic.NET allow us to better utilize object-creational design patterns. As you can see in the last two points, we look at two of the more common design patterns used to create objects: the **Singleton** and **Factory** design patterns. First, however, we will discuss the management of an object's lifecycle.

Object Lifecycle Management

When an object is created in the .NET environment, by using the New keyword in Visual Basic, the CLR first must allocate memory on the managed heap. The managed heap is similar to a C run-time heap, except that the programmer is freed from explicitly having to remove objects. Once the memory is allocated, the object is given an initial state, and a pointer to the object (a reference) is returned to the code. Once the code has finished using the object, any resources used by the object are freed and the object is deleted, freeing the memory.

In many programming languages, object creation, management, and destruction are quite complex. In C++ for example, objects are created, maintained, and destroyed manually. While this gives the programmer ultimate control over the environment, it also proves to be a breeding ground for bugs. If a programmer references an object after it has been destroyed, or neglects to destroy objects entirely, subtle and unpredictable bugs creep into the code.

Correct object lifecycle management is difficult and often non-productive. An abundance of time is spent writing resource managers and reference counters, and on other techniques to assist with resource management. A mechanism to automate the resource management process would mean that these hours could be better spent working on meaningful functionality for the application. Fortunately, with .NET, we have such a mechanism built into the CLR dedicated to resource management. The piece of the CLR responsible for resource management is called the garbage collector (**GC**).

Garbage collection is by no means a new technology. If you came from a VB6 or Java background, you should be familiar with garbage collection. Garbage collection within the CLR implements a generational garbage-collection algorithm. When objects are created, they are put into an area of the managed heap called Generation 0. When Generation 0 is completely filled with object references, the GC executes and deletes any objects that are unreachable by the code. An object is unreachable if no other code has access to the object. All objects in Generation 0 that are still in use when the GC executes, are moved to another area of the managed heap called Generation 1. When Generation 0 is completely empty, the GC has finished with the collection and new objects are again created in it. The GC process repeats whenever Generation 0 becomes full. You can trigger the collection process at any time by calling System.GC.Collect() from within your code, but this isn't advisable as it is time-consuming, and the GC generally knows when best to start the collection process.

In all, the GC maintains three Generations. Generation 0 represents the place where all new objects are created and is very small. If Generation 0 fills up, the GC will remove all references that are no longer active, compact the active objects together, and move them all into the next available space in Generation 1, emptying Generation 0. If Generation 1 fills up, inactive objects are removed, the active objects compacted, and the entire contents moved into Generation 2. If all three generations in the heap are full, the GC will throw an `OutOfMemoryException` on a new attempt at object creation. Generation 0 is incredibly fast, and Generation 2 is quite slow, so that is why it performs this sequence so that the clearing of Generation 2 doesn't happen until necessary. This means that short-lived objects, which are created in Generation 0, and then dereferenced before the next GC cycle, never get moved to Generation 1, and are therefore very cheap to create and destroy. The objects that make it to Generation 2 are the longest lived objects, which generally means they are likely to be around for a long time, so it matters less that they are being moved to a slower area of the heap for cleanup.

While a detailed discussion of garbage collection is beyond the scope of a section on object creation, it is important to know the basics about the underlying services offered by .NET for object lifecycle management. The useful thing about the garbage collection and the managed environment the CLR offers is that they allow us to focus on writing productive code to solve the problem at hand and free us from worrying about the details of writing complex resource managers.

Whenever the programmer loses control of the environment, as is the case with garbage collection, the initial concern is how the performance will be affected. Many of these concerns turn out to be unfounded. When the C run-time heap needs to allocate memory for an object, it must run through a linked list of objects, looking for a block of memory large enough for the new object. Once that memory is located, a portion is used for the new object creation. With a managed heap, the runtime maintains a pointer to the next available memory address within Generation 0. Since there is no search time associated with finding a memory address as there is with the C runtime, storing an object in the managed heap is much faster than with the C runtime. Allocating the object in the managed heap is almost as fast as allocating memory from the stack!

This brief exploration into the world of the CLR and garbage collection does not do justice to these powerful pieces that lie at the heart of the .NET platform. Thankfully, as developers, we can rest assured knowing that these services are built well, and that we can focus on the application logic, and we don't have to worry about our own resource management. Now that we understand a little about what happens behind the scenes when working with .NET, let's turn our attention to the way we programmatically control the object lifecycle.

Object Instantiation

An object is created when the runtime encounters the newobj IL instruction. In Visual Basic .NET, this happens when we use the New keyword. Once the object is created, the fields (class variables) in the object are guaranteed to have a value of 0 or Null. If the field declarations are initialized with a value, the fields assume that value. Let's look at an example of simple field initialization. This example uses public fields, which aren't generally recommended, but they illustrate the point we're trying to make. The following code can be found in field_init.vb:

```
Public Class Programmer
    Public Name As String = "New Programmer"
    Public Address As String
    Public ID As Integer
End Class

Module FieldInit
    Sub Main()
        Dim ProgrammerInstance As Programmer
        ProgrammerInstance = New Programmer()
        Console.WriteLine("Name is: " & ProgrammerInstance.Name)
        Console.WriteLine("Address is: " & ProgrammerInstance.Address)
        Console.WriteLine("ID is: " & ProgrammerInstance.ID)
    End Sub
End Module
```

Compiling and running this code produces the following output:

```
Name is: New Programmer
Address is:
ID is: 0
```

When the ProgrammerInstance = New Programmer() line is reached, the uninitialized fields are given the default values of 0 or Null, depending on type.

Often, default initialization values do not provide enough flexibility to create an object's desired initial state. We need the ability to have more control over how our initial state is obtained, for example, if we wanted to retrieve data from a database, or have the user pass in data when creating the object. Constructors are type members that contain blocks of instructions that are executed when an object is created. When the programmer calls New, a constructor is called. Creating a constructor is comparable to creating a method; in VB.NET you use Sub New to define a constructor. The following example shows how constructors are declared with Sub New. This example declares three different constructors on the CreationExample class. The code for this example can be found in constructor_intro.vb:

```
Public Class CreationExample
   Private MyState As String

   Sub New()
      Console.WriteLine("New() fired")
      MyState = "DEFAULT"
   End Sub

   Sub New(Value As String)
      Console.WriteLine("New(String) fired")
      MyState = Value
   End Sub

   Sub New(Value As String, Value2 as String)
      Console.WriteLine("New(String, String) fired")
      MyState = Value & " " & Value2
   End Sub

   Public ReadOnly Property State As String
      Get
         Return MyState
      End Get
   End Property
End Class

Module ConstructorIntro
   Sub Main()
      Dim C1 As New CreationExample()
      Dim C2 As New CreationExample("Hello World")
      Dim C3 As New CreationExample("Hello", "World")
      Console.WriteLine(C1.State)
      Console.WriteLine(C2.State)
      Console.WriteLine(C3.State)
   End Sub
End Module
```

Compiling and running this code produces the following output:

```
New() fired
New(String) fired
New(String, String) fired
DEFAULT
Hello World
Hello World
```

This example illustrates constructor calling syntax (using New), and definition. We have a constructor that accepts no parameters. This constructor is called the **default constructor** and will be explained in more detail shortly. The other two constructors accept string parameter(s) that are used to give an initial state to the MyState variable. When we create an object with the New keyword, the constructor matching the parameters provided is executed (just as with methods). Before the constructor is entered, the CLR has allocated space for the object, and has set the private variable MyState to the String type's default value of Nothing, which is the same as Null in this case. Once the CLR is finished with the initialization procedure, the statements within the constructor are executed. Once the constructor is finished, the reference to the newly created object is returned to the code instantiating the object.

Constructors are extremely similar to methods on an object. Just like methods, they can be overloaded (although you should note that the Overloads keyword is not required). A constructor that accepts parameters is often referred to as a **_parameterized constructor_**, although there is nothing special about a parameterized constructor. There is no technical need for this special term; it simply provides a brief description for discussing any constructor that accepts parameters.

Constructors differ from methods in that they can only be called during object creation and are not inherited. Once the object is created, the constructor can no longer be called. When using inheritance, constructors are not inherited from a base class to a derived object. The derived object has access into the base class constructors during object creation, but cannot inherit them as other type members are inherited. A new set of constructors must be created within the derived class. We will look at how to implement constructors with inheritance later in this chapter.

Object Destruction

You can explicitly destroy an object (release references to it and allow the memory it was using to be written over), using a variety of methods. The first is the same as was used in VB6: set the variable containing the reference to the object to Nothing. This removes the reference to the object, and so as long as there is no other reference, the memory can be freed when the garbage collector next operates. But doing so doesn't inform the object itself that it is no longer referenced, and the GC will only run when it runs out of memory. In some programs, which don't create many objects, the GC never runs until the program exits. So, if an object has a large amount of memory allocated, and we want to free that memory up as soon as we know we don't need it any more, how can we do so? Well, because of the GC, two methods have been provided to clean up these objects in a standard way.

The first is the Finalize() method. This method is called by the GC before de-allocating the section of memory used by the object. In here, you can put as much cleanup code as necessary, closing database connections and file streams, and calling any other relevant methods. Then when all references to the object have been removed, all of these tasks will be completed, ensuring no unfortunate side effects when the memory is freed. This is a special method, designed only to be executed via the GC. Look at this sample Finalize() method:

```
Protected Overridable Overrides Sub Finalize()
   FS.Close()
   FS = Nothing
   MyBase.Finalize()
End Sub
```

If a file was opened and the reference to its stream was stored in FS, then this would ensure that the file is closed, the `FileStream` object reference is removed, and the base class's `Finalize()` method is called also, as that is likely to have some important cleanup operations too. This method is declared `Protected`, and it overrides the base class's implementation. Making it `Overridable`, means that a sub-class could define its own `Finalize()` method also. Now these various instructions will be executed before destruction of the object, which will ensure that any connections are closed before destroying a connection object, for instance, and that related references are also removed, allowing more objects to be cleaned up during the garbage-collection process.

The other method that can be used comes from the `IDisposable` interface. It is good design practice to close all connections and remove all references to an object when you have finished with it. Certain objects will consume many resources and if the GC isn't certain that the object is finished with them, they will continue to consume those resources until the GC is certain that they are no longer needed. So, a standard method for disposing of objects has been provided within the .NET Framework.

The `IDisposable` interface defines one method, `Dispose()`, with no return value, and you can implement this to finalize anything before the object is dereferenced. The normal execution of this method would be as follows:

```
MyObj.Dispose()
MyObj = Nothing
```

This would perform any final housekeeping on the object before removing its reference, and so (unless there are multiple references in use) allowing the GC to collect it. The fundamental difference between this and the `Finalize()` method is that `Finalize()` is called by the CLR on an object that still exists but the CLR believes will not be reached again in the code, whereas `Dispose()` should be called by your code to safely remove a reference to an object, so that the GC can remove it from the heap during collection.

Below is an example (`dispose.vb`) of how to implement the `Dispose()` method:

```
Class Point
   Implements IDisposable

   Private MX = 3
   Private MY = 4

   Sub New(X As Integer, Y As Integer)
      MX = X
      MY = Y
   End Sub
```

```vb
    Public Property X As Integer
      Get
        Return MX
      End Get

      Set(Value As Integer)
        MX = Value
      End Set
    End Property

    Public Property Y As Integer
      Get
        Return MY
      End Get

      Set(Value As Integer)
        MY = Value
      End Set
    End Property

    Public Overrides Function ToString() As String
      Return "(" & MX & "," & MY & ")"
    End Function

    Public Overridable Overloads Sub Dispose() _
          Implements IDisposable.Dispose
      Console.WriteLine("Point " & Me.ToString() & " disposed of")
    End Sub
End Class

Class PointPair
  Implements IDisposable

  Public First As Point
  Public Second As Point

  Public Sub New()
    First = New Point(1, 2)
    Second = New Point(3,4)
  End Sub

  Public Overrides Function ToString() As String
    Return "(" & First.ToString() & "," & Second.ToString() & ")"
  End Function

  Public Overridable Overloads Sub Dispose() _
                  Implements IDisposable.Dispose
    First.Dispose()
    Second.Dispose()
    First = Nothing
    Second = Nothing
  End Sub
```

```
Protected Overridable Overloads Sub Finalize()
    First.Dispose()
    Second.Dispose()
    First = Nothing
    Second = Nothing
  End Sub
End Class

Module DisposePoint
  Sub Main()
    Dim P As PointPair = New PointPair()
    Console.WriteLine("The object is: " & P.ToString())
    P.Dispose()
    P = Nothing
    Console.WriteLine("The object, after disposal is " & _
      P.ToString())
  End Sub
End Module
```

This example shows that the P object has been destroyed. The references to the two
Point objects are destroyed in this example. In this case, the references to the
Point objects would be destroyed without the use of the Dispose() method, but if
one of these objects had a connection open to a database, for instance, then the
object would not be destroyed so simply. By invoking the Dispose() method, and
having that method invoke it on all objects instantiated within the class, as long as
each Dispose() closes all connections, files, sockets, etc., we can be sure that all
references are safely removed.

We have implemented a Finalize() method here, although it isn't necessary. All
Finalize() does is ensure Dispose() is called on this object, even if the client
coder forgets to do so. This just helps to ensure that the objects will be cleaned up
properly. Other .NET languages, like C#, have mechanisms to call Dispose()
automatically when an object is finished with. By implementing this method, you can
ensure better interoperability with other .NET applications.

Kinds of Constructor

So, having described the role constructors play in the object lifecycle, it's time for us
to look at how we can use different kinds of constructor to control how objects
belonging to our classes are created.

Default Constructor

The default constructor is the term used to define a parameter-less constructor. The
default constructor is a little different from a parameterized constructor because of
how the compiler handles it.

If no constructors are created on an object, the compiler will automatically insert a default constructor into the resulting IL code. If the compiler did not do this, the object could not be created using the New keyword. In the following example (default_contructor.vb), the CreationExample object appears constructor-less; however, a look at the IL shows the presence of a default constructor:

```
Public Class CreationExample
   Private MyState as String = "DEFAULT"

   Public Property State As String
      Get
         Return MyState
      End Get

      Set(Value As String)
         MyState = Value
      End Set
   End Property
End Class

Module DefaultConstructor
   Sub Main()
      Dim C As New CreationExample()
      Console.WriteLine(C.State)
   End Sub
End Module
```

Compiling and running this code produces the following output:

```
DEFAULT
```

If you look at the IL created by the compiler for default_constructor.exe, you will notice a special method on the object called .ctor. .ctor is the CLR internal keyword for designating a constructor. Here, the default constructor has been created automatically by the compiler:

```
CreationExample::.ctor : void()                                          _|□|x|
.method public specialname rtspecialname
        instance void  .ctor() cil managed
{
  // Code size       20 (0x14)
  .maxstack  8
  IL_0000:  ldarg.0
  IL_0001:  call       instance void [mscorlib]System.Object::.ctor()
  IL_0006:  nop
  IL_0007:  ldarg.0
  IL_0008:  ldstr      "DEFAULT"
  IL_000d:  stfld      string CreationExample::MyState
  IL_0012:  nop
  IL_0013:  ret
} // end of method CreationExample::.ctor
```

The compiler will only insert a default constructor if no other constructors exist on the object. This is an important point to remember, especially when adding a constructor. For example, if you add a parameterized constructor to `CreationExample`, any code relying on the default constructor will break because the compiler will not insert a default constructor. In order to prevent code relying on the default constructor from breaking, we must insert a default constructor manually. You may want to explicitly provide an empty default constructor on the object.

The default constructor has special meaning when dealing with interoperability between COM and .NET. If a COM client creates an instance of a .NET object, the .NET object must have a default constructor or COM object creation will fail. A default constructor is one example of requirements COM places on .NET objects. For a more detailed description of COM requirements for .NET objects, refer to *Professional Visual Basic Interoperability*, Wrox Press, ISBN 1-861005-65-2.

If you look closely at the IL in this example, you will notice that the `MyState` variable is initialized in the constructor. Within the beginning of each constructor declared on a class, the class's fields are initialized to their default values. If we included another constructor on the class, it would also initialize the field variables before entering the logic within the constructor. If you have many instance fields, the resulting IL becomes bloated by including the same field initialization logic in every constructor. Instead of providing initialization values on the field declarations, you should consider creating a single constructor that performs the initialization; and have all other constructors call that common constructor. We will illustrate the process of calling constructors within other constructors, also known as *constructor chaining*, in a later section.

Constructors and Optional Parameters

As shown at the start of this section, constructors can be overloaded like methods. Like methods, constructors also support optional parameters. Optional parameters in .NET are similar to their VB6 counterparts, but are not as useful or portable as overloading. Optional parameters in .NET require default values, which is a change from VB6. VB6's `IsMissing()` function is not supported in .NET because each parameter is required to have a value when the function begins. If the caller does not pass in an optional parameter, the compiler will assign the default. Let's look at a constructor defined with two optional parameters (`optional_point.vb`):

```
Public Class Point
   Private MX as Integer
   Private MY as Integer

   Public Sub New(Optional X As Integer = 0, _
               Optional Y As Integer = 0)
     MX = X
     MY = Y
   End Sub
```

```
        Public Overrides Function ToString() As String
            Return "(" & MX & "," & MY & ")"
        End Function
    End Class

    Module OptionalPoint
        Sub Main
            Dim P1 As New Point()
            Console.WriteLine(P1.ToString())

            Dim P2 As New Point(1, 1)
            Console.WriteLine(P2.ToString())

            Dim P3 As New Point(, 1)
            Console.WriteLine(P3.ToString())

            Dim P4 As New Point(9, )
            Console.WriteLine(P4.ToString())
        End Sub
    End Module
```

Here the `Point` constructor is defined with two optional parameters. The default value of each parameter is 0. The compiler will force you to define default values. Compiling and running this code produces the following output:

```
(0,0)
(1,1)
(0,1)
(9,0)
```

Notice the last two constructor invocations of the `Point` objects:

```
Dim P3 As New Point(, 1)
Dim P4 As New Point(9, )
```

While these are possible, they are very confusing and could quite easily lead to bugs. If you are going to use optional parameters, avoid this syntax and explicitly enter the default value.

Overloading Constructors

Optional parameters were provided for flexibility in VB6 as a shortcut for overloading. It was possible to have optional parameters so you could call the same method with different parameter lists. Since the .NET environment and VB.NET support overloading, this is now the preferred technique to employ. Optional parameters are not supported by all other .NET-compatible languages. To see what the compiler does with optional parameters, let's take the above `Point` class and compile it into a DLL. Once we have the DLL created with optional parameters, we will try to instantiate a `Point` object from a C# application, trying to take advantage of the optional parameters. The following snippet can be found in `point.vb`. It makes use of the `Namespace` keyword, which will be covered in detail in Chapter 8:

116

```
Namespace PointClass
   Public Class Point
      Private MX as Integer
      Private MY as Integer

      Public Sub New(Optional X As Integer = 0, _
                Optional Y As Integer = 0)
         MX = X
         MY = Y
      End Sub

      Public Overrides Function ToString() As String
         Return "(" & MX & "," & MY & ")"
      End Function
   End Class
End Namespace
```

Compile this into a DLL with the following command line, if you are using vbc.exe:

```
> vbc /t:library point.vb
```

Now that the point class DLL is created, create the following test program in C# that will attempt to use the default parameters. The code shown below can be found in point.cs:

```
using PointClass;

class TestPoint
{
   public static void Main()
   {
      Point P1 = new Point(4, 4);
      Console.WriteLine(P1.ToString());
      Point P2 = new Point();
      Console.WriteLine(P2.ToString());
   }
}
```

Save the file in the same directory as point.dll. Now compile the C# application, referencing the point.dll assembly, which with the command-line Framework SDK tools, occurs by use of the /r switch on the csc compiler.

Notice that the second Point object created is attempting to use the overload. Because C# does not recognize optional parameters, the compiler will produce the following error message:

```
point.cs(10,16): error CS1501: No overload for method 'Point' takes
'0' arguments
point.dll: (Location of symbol related to previous error)}
```

Even though we cannot use optional parameters, the Point class is not useless to the C# application. When the IL is created for the Point class, a signature is declared with two Int32 optional parameters. Because C# does not recognize the optional parameters, it treats the method signature as a normal signature requiring two parameters. Removing the lines for object P2 would allow us to create an instance of the Point class successfully.

Further to this, if you look at the IL for the constructor of this class, you see the following:

```
Point::.ctor : void(int32,int32)                                        _□×
.method public specialname rtspecialname
        instance void  .ctor([opt] int32 'MX',
                             [opt] int32 'MY') cil managed
{
  .param [1] = int32(0x00000000)
  .param [2] = int32(0x00000000)
  // Code size       24 (0x18)
  .maxstack  8
  IL_0000:  nop
  IL_0001:  ldarg.0
  IL_0002:  call       instance void ['mscorlib']'System'.'Object'::.ctor()
  IL_0007:  nop
  IL_0008:  ldarg.0
  IL_0009:  ldarg.1
  IL_000a:  stfld      int32 'PointClass'.'Point'::'X'
  IL_000f:  ldarg.0
  IL_0010:  ldarg.2
  IL_0011:  stfld      int32 'PointClass'.'Point'::'Y'
  IL_0016:  nop
  IL_0017:  ret
} // end of method 'Point'::.ctor
```

The two parameters contain [opt] attributes, which means that another .NET language that supports optional parameters (Perl.NET, possibly) would understand that these are optional, and an application that uses this DLL could successfully compile against it if it omitted any of the constructor's parameters during object creation.

A better and recommended solution would have been to use overloading and declare multiple constructors that accept different numbers and types of parameters. If we declared a constructor accepting a single Integer parameter, our original C# application (and an application written in any other .NET language that uses the DLL) would compile. Overloading is not always desirable for every problem, however. For instance, to repeat the same functionality in the above example, in addition to the default constructor, you would have to specify an overload for the case of either of the X, or Y parameters being dropped, and a way of specifying which one is missing. Apart from having three constructors as opposed to one, it means you have to pass another parameter on the third, perhaps an enumeration, to specify which parameter is missing.

Chaining Constructors

Instance constructors within a class have the ability to invoke other constructors in the same class. Often, many constructors provide similar functionality. Instead of rewriting the same functionality in every constructor overload, invoking a common constructor allows us to reuse logic found in another constructor. For example, let's assume that New() in SpecificLocation performs detailed initialization instructions. Since our other constructor instances would also benefit from that code, we would need to invoke it from other constructor instances.

The call to another constructor must be the first line of code found in a constructor. In Visual Basic, we use Me.New() to refer to the default constructor; however, any constructor can be called by providing the correct arguments for the constructor we wish to invoke. The first line in New(String, String) must invoke the Me.New() constructor before processing the logic found in its body. The New() constructor executes and returns execution to the calling constructor. The following example illustrates this process:

```
Public Class SpecificLocation
   Private MAddress as String = "Default"
   Private MCity As String = "Default"

   Sub New()
      MyBase.New()
      Console.WriteLine("SpecificLocation Created")
   End Sub

   Sub New(Address as String, City As String)
      Me.New()

      MAddress = Address
      MCity = City
      Console.WriteLine("SpecificLocation.Address and Set")
   End Sub

   Public Property Address as String
      Get
         Return MAddress
      End Get

      Set(Value As String)
         MAddress = Value
      End Set
   End Property

   Public Property City as String
      Get
         Return City
      End Get
```

```
        Set(Value As String
            MCity = Value
        End Set
    End Property
End Class

Module ConstructorChain
    Sub Main()
        Dim SL As New SpecificLocation("123 First Street", "Somewhere")
    End Sub
End Module
```

Compiling and running this code produces the following output:

```
SpecificLocation Created
SpecificLocation.Address and Set
```

Here, New(String, String) uses the services of New() by calling Me.New().
Calling another instance of a constructor must be the first instruction found in the
constructor body. Compilation will fail if the constructor invocation instruction is not
the first call found. The Visual Studio.NET IDE and the compiler will give the
following error message if we try to call another constructor in any position other
than the first statement:

"Constructor call is only valid in the first statement in an instance constructor"

Constructors and Inheritance

Whenever we create an object within the .NET platform, it inherits from a base class.
We can specifically derive from a base class or we can default to the .NET base class
of System.Object. Either way, our class will have a base class. Since an instance of
a type that inherits from a particular base type can be treated as if it were an instance
of the base type, we need to ensure that any initialization the base type needs to
undergo is performed, so that any inherited functionality can work. Before our object
is created, the instance state pertaining to the base class must be created. Before our
base class is created, its base class must be created. This process continues until
System.Object is created. Because the base class must be created before our
object, we must first call into our base class constructor. Within Visual Basic, the
keyword MyBase is used to refer to the class's immediate base class, as shown in the
previous code.

The first line of our constructor is important because it must always call another
constructor. In the constructor chaining example, we called Me.New() to get the
default constructor. Within the IL of the default constructor, having System.Object
as the base class, we notice the first instruction is to call into
System.Object::.ctor. This is the call into the base class constructor. In this
case, the object inherited from System.Object.

120

Since we did not create the code to call the base's constructor, why is it present in the IL? Just as the compiler will insert a default constructor for a class, it will also insert a call to MyBase.New() to call the default base class constructor if another constructor invocation is not present.

We can manually call MyBase.New() by including this as the first line within the constructor. If we omit the call to MyBase.New(), the compiler will always generate the call to the base class's default constructor. With MyBase.New(), we can call into any constructor on the base class – not only the default constructor. If the base class has a constructor accepting a string parameter, we can call into the base class constructor by issuing the call to MyBase.New("someString").

By default, the compiler will only insert calls to the default base class constructor MyBase.New(). You must explicitly call another overloaded version to call a parameterized constructor instance. If the base class does not implement a default constructor, you must explicitly call another constructor the base class provides.

The following example (constructor_inheriting.vb) shows the class with the explicit calls into MyBase.New(). If these lines were commented out, the resulting IL would be the same, since the compiler would generate these calls automatically:

```vb
Public Class Location
   Private MyState as String = "DEFAULT"

   Sub New()
     MyBase.New()
     Console.WriteLine("Location Created")
   End Sub

   Public Property State As String
     Get
        Return MyState
     End Get

     Set(Value As String)
        MyState = Value
     End Set
   End Property
End Class

Public Class SpecificLocation
   Inherits Location

   Private MyAddress as String

   Sub New()
     MyBase.New()
     Console.WriteLine("SpecificLocation Created")
   End Sub
```

```
    Public Property Address as String
       Get
          Return MyAddress
       End Get

       Set(Value As String)
          MyAddress = Value
       End Set
    End Property
  End Class

  Module ConstructorCalling
    Sub Main()
       Dim SL As New SpecificLocation()
       SL.State = "CANADA"
       SL.Address = "123 Winnipeg Way"
    End Sub
  End Module
```

Compiling and running this code produces the following output:

```
Location Created
SpecificLocation Created
```

This example illustrates the instantiation hierarchy. Instances of the base type must be created before the derived type. In this example, creating a new SpecificLocation object must first create an instance of its base class, the Location object. Before the Location object is created, it must first create an instance of its base class, System.Object. Once System.Object has been created, Location is created followed by our requested type SpecificLocation.

Because the base class must be created before the derived type, the call to MyBase.New() must be the first call within the constructor. If MyBase.New() is omitted, the compiler will insert the call to ensure proper base class creation takes place.

To show how MyBase.New() works within a class hierarchy, let's look at the IL instructions for the Location and the SpecificLocation constructors, respectively:

```
Location::.ctor : void()                                              _ □ X
.method public specialname rtspecialname
         instance void  .ctor() cil managed
{
  // Code size          32 (0x20)
  .maxstack  8
  IL_0000:  nop
  IL_0001:  ldarg.0
  IL_0002:  call          instance void [mscorlib]System.Object::.ctor()
  IL_0007:  nop
  IL_0008:  ldarg.0
  IL_0009:  ldstr         "DEFAULT"
  IL_000e:  stfld         string Location::MyState
  IL_0013:  ldstr         "Location Created"
  IL_0018:  call          void [mscorlib]System.Console::WriteLine(string)
  IL_001d:  nop
  IL_001e:  nop
  IL_001f:  ret
} // end of method Location::.ctor
```

```
SpecificLocation::.ctor : void()                                      _ □ X
.method public specialname rtspecialname
         instance void  .ctor() cil managed
{
  // Code size          21 (0x15)
  .maxstack  8
  IL_0000:  nop
  IL_0001:  ldarg.0
  IL_0002:  call          instance void Location::.ctor()
  IL_0007:  nop
  IL_0008:  ldstr         "SpecificLocation Created"
  IL_000d:  call          void [mscorlib]System.Console::WriteLine(string)
  IL_0012:  nop
  IL_0013:  nop
  IL_0014:  ret
} // end of method SpecificLocation::.ctor
```

Notice the call to System.Object::.ctor() in Location. This line represents the MyBase.New() call translated into IL to Location's immediate base class: System.Object.

```
IL_0002:  call    instance void [mscorlib]System.Object::.ctor()
```

Likewise, the call in MyBase.New() from the SpecificLocation class will invoke the constructor on its base object, Location. The instruction IL_0002 is responsible for the MyBase.New() call here as well. The SpecificLocation's immediate base class is Location, so MyBase.New() will call the constructor on the Location object:

```
IL_0001:  call        instance void Location::.ctor()
```

123

Protected Constructors and MustInherit Classes

If you define a class as `MustInherit`, then there seems little point in giving it a public constructor, since a `MustInherit` class cannot, in itself, be instantiated. However, it will have to be constructed if we instantiate a class that inherits from it, so it makes sense to provide a `Protected` constructor. Using constructor chaining, we can call into a `Protected` constructor, that could define some characteristics that classes that inherit from this class could specify through the constructor. The simplest way to show this in use is to include an example. Look at the following code, located in `mustinherit_constructor.vb`:

```
Public MustInherit Class Stock
   Private MPrice As Single
   Private MLocation As String = "Unshelved"
   Private MDummy As Boolean = False
   Private MType As String = "Not Defined"

   Public ReadOnly Property Dummy As Boolean
     Get
        Return MDummy
     End Get
   End Property

   Public Property Price As Single
     Get
        Return MPrice
     End Get

     Set(Value As Single)
        If Value > 0 Then MPrice = Value
     End Set
   End Property

   Public Property Location As String
     Get
        Return MLocation
     End Get

     Set(Value As String)
        MLocation = Value
     End Set
   End Property

   Public ReadOnly Property Type As String
     Get
        Return MType
     End Get
   End Property
```

```
        Protected Sub New(Type As String, _
                          Optional Dummy As Boolean = False)
            If Dummy Then MDummy = True
            MType = Type
        End Sub
End Class
```

Here we have defined a class that cannot be instantiated and can only be inherited from. In here, we have defined a protected constructor, which will set two private fields specifying whether the object in question actually exists, or is a dummy used for testing purposes (Dummy), and the type of the object (Type), which could be CD, Cassette, VHS, etc.

```
Class CDType
    Inherits Stock

    Private MTitle = "Test Title"

    Public Sub New()
        MyBase.New("CD")
    End Sub

    Public Sub New(Dummy As Boolean)
        MyBase.New("CD", Dummy)
    End Sub

    Public Sub New(Title As String, Optional Dummy As Boolean = False)
        Me.New(Dummy)
        MTitle = Title
    End Sub

    Public ReadOnly Property Title As String
        Get
            Return MTitle
        End Get
    End Property
End Class
```

The above class inherits from Stock, and passes data to the protected constructor of the Stock class through its own overloaded constructors.

```
Module CreateCDs
    Sub Main()
        Dim C1 = New CDType("Show of Hands - Live")
        Dim C2 = New CDType("Hourglass", True)

        C1.Price = 9.99
        C2.Price = 12.99

        Console.WriteLine("Please Enter the shelving location of " & _
            C1.Title & ":"
```

```
        C1.Location = Console.ReadLine()
        Console.WriteLine("Please Enter the shelving location of " & _
          C2.Title & ":"
        C2.Location = Console.ReadLine()

        Console.WriteLine(C1.Title & " is shelved at " & C1.Location & _
          " and costs " & C1.Price & ".")
        Console.WriteLine(C2.Title & " is shelved at " & C2.Location & _
          " and costs " & C2.Price & ".")
      End Sub
    End Module
```

Finally, we implement the class here. If you tried to instantiate an instance of the Stock class, it would fail, but we can inherit all of its members for the CDType class. If you look in the MSIL for the Stock class, you will find that there is no default constructor, and that the parameterized constructor is declared as a family constructor, which in VB.NET we call Protected.

Private Constructors

Not all classes should be instantiated; the System.Console class, for example. It simply provides functionality for interacting with the console standard input, output, and error streams. All methods on the System.Console class are shared, which provides the necessary functionality without needing an instance of the class. A compiler error will be thrown if you try to create a new instance of System.Console.

The System.Console class is a group of functions with a common purpose of interacting with the I/O streams. Instead of creating an instance of the System.Console class, we call the functions directly. The functions on System.Console are declared as Shared, meaning they are available without instantiating a reference to the class. In your applications, if you have a set of functions you want to call directly, you could implement them as shared members on a class and prevent the class from being instantiated. In the example you will see shortly, we have a set of string formatting functions we implement together in a class, and instantiation of the class is prevented.

How can we prevent instantiation of our custom classes? The answer lies in combining what we know about constructors and accessibility levels. To this point, all the constructors have been declared (implicitly or explicitly) as public. If we give a constructor private accessibility, the class cannot be instantiated. Private constructors are simply declared, like other VB.NET constructs, with the Private keyword, thus making the constructor inaccessible outside the current class and so preventing instantiation. If a private constructor is created, the compiler will not insert a default constructor.

In the following example, the CustomPrinter class contains functionality that does not require instantiation. We declare these members as Public Shared. In general, if a function does not require instance state to perform its functionality, it becomes a candidate to be a shared method. The code below is taken from private_constructor.vb:

```
Public Class CustomPrinter
  Private Sub New()
  End Sub

  Public Shared Function QuoteIt(ToQuote as String, _
                              Author As String) As String
    Return """" & ToQuote & """"  - " & Author
  End Function

  Public Shared Function UpperLower(ToChange as String) As String
    Dim CharacterPointer as Integer
    Dim SB as New Text.StringBuilder(ToChange)

    For CharacterPointer = 0 To ToChange.Length - 1
      If CharacterPointer Mod 2 = 0 Then
        SB.Chars(CharacterPointer) = SB.Chars( _
          CharacterPointer).ToUpper(SB.Chars(CharacterPointer))
      Else
        SB.Chars(CharacterPointer) = SB.Chars( _
          CharacterPointer).ToLower(SB.Chars(CharacterPointer))
      End If
    Next

    Return SB.ToString()
  End Function
End Class

Module PrivateConstructor
  Sub Main
    Console.WriteLine(CustomPrinter.QuoteIt( _
      "640K ought to be enough for anybody.", "Bill Gates"))
    Console.WriteLine(CustomPrinter.UpperLower("Wrox Press"))
  End Sub
End Module
```

Compiling and running this code produces the following output:

```
"640K ought to be enough for anybody." - Bill Gates
WrOx pReSs
```

The CustomPrinter class prevents instantiation by providing a private constructor. To provide its functionality, all its members must be shared. You could create non-shared type members on the CustomPrinter class, but since the object cannot be instantiated, the methods could not be called outside the class.

If you tried to create an instance of `CustomPrinter`, you would get a detailed compiler error stating the constructor that you tried to call is inaccessible. Here is the message that would be generated by the compiler:

```
c:\custom\customprinter.vb(7) : error BC30390:
'CustomPrinter.Private Sub New()' is not accessible in this context
because it is 'Private'.

    Dim i as New CustomPrinter()
    ~
```

Deciding when to prevent instantiation depends on the software you are designing. Helper classes, or classes containing functions not requiring instance state, such as mathematical functions, are candidates for preventing instantiation. In our example, there would be no reason to instantiate the `CustomPrinter` type, because the instance would not provide any benefit over using the shared methods. The constructor is present in the IL; however, it is defined as private, indicating that it cannot be instantiated.

It's also not possible to create an instantiable class that inherits from a class that only provides a private default constructor, since it isn't possible for its constructors to be chained.

It's worth noting that VB.NET allows us to easily create .NET classes that can't be instantiated, and only contain shared logic, in the form of modules.

Private constructors do have one other important use, in that they can be used to limit the right to create instances of the class to code contained within the class itself. For example, here's a class that allows us to build a tree of connected nodes:

```
Imports System
Imports System.Collections
Imports System.Text

Public Class Node

  Private Shared rootNode As Node

  Shared Sub New()
    rootNode = New Node(Nothing, "Root")
  End Sub

  Private parentNode As Node
  Private nodeName As String
  Private children As IList

  Private Sub New(parent As Node, name As String)
    Me.parentNode = parent
    Me.nodeName = name
    Me.children = New ArrayList()
```

```
    If Not (parentNode Is Nothing) Then parentNode.AddChild(Me)
End Sub

Public Shared ReadOnly Property Root As Node
  Get
    Return rootNode
  End Get
End Property

Public ReadOnly Property Parent As Node
  Get
    Return parentNode
  End Get
End Property

Public ReadOnly Property Name As String
  Get
    Return nodeName
  End Get
End Property

Public Function CreateChild(name As String) As Node
  Return New Node(Me, name)
End Function

Private Function AddChild(child As Node)
  children.Add(child)
End Function

Public Default ReadOnly Property Child(i As Integer) As Node
  Get
    Return children(i)
  End Get
End Property

Public ReadOnly Property CountOfChildren As Integer
  Get
    Return children.Count
  End Get
End Property

Public Overrides Function ToString() As String
  Dim sb As New StringBuilder()
  sb.Append("<")
  sb.Append(nodeName)
  sb.Append(">")
  Dim c As Node
  For Each c In children
    sb.Append(c.toString())
  Next
  sb.Append("</")
  sb.Append(nodeName)
  sb.Append(">")
```

```
        Return sb.ToString()
      End Function

   End Class

   Public Module MainModule
      Public Sub Main()
         Node.Root.CreateChild("Child1")
         Node.Root.CreateChild("Child2")
         Node.Root(1).CreateChild("Child3")

         Console.WriteLine(Node.Root)
      End Sub
   End Module
```

A Node instance has a set of children, and a parent. The only way to create a node is by calling the private constructor, Private Sub New(parent As Node, name As String). This constructor can only be called by code inside the class, and it is in fact only called in two places: first, in the shared constructor, which creates a node called Root; and second, in the CreateChild() function, which is used to create a node whose parent is the node on which it is called. This constrains the ways the class can be instantiated, and restricts users to creating nodes that belong to a tree of children whose ultimate parent is the root node. It isn't possible to create a detached node using this class.

We'll look at two common patterns of restricted object creation – Singleton and Factory – later on in the chapter.

Shared Constructors

The constructors we have discussed thus far have all been instance constructors. Instance constructors are executed when new object instances are created. In the case of private constructors, they are inaccessible instance constructors.

Some objects define shared type members, such as fields, which can be used without any explicit object instance being instantiated. Shared type members are created exactly once, regardless of how many (if any) instances of the class are created. In order to create shared fields, shared constructors are used.

Shared constructors are similar to instance constructors in that they are used to initialize state, but that is where similarities between shared and instance constructors end. Unlike instance constructors, shared constructors cannot be overloaded, cannot have parameters, must have public access, and are not allowed to call other constructors. Shared constructors are called by the CLR – we cannot call shared constructors from our code. The exact time the shared constructor executes is not fixed; however, the CLR guarantees shared members are initialized, and shared constructors are executed, before any shared members on the type are referenced, or any instances of the type are created. The following example (shared_constructor.vb) illustrates the use of a shared constructor.

```
Public Class Employee
   Private Shared EmpID as Integer = 10

   Public Shared ReadOnly Property CurrentID as Integer
      Get
         Return EmpID
      End Get
   End Property

   Public Shared Function GetEmployeeID() as Integer
      EmpID += 1
      Return EmpID
   End Function

   Shared Sub New()
      Console.WriteLine("Before init: " & EmpID)
      EmpID = 100
      Console.WriteLine("After init: " & EmpID)
   End Sub
End Class

Module SharedConstructor
   Sub Main()
      Dim CountValue As Integer
      For CountValue = 1 to 10
         Console.WriteLine(Employee.GetEmployeeID())
      Next
   End Sub
End Module
```

Compiling and running this code produces the following output:

```
Before init: 10
After init: 100
101
102
103
104
105
106
107
108
109
110
```

We learn a number of details about shared initialization from this example. First, we learn that like instance variables being initialized before their class constructor is executed, shared variables are initialized before the shared constructor is executed. The **Before init: 10** line shows EmpID was initialized. Second, we learn that that the CLR is true to its word: shared constructors are executed sometime prior to referencing shared members. Again, we cannot explicitly call the shared constructor, but the CLR guarantees its execution.

When would we use shared constructors? If we have shared variables that we want to initialize with an initial state (say from a database), we would put the initialization routines in the shared constructor.

Copy Constructors and Object Cloning

At times, we would like the ability to create a new object with exactly the same values as another instance. One possible way to copy an object would be to create a constructor that accepts another instance of the class. We would then copy the state from the passed instance into our current instance, effectively cloning the object passed in. The term for such a constructor is called a ***copy constructor***. Here is an example of a copy constructor, `copy_constructor.vb`:

```
Public Class Point
  Private MX as Integer
  Private MY as Integer

  Sub New(X As Integer, Y As Integer)
    MX = X
    MY = Y
  End Sub

  Sub New(ToCopy As Point)
    MX = ToCopy.X
    MY = ToCopy.Y
  End Sub

  Public ReadOnly Property X as Integer
    Get
       Return MX
    End Get
  End Property

  Public ReadOnly Property Y as Integer
    Get
       Return MY
    End Get
  End Property

  Public Overloads Function ToString() As String
    Return "(" & MX & "," & MY & ")"
  End Function
End Class

Module CopyConstructor
  Sub Main()
    Dim P1 as New Point(5, 5)
    Dim P2 as New Point(P1)
```

```
      Console.WriteLine("First Object: " & P1.ToString())
      Console.WriteLine("Cloned Object: " & P2.ToString())
   End Sub
End Module
```

Compiling and running this code produces the following output:

```
First Object: (5,5)
Cloned Object: (5,5)
```

The copy constructor in the `Point` class takes an instance of the `Point` type and populates the state with the state from the instance passed in.

The ICloneable Interface

While copy constructors are possible, the .NET Framework guidelines suggest you avoid using copy constructors. In order to copy objects, the .NET Framework provides the `ICloneable` interface. Implementing `ICloneable` is the .NET preferred way to clone objects and it is implemented by many objects within the .NET Framework. Implementing `ICloneable` will enable your object to work with any .NET object expecting `ICloneable`-capable objects as parameters. It will also assist future maintainers of the code in recognizing and understanding it.

`ICloneable` is an interface defined in the `System` namespace (`System.ICloneable`). `ICloneable` provides a single method, `Clone()`, which is implemented to return a copy of the current object instance. Let's look at implementing `ICloneable` in `icloneable_constructor.vb`:

```vb
Public Class Point
   Implements ICloneable

   Private MX as Integer
   Private MY as Integer

   Sub New(X as Integer, Y as Integer)
      MX = X
      MY = Y
   End Sub

   Public ReadOnly Property X as Integer
      Get
         Return MX
      End Get
   End Property

   Public ReadOnly Property Y as Integer
      Get
         Return MY
      End Get
   End Property
```

```
    Public Overloads Function ToString() As String
        Return "(" & MX & "," & MY & ")"
    End Function

    Public Overridable Function Clone() As Object _
                    Implements ICloneable.Clone
        Return New Point(MX, MY)
    End Function
End Class

Module ICloneableConstructor
    Sub Main()
        Dim P1 As New Point(5, 5)
        Dim P2 As Point

        P2 = P1.Clone()
        Console.WriteLine("First Object: " & P1.ToString())
        Console.WriteLine("Cloned Object: " & P2.ToString())
    End Sub
End Module
```

Compiling and running this code produces the following output:

```
First Object: (5,5)
Second Object: (5,5)
```

Implementing ICloneable requires providing an implementation of ICloneable's only member, Clone(). Clone returns a new object reference with an exact replica of the current instance.

If you implement Clone() in your code, you should be aware of two different styles of cloning, called **shallow** and **deep** cloning. In the above example, the Clone method just returns a new Point object, initialized by passing the current property values, from the private variables MX and MY, as the arguments. In this example, only one object is used, the Point object, and its properties all return integers, or value types. What would happen if we created a new class that inherited from Point, and defined an Other property that also contained a Point object (perhaps to draw a line)?

Make the following changes to the above code, which can be found in shallow_clone.vb:

```
Public Class Point
    ...
    Public Property X as Integer
        Get
            Return MX
        End Get
```

```
        Set(Value As Integer)
          MX = Value
        End Set
      End Property

   Public Property Y as Integer
      Get
         Return MY
      End Get

      Set(Value As Integer)
         MY = Value
      End Set
   End Property
      ...
   Public Overridable Function Clone() As Object _
                      Implements ICloneable.Clone
      Return New Point(MX, MY)
   End Function
End Class

Public Class Line
   Inherits Point

   Private MPoint As Point

   Sub New(X As Integer, Y As Integer, Other As Point)
      MyBase.New(X, Y)
      MPoint = Other
   End Sub

   Public Property Other As Point
      Get
         Return MPoint
      End Get

      Set(Value As Point)
         MPoint = Value
      End Set
   End Property

   Public Overloads Function ToString() As String
      Return "(" & Me.X & "," & Me.Y & ")" & _
         " Other: " & MPoint.ToString()
   End Function

   Public Overrides Function Clone() As Object
      Return New Line(Me.X, Me.Y, MPoint)
   End Function
End Class

Module ICloneableConstructor
   Sub Main()
```

135

```
      Dim P as New Point(4, 5)
      Dim P1 As New Line(3,4, P)
      Dim P2 As Line
      P2 = P1.Clone()
      Console.WriteLine("Object Cloned, now changing the Other " & _
         "property on clone")
      P2.Other.X = 5
      P2.Other.Y = 4
      Console.WriteLine("First Object: " & P1.ToString())
      Console.WriteLine("Cloned Object: " & P2.ToString())
   End Sub
End Module
```

Now, if you compile and execute this, you will get unexpected results as shown below:

```
Object Cloned, now changing the Other property on clone
First Object: (3,4) Other: (5,4)
Cloned Object: (3,4) Other: (5,4)
```

Supposedly, only the Other property on the clone, P2, should have changed, but they have changed on both objects. This is an example of shallow cloning, because no objects inside of the class have been cloned correctly. What has happened is that the Other property contains a reference to an object and when the Line object was copied, the reference to the original object was copied with it.

This problem can be remedied simply with a change to two lines, which can be found in deep_clone.vb. The first is in the constructor for the Line class:

```
Sub New(X As Integer, Y As Integer, Other As Point)
   MyBase.New(X, Y)
   MPoint = Other.Clone()
   End Sub
```

The second amendment is in the overridden Clone() method:

```
Public Overrides Function Clone() As Object
      Return New Line(Me.X, Me.Y, MPoint.Clone())
   End Function
```

These lines now produce the expected results, as shown:

```
Object Cloned, now changing the Other property on clone
First Object: (3,4) Other: (4,5)
Cloned Object: (3,4) Other: (5,4)
```

What is happening here is that the `Clone()` method is being called on every instance of an object present as one of the members of an object instance, in this case, just one, when passed to the constructor of the new object instance. In the code above, we also notice a potential bug that could creep into the program that may be difficult to track down. In the constructor call, it was originally setting `MPoint` to the reference passed in via `Other`. This could cause code to fail later if the `Other` coordinate is ever garbage-collected or amended later. By creating a clone, we ensure that `MPoint` contains a clone of `Other` and so amending `MPoint` will not amend any other object.

In some cases, it isn't desirable to deep-clone an object. Classes representing a physical object often shouldn't be deep cloned – different copies of the object should reference the same underlying data structures. A `PassengerList` object, for example, containing a set of references to `Passenger` entities, might be cloned as the basis for building a new passenger list. But we shouldn't clone every passenger, since the passengers making up both lists will be the same people, and changes to the person made through one list (perhaps a change of address) should be visible when the same person is viewed through the other passenger list. In these cases, ensure any implementation of the `Clone()` method for these objects is only a shallow clone, and don't set it `Overridable`.

To prevent cloning altogether, don't provide a copy constructor, and don't implement `ICloneable`.

Deserialization

Serialization is a technique used to save the state of an object to a stream or data source so the object can be readily recreated at a later time and potentially different place. Within the .NET Framework, whenever an object needs to be passed by value between application domains, it must be serialized. When persisting an object to disk, or saving the instance state to database, serialization is used to perform the persistence. Likewise when retrieving the object from disk or database, and populating the object from the data, we use deserialization. *Deserialization* can be considered as reversing the serialization process. Serialization occurs when you want to save an object, deserialization occurs when you want to create an object from that serialized state.

Why discuss deserialization in conjunction with constructors and object creation? Deserialization as a process creates a new object. Consider the situation where we serialize an object, and then deserialize it several times. Obviously, we'll have several references to identical objects. What we won't have is several references to the same object – each deserialized object will be created separately on the heap, and will be a different instance of the same type. Deserialization is an object creation process. What's even stranger is, it doesn't use constructors.

The serialization process is used to store objects for use by other .NET applications, and can even be used by non-.NET applications. Perhaps the most interesting use of serialization is in conjunction with SOAP and Web Services. Serialized objects can be packaged in SOAP messages, sent across a network, and be deserialized back into objects when reaching their destination. The application accepting the object on the other end of the Web Service could easily be a .NET-incompatible application, such as a Java servlet.

The promise of Web Services has been heavily promoted within the IT industry. Microsoft in particular has pushed the promise of Web Services to integrate applications and standardize data transfer. Object serialization plays a big part in the creation and consumption of Web Services. Serialization can be used to create the outbound SOAP messages, and deserialization can be used to populate an object from the inbound SOAP message.

.NET defines two major forms of serialization: Binary and XML (which includes SOAP). Binary serialization offers the most complete serialization in terms of what can be serialized. Binary serialization can serialize private fields, properties (except read-only collections), and public fields. XML serialization serializes only the public members, and it cannot be used if the object model contains circular references. Binary serialization serializes the object into a concise binary stream, while XML is more verbose. Binary serialization is most advantageous where speed and power is important, while XML is powerful when working with distributed, heterogenous systems, or to save object state in a very flexible format.

XML Serialization

In the following example, xml_serialization.vb, we will examine serialization by serializing our object to an XML file and retrieving the XML to populate a new instance of the object.

```
Public Class Point
  Private MX As Integer
  Private MY As Integer

  Public Property X as Integer
    Get
      Return MX
    End Get

    Set(Value As Integer)
      MX = Value
    End Set
  End Property

  Public Property Y as Integer
    Get
      Return MY
    End Get
```

```
      Set(Value As Integer)
         MY = Value
      End Set
   End Property

   Public Overrides Function ToString() As String
      Return "(" & MX & "," & MY & ")"
   End Function
End Class

Module XMLSerialization
   Sub Main()
      Dim P1 As New Point()
      P1.X = 6
      P1.Y = 4
      SaveToFile(P1)

      Dim P2 As Point = RetrieveFromFile()
      Console.WriteLine(P2.ToString())
   End Sub

   Sub SaveToFile(P as Point)
      Dim Serializer As New XmlSerializer(GetType(Point))
      Dim Writer As StreamWriter = New StreamWriter("point.xml")
      Serializer.Serialize(Writer, P)
   End Sub

   Function RetrieveFromFile() As Point
      Dim ReturnObject As Point
      Dim Serializer As New XmlSerializer(GetType(Point))
      Dim FS As FileStream = New FileStream("point.xml", _
         FileMode.Open)

      ReturnObject = CType(Serializer.Deserialize(FS), Point)
      FS.Close()
      Return ReturnObject
   End Function
End Module
```

Compiling and running this code produces the following output:

```
(6, 4)
```

The XML serialization object is responsible for serializing object references to and from XML. Since we want to persist the Point object to hard disk, we create an instance of System.IO.StreamWriter() to perform the interaction with the hard drive. SaveToFile() creates an XML document with the P1 instance state. The file, point.xml, has the following contents:

```
<?xml version="1.0" encoding="utf-8"?>
<Point xmlns:xsd="http://www.w3.org/2001/XMLSchema"
```

```
        xmlns:xsi="http://www.w3.org/2001/XMLSchema-instance">
   <X>6</X>
   <Y>4</Y>
 </Point>
```

Once the file is persisted, the `RetrieveFromFile()` function creates a new `Point` instance by deserializing the `point.xml` file into a new object instance.

Behind the scenes, some powerful work is taking place because of the `XMLSerializer` object. The `XMLSerializer` object first reads the interface of the type it is going to serialize. Since it now understands the type interface, it is ready to create an XML document based on that interface. In this case, we use the `Point` type, so the `XMLSerializer` knows it will have to output an `X` field and a `Y` field into XML, because those two fields are public on the `Point` type. Once the serialization takes place, it accepts an instance of the `Point` type and a serialization stream and is able to convert the instance into the XML and push that XML into the stream.

Much the same process is used by the `XMLSerializer` for deserialization. In this case, instead of moving the state from the object into the stream, it moves the state from the stream into the object instance.

We need to be careful when designing objects to be serializable for all kinds of reasons. In particular, if we are trying to control the number of instances of the type that exist (as in our nodes example above), if we made the node serializable, we would find that on deserialization, we had nodes not connected to our root node.

It's also worth bearing in mind that making an object serializable places constraints on anybody who extends your class as well. They must ensure that their classes can be serialized too, which may force them into design compromises, or mistakes that are hard to track down. For this reason, serialization is something you should only use if you are certain you understand all the consequences.

Singleton

At times, it becomes important for classes to have exactly one instance. For example, we can have many connections to a database, but we only want one database connection manager, to mediate creation of connections. To ensure that a class has at most one instance created, we could create a shared variable of the type. A shared variable provides a common instance we can use throughout our code; however, it does not guarantee that we will only create one connection pool instance. Our code, either inadvertently or on purpose, can create another instance of the shared variable's type.

In order to ensure that we create a maximum of one object instance, we create a class dedicated to the creation of a sole object instance. In OO terminology, we refer to such an object as a **_Singleton_** object.

Let's look at an example of a Singleton object in VB.NET. The Singleton object in our example is called `StringPooler`, and has two public members called `Create()` and `Pool`. The purpose of `StringPooler` is to ensure we only have one instance of the `StringPooler` class that contains the strings we are pooling. As you will see, the constructor has to be declared as `Private` here. See the code in `singleton_example.vb`, below:

```
Public Class StringPooler
    Private Shared SP As StringPooler
    Private Pool as New Collections.ArrayList()

    Private Sub New()
    End Sub

    Public Shared Function Create() As StringPooler
        If SP is Nothing Then SP = New StringPooler()
        Return SP
    End Function

    Public ReadOnly Property Pool As Collections.ArrayList
        Get
            Return Pool
        End Get
    End Property
End Class

Module SingletonExample
    Sub Main
        Dim CountValue as Integer
        Dim SP As StringPooler = StringPooler.Create()
        Dim SP2 As StringPooler = StringPooler.Create()

        SP.Pool.Add("First")
        SP.Pool.Add("Second")
        SP.Pool.Add("Third")

        For CountValue = 0 To SP2.Pool.Count - 1
            Console.WriteLine(SP2.Pool.Item(CountValue).ToString())
        Next
    End Sub
End Module
```

Compiling and running this code produces the following output:

```
First
Second
Third
```

The `StringPooler` is a Singleton object. Since there is no public constructor on `StringPooler`, the only way to return a reference to an instance of `StringPooler` is by calling the `Shared Create()` method. The simple logic of the `Create()` method will always return a reference to the same object (`SP`). We can prove that `SP` and `SP2` are referencing the same object by adding data to the `SP` reference and printing the contents through the `SP2` reference.

The `StringPooler` object contains one piece of data, that is `Pool` itself, which is implemented as a simple `ArrayList` object.

It should be clear from this that by using a private constructor, and mediating construction through a public shared method, we can ensure that only a single instance is ever created. Obviously, we need to be careful to prevent other techniques overcoming our efforts to keep only one instance in existence: we mustn't make the singleton class serializable, or cloneable, and we should really explicitly prevent it being extended (although the private constructor effectively prevents this).

Factory

In our discussion about object creation, we have presented many different techniques to create an object. All of the previous examples take one major point for granted: they all know what type of object to create. What would happen if we were unable to determine which type of object we needed to create until run time; perhaps because the type of object created depended on user input? What we need is the ability to create an instance of an object whose type is not defined until run time.

A *Factory* is an OO design pattern frequently used to create objects based on dynamic criteria. The factory is an object solely responsible for creating instances of other objects. As a computer factory produces computers, an OO factory produces objects. You instruct the factory what object to create by sending it data through its parameters. The factory interprets the input, creates the desired object, and returns the object reference to the caller.

In the following example, we have a `SodaFactory` class that returns soda objects (cans of soft drinks). Since this factory produces only soda objects, each type of soda (`MountainDew` and `Coke`) implements an interface `ISoda`. By implementing a common interface, we gain the flexibility of being able to return a common `ISoda` interfaced object. The code listing from `factory_example.vb`, is shown below, broken up into sections:

```
Module FactoryExample
  Sub Main()
    Dim SF As New SodaFactory()
    Dim Pop As ISoda
    Dim AnotherPop As ISoda

    Pop = SF.GetSoda("MountainDew")
    AnotherPop = SF.GetSoda("Coke")
    Pop.Drink(10)
    AnotherPop.Drink(10)

    Console.WriteLine(Pop.Name & " has " & _
      Pop.Remaining & " gulps left.")
    Console.WriteLine(AnotherPop.Name & " has " & _
      AnotherPop.Remaining & " gulps left")
  End Sub
End Module
```

The above `Main()` method simply creates an instance of each beverage, each of type `ISoda`. In reality, we would have retrieved the types of sodas to create based on run-time information, user preferences stored in databases, or supplied by the user.

The factory object is responsible for creating the requested drink. The factory does not know what object will be created until it is called. Depending on the parameter information, the correct object is created and returned.

```
Public Class SodaFactory
   Public Function GetSoda(Name As String) As ISoda
      If Name.ToUpper() = "MOUNTAINDEW" Then
         Return New MountainDew("DEW")
      Elseif Name.ToUpper() = "COKE" Then
         Return New Coke("COKE")
      Else
         Throw New ArgumentOutOfRangeException("Name", _
            "We do not carry " & Name)
      End If
   End Function
End Class
```

The above class contains one method, `GetSoda()`, which returns the required object, of type `ISoda`:

```
Public Interface ISoda
   ReadOnly Property Name as String
   ReadOnly Property Remaining As Integer
   Sub Drink(Gulps as Integer)
End Interface
```

`ISoda` is the interface all objects returned by the factory must implement. The factory will return a reference to this interface when a new soda is requested.

The `MountainDew` and `Coke` classes are the actual objects we want to create:

```
Public Class MountainDew
   Implements ISoda

   Private MName as String
   Private MRemaining as Integer = 100

   Public Sub New(Name As String)
      MName = Name
   End Sub

   Public ReadOnly Property Name As String Implements ISoda.Name
      Get
         Return MName
      End Get
   End Property
```

```
      Public ReadOnly Property Remaining As Integer _
                            Implements ISoda.Remaining
        Get
          Return MRemaining
        End Get
      End Property

      Sub Drink(Gulps as Integer) Implements ISoda.Drink
        If Gulps < 0 Then
          Throw New ArgumentOutOfRangeException("Gulps", _
            "Cannot drink negative gulps")
        ElseIf Gulps * 2 > MRemaining Then
          MRemaining = 0
        Else
          MRemaining -= Gulps * 2
        End If
      End Sub
    End Class

    Public Class Coke
      Implements ISoda

      Private MName As String
      Private MRemaining As Integer = 100

      Public Sub New(Name As String)
        MName = Name
      End Sub

      Public ReadOnly Property Name As String Implements ISoda.Name
        Get
          Return MName
        End Get
      End Property

      Public ReadOnly Property Remaining As Integer _
                    Implements ISoda.Remaining
        Get
          Return MRemaining
        End Get
      End Property

      Sub Drink(Gulps As Integer) Implements ISoda.Drink
        If Gulps < 0 Then
          Throw New ArgumentOutOfRangeException("Gulps", _
            "Cannot drink negative gulps")
        ElseIf Gulps > MRemaining then
          MRemaining = 0
        Else
          MRemaining -= Gulps
        End If
      End Sub
    End Class
```

144

Both objects are very similar, except in this example, whenever someone takes a gulp of the Mountain Dew, they always end up taking two!

Compiling and running this code produces the following output:

```
DEW has 80 gulps left
COKE has 90 gulps left
```

In our application, we do not know what type of soda the user wants to drink until run time. Perhaps we would pull this information out of a user preferences data store, or prompt the user to select a cola. How we determine the object to create isn't of much importance; the important point is that the Main() method doesn't have this information until run time, so it cannot create a Coke or MountainDew object at compile time. Our example is simplified for brevity; we simply create one instance of each object to illustrate the use of the factory. An elaborate example could be created where hundreds of objects are requested depending on requirements. Coke and MountainDew objects are the ultimate products the factory produces.

The implementations of the MountainDew and Coke classes are irrelevant, as long as they adhere to the ISoda interface. MountainDew, for example, could define a completely different default interface from the Coke class and define completely different algorithms for how it manipulates its state. However different, as long as both classes are both bound to the ISoda interface contract, they are guaranteed to expose a common set of functionality and can be created via the SodaFactory factory.

The difference between the MountainDew and Coke classes is that the Drink(Gulps As Integer) method, Drink(), is implemented differently to suggest that different classes created by the factory can have very different implementations.

Summary

.NET, or more specifically the CLR, provides a managed environment, which frees us from having to manage our object's lifecycle. The CLR implements a generational garbage collector to provide an efficient mechanism for controlling the lifetime of our objects and releasing the objects from memory. Garbage collection allows us to focus on the problem at hand, not having to worry about writing our own object management code.

With the improvements in VB.NET, the Visual Basic language has taken a giant step forward with its abilities to create objects. The most fundamental advance in the language is the ability to define constructors. In the vast majority of object creation cases, objects will be created with the New keyword, calling one of possibly many constructors on an object.

In this chapter you have learned about:

- ❑ Object lifecycle management with how and when the garbage collector removes references to an object, freeing the memory it is using when it is no longer needed.

- ❑ What exactly a constructor is, and how it relates to object management.

You have also learned how to:

- ❑ Define the default constructor, and how it is created by the compiler if not explicitly included in the code.

- ❑ Use optional parameters in the constructor, although this isn't advisable, as other .NET languages may not support them.

- ❑ Call constructors from other constructors, including calling those in the current and base classes. However, the compiler will automatically call the base classes constructors on instantiation of the object, all the way back to `System.Object.New()`.

- ❑ Create objects that don't need to be instantiated with private default constructors, and create shared constructors to initialize shared type members.

- ❑ Use the `ICloneable` interface, rather than a copy constructor, to create exact copies of another object. This is advisable as .NET recommends that applications should use this interface so that other .NET applications know how to clone them.

- ❑ Use serialization and deserialization to save or transmit an object and its values so that it can be used in a different application.

- ❑ Create a Singleton object, so that when different instantiations exist, they point to the same object.

- ❑ Create a Factory object, where a method can return a different kind of object depending on the parameters passed to one of its methods.

This chapter has covered the various different kinds of objects, as defined through their constructors, and how an object is managed through its lifecycle, knowing when it is destroyed. This should allow you to confidently create all kinds of objects within Visual Basic .NET, knowing how it will be managed by the Common Language Runtime.

VB.NET

Class Design

Handbook

5

Properties

Properties have been part of Visual Basic for a long time. In this chapter, we describe how Visual Basic .NET extends the support for properties found in earlier versions of the language. We'll see plenty of examples along the way, to illustrate how properties can improve the encapsulation, usability, and robustness of our classes. In this chapter we will cover:

- ❑ The implementation of properties in VB.NET

- ❑ Scalar properties, and their advantages over fields and methods

- ❑ How properties look when compiled to MSIL

- ❑ Read-only and write-only properties, and when to use them

- ❑ Shared properties and when to use them

- ❑ Indexed properties, including default properties and overloading

So, let's start by defining how properties are implemented in Visual Basic .NET.

Properties in Visual Basic .NET

Let's begin with a brief overview of properties in Visual Basic .NET. If you're already familiar with these basic issues, feel free to skip ahead to the next section where we discuss scalar properties.

A property behaves, from the perspective of a programmer using a class, like a piece of data in a class. Users of the class can access the property name directly, as if the class really contains a data item with that name. However, inside the class the property is implemented as a pair of **property procedures**; the get property procedure gets the value of the property, and the set property procedure sets the value of the property. The property procedures perform whatever processing is required to get or set the property value.

Properties are an important part of our class design.For example, the following diagram shows a small part of an object model for people that work in a company. The Unified Modeling Language (**UML**) notation is used to express the design decisions:

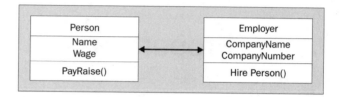

The Person class has two attributes, called Name and Wage. During design, we identify the need for these two attributes in the Person class. When we implement this design in Visual Basic .NET, we must decide how to represent Name and Wage in our code. One option would be to define Name and Wage as Private fields in the Person class; however, this will prevent the information from being accessed elsewhere in the program. How about declaring Name and Wage as Public fields? That's not a good idea at all, because it breaks the encapsulation of the class. It exposes the data so that it can be read and modified by any other part of the program – so much for data hiding.

In these sorts of situations, properties can be the ideal solution. Properties enable us to expose data to the client code, while at the same time preserving the encapsulation of how that data is represented within the class. For example, we can write validation code in the set property procedure to ensure the user doesn't assign an illegal value to the property. Likewise, we can perform computations in the get property procedure to recalculate the value of the property on request.

We can omit either the get or set procedure for a property:

❑ If we omit the set property procedure, and apply the ReadOnly keyword to the property, it, unsurprisingly, becomes read-only. This can be useful for properties that might need to be recalculated each time they are used, such as the days a person has worked at a company. Another use for read-only properties is to achieve lazy initialization, where we don't get the value for a property until it is specifically requested by the client code; this is a useful optimization feature for applications that do a lot of database access.

❑   If we omit the get property procedure, and apply the WriteOnly keyword to the property, the property becomes write-only; this can be useful if the class has an internal configuration flag that we want to set but never need to query. However, since making the property readable is rarely a bad idea (you never know when someone might need to query it), this situation will not be common.

As it happens, read-only properties are quite commonplace, but write-only properties are relatively rare.

The Common Language Specification (CLS) in the .NET Framework supports two different kinds of properties:

❑   **Scalar properties**

A scalar property represents a single value. The value could be a simple value such as an Integer or String, or a more complex value such as a DateTime, a Color, or a BankAccount object.

❑   **Indexed properties**

An indexed property represents a collection of values. The client code uses array syntax to access a specific value in the collection.

We'll examine both kinds of property in detail during this chapter. During these discussions, remember that properties are a standard feature in the .NET Framework. This means client code written in any CLS-compliant language can use the properties defined in our Visual Basic .NET classes.

> *If you are familiar with properties in Visual Basic 6.0, there are some notable differences with how properties work in Visual Basic .NET. For example, Visual Basic 6.0 allows us to define a default property in a class; if we omit a property name when we use the class, the compiler assumes we are using the default property. In Visual Basic .NET, we can only designate an indexed property as the default property; we cannot designate a scalar property as the default property. We'll see examples of how to define and use default properties later in this chapter, when we discuss indexed properties.*

Scalar Properties

Let's start with scalar properties. The following example shows a simple read-write property called Name, in a class called Person. We'll explain how this property can be used, after the code listing. The source code for this example is located in the file simple_scalar_property.vb:

```
Class Person
   Private MName As String

   Public Property Name() As String
      Get
         Return MName
      End Get

      Set(ByVal Value As String)
         MName = Value
      End Set
   End Property
End Class
```

Note the following points in this example:

❏   The Person class has a field called MName, which holds the person's name. This field is declared as Private, to prevent direct access by client code. As we've said several times already, one of the most important aims of object-oriented development is to preserve the encapsulation of the class. Or to put it another way, "Don't declare Public fields."

❏   The Person class has a property called Name, to get and set the person's name. The property acts as a wrapper for the MName field. The Name property is declared as Public, so that it can be used in client code. Most properties tend to be Public, because the essence of properties is to provide a convenient public interface to a class. Nevertheless, situations do arise where a Private, Protected, or Friend property might be required. For example, we can define a Private field that can only be accessed by the other members in the same class. We investigate Private properties later in the chapter.

> *When you define a property, specify the type of the property by appending the syntax As ReturnType at the end of the Property statement. If you omit the return type, the default return type is Object, which is usually not what you want. The Set property procedure requires a single parameter, to specify the new value of the property. The parameter must have the same type as the property. The parameter must be defined as ByVal, which means the parameter value is passed by value rather than by reference.*

It is important to devise a consistent naming scheme that differentiates between fields and properties in a class. This will make the code more self-documenting, which will make it easier to write and (hopefully) reduce the bug count. Also, our code will be easier to maintain because our intentions are clearer for the maintenance programmer.

Defining a naming scheme for properties is more difficult in Visual Basic .NET than in case-sensitive languages such as C# and Managed Extensions for C++; in these other languages, developers often use a lowercase letter at the start of fields (for example, name) and an uppercase letter at the start of properties (for example, Name). This isn't an option in VB.NET, because it is not case-sensitive. The approach we've taken in this chapter is to use MXxxx for fields (for example, MName) and Xxxx for properties (for example, Name). Some developers prefer to use a leading underscore for fields (for example, _Name). It really doesn't matter what naming convention you choose, as long as you use it consistently within and across classes.

> *There is a common notation for .NET Framework applications, available at the following MSDN link:* ms-help://MS.MSDNQTR.2002JAN.1033/cpgenref/html/cpconnamingguid elines.htm, *or at* http://msdn.microsoft.com/net/ecma/.

The following code snippet shows how to use the Name property defined in the Person class:

```
Sub Main()
    Dim APerson As New Person()

    APerson.Name = "Roger"
    Console.WriteLine("{0}", APerson.Name)
End Sub
```

Note the following in the Main() method:

❑ The client code has no direct access to the MName field; all access to this data must be made indirectly through the Name property. This means the class author for Person retains control over how the data is implemented in the class.

❑ The client code uses field-like syntax to access the property. This is more convenient than method-call syntax. For example, if Person defined a pair of methods called GetName() and SetName(), the client code would have to use the following syntax to get and set the person's name:

```
APerson.SetName("Roger")
Console.WriteLine("{0}", APerson.GetName())
```

Now that we've seen how to define and use a simple property, it's time to roll up our sleeves and discuss the design and implementation issues that enable us to use properties correctly in our classes.

153

Compiling Properties into MSIL

When we define a read/write property in a class, the Visual Basic .NET compiler generates a pair of methods for the MSIL code. For example, if our property is called Name, the compiler generates methods called get_Name() and set_Name() in the MSIL code. Whenever these properties are used in client code, the compiler implicitly generates code to invoke the get_Name() and set_Name() MSIL methods.

We can use the MSIL Disassembler tool to illustrate this behavior. Follow these steps:

❑ Build the sample Visual Basic .NET program for this section (simple_scalar_property.vb). If using vbc.exe, use the /debug:full compiler switch to generate full debugger information for the variables in the code. Without this switch, the private fields will not have their original names in MSIL. Visual Studio .NET will add this information by default.

❑ At the command prompt, in the same folder as the new executable, type the following command, to run the MSIL Disassembler:

```
> ildasm simple_scalar_property.exe
```

The MSIL Disassembler window appears, displaying information about the MSIL code in our executable file. Expand the entries as follows in the MSIL window:

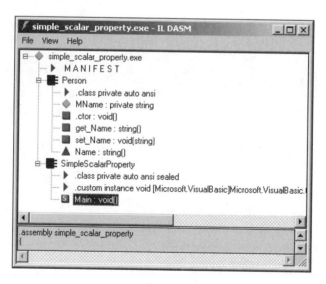

Notice the following members of the Person class:

Member name	Description
MName	This is a private field, to hold the person's name
get_Name	This method is generated by the compiler, to get the Name property as a String
set_Name	This method is generated by the compiler, to set the Name property as a String
Name	This is the Name property itself, which contains the get and set methods

Double-click the Name property, to see how it is implemented in MSIL code. The following window appears:

```
Person::Name : string()                          _ | □ | ×
.property string Name()
{
  .get instance string Person::get_Name()
  .set instance void Person::set_Name(string)
} // end of property Person::Name
```

Notice that the Name property contains two MSIL statements that identify the get and set methods for this property. In the MSIL Disassembler window, double-click the Main() method to see how it is implemented in MSIL code. The following window appears:

```
SimpleScalarProperty::Main : void()                                        _ | □ | ×
.method public static void  Main() cil managed
{
  .entrypoint
  .custom instance void [mscorlib]System.STAThreadAttribute::.ctor() = ( 01 00 00 00 )
  // Code size       38 (0x26)
  .maxstack  2
  .locals init ([0] class Person APerson)
  IL_0000:  nop
  IL_0001:  newobj      instance void Person::.ctor()
  IL_0006:  stloc.0
  IL_0007:  ldloc.0
  IL_0008:  ldstr       "Roger"
  IL_000d:  callvirt    instance void Person::set_Name(string)
  IL_0012:  nop
  IL_0013:  ldstr       "{0}"
  IL_0018:  ldloc.0
  IL_0019:  callvirt    instance string Person::get_Name()
  IL_001e:  call        void [mscorlib]System.Console::WriteLine(string,
                                                                 object)
  IL_0023:  nop
  IL_0024:  nop
  IL_0025:  ret
} // end of method SimpleScalarProperty::Main
```

Notice the following statements in particular:

- ❑ Statement IL_000d sets the Name property. To achieve this effect, the compiler generates code to invoke the set_Name() method.

- ❑ Statement IL_0019 gets the Name property. To achieve this effect, the compiler generates code to invoke the get_Name() method.

By understanding how our code is compiled into MSIL, we can use language features effectively and appropriately in our code. For example, we have just seen that properties are implemented as methods in MSIL code. Whenever client code uses a property, the compiler uses a method call. This can have implications for the run-time efficiency of the code. On balance, however, properties are still preferable to the alternative Public fields; if we define Public fields, we cannot change our minds on how to implement these fields in the future, without potentially breaking any code that uses these fields.

Some .NET Framework languages are much more explicit about the way properties map to methods. A good example is Managed Extensions for C++; to create a read/write property called Name, we would explicitly define separate property functions called get_Name() and set_Name(). However, these differences at the source code level are smoothed out when we compile our code into IL. MSIL code always looks the same, regardless of which programming language we use to write the source code.

Read/Write, Read-Only, and Write-Only Properties

The Name property in the previous example was a read/write property. We can also define read-only properties and write-only properties. Read-only properties are quite useful, because they enable us to expose data without allowing the client code to modify the data. For example, we might want to provide a read-only property to get a person's date of birth. Conversely, write-only properties are used much less often; an example of a write-only property might be to set a value that is used as part of another calculation within the class.

The following example illustrates read/write properties, read-only properties, and write-only properties. The Person class has the following properties:

- ❑ A Name property, to get and set the person's name. The person's name is allowed to change, for example if the person gets married or decides they don't like the name they were born with.

- ❑ A DOB property, to get the person's date of birth. The person's date of birth must be set in the constructor, and cannot change thereafter (a person's date of birth cannot change after the person has been born).

❏ An `EmailAlias` property, to set the person's e-mail alias. The e-mail alias represents the first part of an employee's e-mail address, before the domain name. The e-mail alias can be modified, but it can never be retrieved on its own (instead, the client program retrieves the full e-mail address – see below).

❏ An `EmailAddress` property, to get the person's full e-mail address. The e-mail address is computed every time it is requested, by appending the company's domain name to a person's e-mail alias.

The source code for this example is located in the file
readable_and_writable.vb:

```
Class Person
    Private MName As String
    Private MDob As DateTime
    Private MEmailAlias As String

    Public Sub New(ByVal Name As String, _
                   ByVal Dob As DateTime)
        MName = Name
        MDob = Dob
    End Sub

    Public Property Name() As String
        Get
            Return MName
        End Get

        Set(ByVal Value As String)
            MName = Value
        End Set
    End Property

    Public ReadOnly Property DOB() As DateTime
        Get
            Return MDob
        End Get
    End Property

    Public WriteOnly Property EmailAlias() As String
        Set(ByVal Value As String)
            MEmailAlias = Value
        End Set
    End Property

    Public ReadOnly Property EmailAddress() As String
        Get
            Return MEmailAlias & "@MyCompany.com"
        End Get
    End Property
End Class
```

```
Module ReadableAndWritable
  Sub Main()
    Dim APerson As New Person( _
      "Thomas Peter", New DateTime(1997, 7, 2))

    APerson.Name = "Tom"
    Console.WriteLine("Name: {0}", APerson.Name)

    Console.WriteLine("Date of birth: {0}", _
      APerson.DOB.ToLongDateString)

    APerson.EmailAlias = "Tom.Pete"

    Console.WriteLine("Email address: {0}", _
      APerson.EmailAddress)
  End Sub
End Module
```

When we run the program, we get the following output in the console window:

```
Name: Tom
Date of birth: 02 July 1997
Email address: Tom.Pete@MyCompany.com
```

We can use the MSIL Disassembler tool to investigate how read-only and write-only properties are compiled into MSIL code. Run the MSIL Disassembler on readable_and_writable.exe and you should see the following:

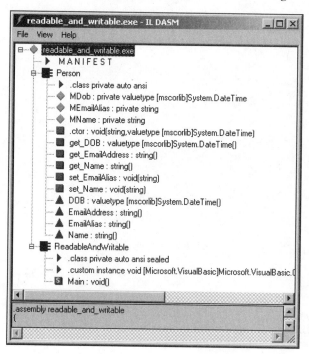

Notice the following items in the MSIL Disassembler window:

- ❑ The get_Name() and set_Name() methods get and set the Name property
- ❑ The get_DOB() method gets the DOB property
- ❑ The set_EmailAlias() method sets the EmailAlias property
- ❑ The get_EmailAddress() method gets the EmailAddress property

Defining Shared Properties

A shared property represents a piece of class-wide information that we want to expose as part of the class, rather than as part of a particular instance. Client code accesses shared properties through the class, rather than through an instance of the class.

The following example shows how to define a shared property named Domain, to represent the domain name used as part of a person's e-mail address. The assumption here is that all people in our system have the same domain name, as might happen in an in-house application.

The source code for this example is located in the file shared_properties.vb:

```
Class Person
    Private Shared MDomain As String

    Private MName As String
    Private MDob As DateTime
    Private MEmailAlias As String

    Public Shared Property Domain() As String
        Get
            Return MDomain
        End Get

        Set(ByVal Value As String)
            MDomain = Value
        End Set
    End Property

    . . .

    Public ReadOnly Property EmailAddress() As String
        Get
            Return MEmailAlias & "@" & MDomain
        End Get
    End Property
End Class

Module SharedProperties

    Sub Main()
        Dim APerson As New Person( _
            "Thomas Peter", New DateTime(1997, 7, 2))
```

159

```
Person.Domain = "MyCoolSite.com"

        APerson.EmailAlias = "Tom.Pete"

        Console.WriteLine("Email address: {0}", _
            APerson.EmailAddress)
    End Sub
End Module
```

Note the following points with this example:

- ❏ The `Domain` property is `Shared`

- ❏ The `EmailAlias` property uses the domain name to generate the full e-mail address for the person

- ❏ The `Main` subroutine sets the `Domain` property by using the class name (`Person`) rather than an instance (such as `APerson`)

Guidelines for Writing Get Procedures

When we define a read/write or read-only property, we need to consider how to write the `get` property function.

Our first recommendation is that a `get` function should not have any observable side effects. That is, the `get` function shouldn't make any changes that affect the state of the object in any way. This is because calling a `get` procedure is logically comparable to accessing a field. If we find ourselves updating state in our `get` function, we should implement it as a method instead. Methods may, and often do, have side effects.

We suggest three distinct scenarios where `get` functions are useful:

- ❏ To get the value of an existing field in the class. In this scenario, the `get` function simply acts as a wrapper for a piece of data that is already present in the class. The `get` function returns the value directly.

- ❏ To calculate a derived value in the class. In this scenario, the `get` procedure uses data in the class to compute the new value. In UML, for object-oriented analysis and design, this is known as a *derived attribute*.

- ❏ To perform *lazy initialization*. In this scenario, the class has a field that is rarely used or is expensive to calculate. For efficiency, we defer initializing this field until it is actually requested through the `get` property function. If the client application never asks for the field, we never have to calculate it. This can improve performance by avoiding unnecessary calls in our code. At the same time, it is not observably any different to returning a value that was already calculated.

The following example illustrates all of these scenarios. The source code for this example is located in the get_procedures.vb file.

This example uses a Microsoft Access database called Northwind. This database is included in the Microsoft Office samples folder. For simplicity, our example assumes Northwind.mdb is located in the same folder as our application's executable file. You will need to copy Northwind.mdb (normally located in C:\Program Files\Microsoft Office\Office\Samples\Northwind.mdb) into this folder before you run this application.

```vb
Imports System.Data.OleDb
Imports System.ComponentModel.Component

Class Person
    Private MName As String
    Private MDob As DateTime
    Private MCompany As String

    Public Sub New(ByVal Name As String, ByVal Dob As DateTime)
        MName = Name
        MDob = Dob
        MCompany = "<not read>"
    End Sub

    Public Property Name() As String
      Get
         Return MName
      End Get

      Set(ByVal Value As String)
         MName = Value
      End Set
    End Property

    Public ReadOnly Property Age() As Integer

      Get
         Dim Today As DateTime = DateTime.Now
         Dim Years As Integer = DateTime.Now.Year - MDob.Year

         If (Today.Month < MDob.Month) Or _
            (Today.Month = MDob.Month And _
            Today.Day < MDob.Day) Then
           Years -= 1
         End If

         Return Years
      End Get
    End Property

    Public ReadOnly Property Company() As String
```

```
    Get

        If MCompany = "<not read>" Then
            Dim Con As OleDbConnection
            Dim Cmd As OleDbCommand

            Try
                Con = New OleDbConnection( _
                    "Provider=Microsoft.Jet.OLEDB.4.0;" & _
                    "Data Source=Northwind.mdb;")
                Con.Open()

                Cmd = New OleDbCommand( _
                    "SELECT CompanyName FROM Customers " & _
                    "WHERE ContactName='" & MName & "'", Con)

                MCompany = Cmd.ExecuteScalar()

                If MCompany Is Nothing Then
                    MCompany = "<unknown>"
                End If
            Catch Ex As OleDbException
                Console.WriteLine("Error occurred: {0}", Ex.Message)
            Finally
                If Not Con Is Nothing Then
                    Con.Close()
                End If
            End Try
        End If

        Return MCompany
    End Get
    End Property
End Class

Module GetProcedures
    Sub Main()
        Dim APerson As New Person( _
            "Ann Devon", New DateTime(1964, 12, 3))

        Console.WriteLine("{0} is {1}, works for {2}", _
            APerson.Name, APerson.Age, APerson.Company)
    End Sub
```

To compile this example using vbc.exe, type the following command:

```
> vbc /r:System.dll /r:System.Data.dll get_procedures.vb
```

The /r:System.dll and /r:System.Data.dll compiler options tell the compiler which assemblies we reference in our program. These are necessary for the Imports statements at the top of the above code listing. Consider the following points in this code:

❑ Firstly, we import the `System.Data.OleDb` namespace. This namespace contains classes and other types for accessing databases such as Microsoft Access, Oracle, and Microsoft Access 6.5 (and earlier). To access SQL Server 7.0 databases (and above), import the namespace `System.Data.SqlClient` instead.

❑ The `Person` class has `Private` fields for the person's name, date of birth, and company name.

❑ The constructor initializes the name and date of birth. The constructor also sets the company name to `"<not read>"`, to indicate that this information has not yet been read from the database (this information will be read from the database when it is first requested).

❑ The `Name` property gets and sets the `MName` field, without any further processing. This property provides wafer-thin encapsulation of `MName`.

❑ The `Age` property calculates the person's age, based upon their date of birth and the current system date. This is an example of a derived attribute. It seems more appropriate to recalculate the age every time, rather than to store it in a field; if we stored the age in a field, we'd have to write supporting code to ensure the field was always kept up-to-date.

❑ The `Company` property illustrates lazy initialization. In this example, the person's company name is held in a database. The `get` procedure queries the database, to get this piece of information. Specifically, we query the `Customers` table in the `Northwind` database. We use the person's name to look up the `ContactName` column, and get the associated `CompanyName` column for this person. Once we've retrieved the company name, we store this information in the `MCompany` field so we don't have to query the database every time.

Notice the error handling strategy in this example. If we cannot find the person's name in the database table, we set `MCompany` to `"<unknown>"` so that we don't try to find it again later. However, if there is an exception, we leave the person's name as `"<not read>"` in case the error was due to a transient problem such as an unplugged network cable; next time the client code asks for the person's company name, we'll repeat the database query in the hope that it works this time.

❑ The `Main()` method uses the `Name`, `Age`, and `Company` properties to get information about a person. The client code is entirely unaware of the amount of processing required to get each property. This is as it should be in an object-oriented application.

Guidelines for Writing Set Procedures

When we define a read/write or write-only property, we need to consider how to write the set property procedure. Perhaps the most important decision is how to handle illegal values. We suggest three possible solutions to this problem:

❏   Do nothing. Ignore the illegal value, and leave the underlying field with its previous value.

❏   Ignore the illegal value, and assign a suitable default value instead.

❏   Throw an exception, to indicate to the client code that an illegal value is unacceptable.

The following example illustrates all of these techniques. The MyColor class has three properties representing the amount of redness, greenness, and blueness in a color. Each set procedure highlights a different technique for data validation.

The source code for this example is located in the set_procedures.vb file:

```
Class MyColor
   Private MRed, MGreen, MBlue As Short

   Private Const Min As Short = 0
   Private Const Max As Short = 255
   Private Const Def As Short = 128

   Public Property Red() As Short
     Get
        Return MRed
     End Get

     Set(ByVal Value As Short)
        If Value >= Min And Value <= Max Then
          MRed = Value
        End If
     End Set
   End Property

   Public Property Green() As Short
     Get
        Return MGreen
     End Get

     Set(ByVal Value As Short)
        If Value >= Min And Value <= Max Then
          MGreen = Value
        Else
          MGreen = Def
        End If
     End Set
   End Property

   Public Property Blue() As Short
     Get
        Return MBlue
     End Get
```

```
      Set(ByVal Value As Short)
        If Value >= Min And Value <= Max Then
          MBlue = Value
        Else
          Throw New ArgumentException( _
            "Illegal color value: " & Value)
        End If
      End Set
    End Property
End Class

Module SetProcedure
  Sub Main()
    Dim AColor As New MyColor()

    Try
      AColor.Red = 400
      AColor.Green = 500
      AColor.Blue = 600
    Catch Ex As Exception
      Console.WriteLine(Ex.Message)
    End Try

    Console.WriteLine("Color is {0},{1},{2}", _
      AColor.Red, AColor.Green, AColor.Blue)
  End Sub
End Module
```

Note the following points in this example:

❑   MyColor defines fields named MRed, MGreen, and MBlue to represent the constituent colors.

❑   The Min and Max constants specify the minimum and maximum allowable values for each color. Def specifies the default value to use in the event of an illegal value assignment.

❑   The set procedure for the Red property ignores illegal values.

❑   The set procedure for the Green property uses the default value if it detects an illegal value assignment.

❑   The set procedure for the Blue property throws an exception if it detects an illegal value assignment.

❑   The Main() method deliberately assigns illegal values to each of the properties Red, Green, and Blue, to test the validation code in these properties.

When we run this application, the application displays the following output on the console window:

```
Illegal color value: 600
Color is 0,128,0
```

Complete Example of Scalar Properties

The following example illustrates all of the issues we've discussed in this section on scalar properties. In this example, we define a class named FootballTeam to represent a football (soccer) team. Among other members, the class has properties for the soccer team's name, the color of their jerseys, and the number of points the team has earned so far (3 points for a win, 1 point for a draw, and 0 points for a defeat).

Read through the code to understand how the properties are defined in the class. The System.Drawing class is used for the Color class, whereas System.IO is used for file handling classes. The source code for this example is located in scalar_properties_complete_example.vb:

```vb
Imports System.Drawing
Imports System.IO

Class FootballTeam
    Private MName As String
    Private MJerseyColor As Color
    Private MWins, MDraws, MDefeats As Short
    Private MLogging As Boolean

    Public Sub New(ByVal Name As String, ByVal Jersey As Color)
        MName = Name
        MJerseyColor = Jersey
    End Sub

    Public ReadOnly Property Name() As String
        Get
            Return MName
        End Get
    End Property

    Public ReadOnly Property Points() As Short
        Get
            Return (MWins * 3) + (MDraws * 1)
        End Get
    End Property

    Public Property JerseyColor() As Color
        Get
            Return MJerseyColor
        End Get

        Set(ByVal Value As Color)
            If Value.Equals(Color.Black) Then
                Throw New ArgumentException("Cannot have black jerseys")
            End If
            MJerseyColor = Value
        End Set
    End Property
```

```
Public WriteOnly Property Logging() As Boolean
   Set(ByVal Value As Boolean)
      MLogging = Value
   End Set
End Property

Private ReadOnly Property LogStream() As FileStream
   Get
      Try
         Return New FileStream( _
            MName & ".log", FileMode.Append, FileAccess.Write)
      Catch Ex As Exception
         Return New FileStream("Default.log", FileMode.Append, _
                               FileAccess.Write)
      End Try
   End Get
End Property

Public Sub PlayGame(ByVal Opponent As String, _
                    ByVal GoalsFor As Short, _
                    ByVal GoalsAgainst As Short)
   If GoalsFor > GoalsAgainst Then
      MWins += 1
   ElseIf GoalsFor = GoalsAgainst Then
      MDraws += 1
   Else
      MDefeats += 1
   End If

   If MLogging Then
      Dim Writer As New StreamWriter(LogStream)
      Writer.WriteLine("{0} {1}-{2} {3}", _
                  MName, GoalsFor, GoalsAgainst, Opponent)
      Writer.Flush()
      Writer.Close()
   End If
End Sub
End Class
```

Note the following design points in the FootballTeam class:

❑   The class has several fields to maintain the state of a football team. We use the naming convention MXxxx for these members.

❑   The constructor explicitly initializes MName and MJerseyColor. The other fields are initialized implicitly; MWins, MDraws, and MDefeats are implicitly initialized to 0, and MLogging is implicitly initialized to False. Generally, it's good practice to rely on implicit initialization where it is suitable; in our example, the implicit initialization for MWins, MDraws, MDefeats, and MLogging is fine.

- The Name property gets the name of the soccer team. There is no set property procedure for Name, because a soccer team cannot change its name once it has been created (this is unlike US football teams, where the name of a team can change when the franchise is sold to another city).

- The Points property calculates and returns the number of points earned by the team so far. This property is never stored in the object: it is always recalculated on demand. An alternative strategy would be to have an MPoints field that is updated every time a game is played. If the Points property is accessed frequently, this might be a more efficient approach. However, if the Points property is seldom used, the overhead of keeping the value up-to-date might not be worth the effort; this is the design assumption that led us to recalculate the Points value only when requested. MDraws is multiplied by 1 in this example, just to explicitly show that there is only one point achieved for a draw.

- The JerseyColor property gets and sets the color of the team's jerseys. The set property procedure includes validation, to prevent teams from having black jerseys (only referees can wear black). An ArgumentException is thrown in this case. An alternative approach might be to ignore the new color and retain the original color, or maybe assign a suitable default color instead. On balance, it was decided that an exception is the best way to indicate an invalid color.

- The Logging property is a rare example of a write-only property. This property enables client code to enable or disable logging of results to a file. If this property is True, we write the result of every game the team plays to a log file. There is no get property procedure for the Logging property; the client program should never need to query whether logging is enabled or disabled.

- The LogStream property is a Private property. This means it can only be used within the FootballTeam class. The purpose of the property is to create and return a FileStream object, which can be used to write results to a log file. The property procedure encapsulates logic that decides which file to use for logging. This is a good example of where a property is more appropriate than a field.

- The PlayGame() method increments MWins, MDraws, or MDefeats. The subroutine also tests the Logging property to see if logging is enabled; if it is, the subroutine uses the LogStream property to get a FileStream object to use to log the result to file.

We can use the FootballTeam properties (and other members) as shown in the following client code. The example uses some soccer teams from the UK; if you follow a different team, please accept my apologies in advance!

```
Module ScalarProperties
  Sub Main()
    Dim MyTeam As New FootballTeam( "Swansea", Color.White)

    Console.WriteLine("Team: {0}", MyTeam.Name)

    MyTeam.JerseyColor = Color.Yellow
    Console.WriteLine("Jerseys: {0}", MyTeam.JerseyColor)

    MyTeam.Logging = True

    MyTeam.PlayGame("Liverpool", 1, 1)
    MyTeam.PlayGame("Chelsea", 3, 1)
    MyTeam.PlayGame("Manchester United", 0, 4)
    MyTeam.PlayGame("Everton", 2, 0)

    Console.WriteLine("Points: {0} ", MyTeam.Points)
    Console.ReadLine
  End Sub
End Module
```

Note the following points about the `Main()` method:

❑ We use the `Name` read-only property to display the name of the soccer team

❑ We use the `JerseyColor` read/write property to change the color of the team's jerseys, and then display the new jersey color

❑ We use the `Logging` write-only property to enable file logging

❑ We use the `Points` read-only property to calculate the number of points earned by the team

To compile this example from the command prompt, because it uses the `System.Drawing` assembly, you need to specify the `/r:System.Drawing.dll` switch for the command-line `vbc.exe` compiler, or import it into your project in Visual Studio .NET.

When you run the application, it should display the following output in the console window:

```
Team: Swansea
Jerseys: Color [Yellow]
Points: 7
```

The application also logs the football results to a file named `Swansea.log`. The file contains the following:

```
Swansea 1-1 Liverpool
Swansea 3-1 Chelsea
Swansea 0-4 Manchester United
Swansea 2-0 Everton
```

Indexed Properties

Now that we've seen how to use scalar properties, let's take a look at *indexed properties*. As we mentioned earlier, an indexed property behaves like an array of values in a class. We use indexed properties to encapsulate getting and setting items in a collection in our class. The client code uses array syntax to access items in the indexed property.

Indexed Properties in .NET Framework Classes

There are many examples of indexed properties in the .NET Framework class library, particularly in the collection classes. For example, the Hashtable class has an indexed property named Item that allows us to insert and retrieve items in the collection.

The following example shows how to get and set items in a Hashtable object. In this example, the Hashtable key is a String representing a country name. The Hashtable value is an Integer representing the international dialing code for the country. The source code for this example is located in hashtable_properties.vb.

```
Imports System.Collections

Class HashtableProperties
   Shared Sub Main()

      Dim DialCodes As New Hashtable()

      DialCodes.Item("USA") = 1
      DialCodes.Item("UK") = 44
      DialCodes.Item("Austria") = 43
      DialCodes.Item("France") = 33
      DialCodes.Item("Italy") = 39

      Console.Write("Please enter a country name: ")
      Dim Country As String = Console.ReadLine()

      Dim Code As Integer = DialCodes.Item(Country)
      If Code = 0 Then
         Console.WriteLine("Code for {0} is not known", Country)
      Else
         Console.WriteLine("Code for {0} is {1}", Country, Code)
      End If
   End Sub
End Class
```

Note the following points in this example:

❑   We import the System.Collections namespace, which contains Hashtable and all the other collection classes in the .NET Framework class library.

❑   We use the Item property in Hashtable to insert new entries into the collection.

❑   We ask the user to enter the name of a country. We use this name with the Index property, to retrieve the international dialing code for that country. Note that Index returns 0 if the specified country is not in the Hashtable.

If we run the program and enter a recognized country name, the application displays a message such as the following:

```
Please enter a country name: France
Code for France is 33
```

If we enter an unrecognized country name (a country that isn't in the Hashtable), the application displays a message such as the following:

```
Please enter a country name: Wessex
Code for Wessex is not known
```

In the following pages, we'll investigate how to define and use indexed properties in our own classes. We'll consider the following issues:

❑   Defining a single indexed property in a class

❑   Defining a default indexed property

❑   Defining overloaded indexed properties

❑   Defining indexed properties with multiple keys

Defining a Single Indexed Property in a Class

To define an indexed property, we use the Property keyword as for scalar properties. Unlike scalar properties, however, we provide one or more arguments to the indexed property. These arguments enable us to find the required item in the underlying collection used by the property.

In the first example, you'll see a simple scenario where you only need a single argument to find the required item in the collection. Later you'll see a more complex example that requires multiple arguments to find the required item.

Our first example shows how to keep a collection of Person objects in an Employer object. The Employer class will define an indexed property named Employee, which will access a Person object with a particular ID. The source code for this example is located in single_indexed_property.vb.

Let's look at the Person class first. This class is fairly straightforward: it has property procedures to get and set fields in the Person class:

```vb
Imports System
Imports System.Collections

Class Person
  Private MName As String
  Private MWage As Double

  Public Sub New(ByVal Name As String, ByVal Wage As Double)
    MName = Name
    MWage = Wage
  End Sub

  Public Property Name() As String
    Get
      Return MName
    End Get

    Set(ByVal Value As String)
      MName = Value
    End Set
  End Property

  Public ReadOnly Property Wage() As Double
    Get
      Return MWage
    End Get
  End Property

  Public Sub PayRaise(ByVal Amount As Double)
    MWage += Amount
  End Sub

  Public Overrides Function ToString() As String
    Return MName & " " & MWage
  End Function
End Class
```

Now look at the Employer class. This code is discussed at the end of the listing:

```
Class Employer
  Private MEmployees As Hashtable

  Public Sub New()
    MEmployees = New Hashtable()
  End Sub

  Public Property Employee(ByVal ID As Integer) As Person
    Get
        Dim TheObject As Object
        TheObject = MEmployees.Item(ID)
        Return CType(TheObject, Person)
    End Get

    Set(ByVal Value As Person)
        MEmployees.Item(ID) = Value
    End Set
  End Property
End Class
```

Note the following points regarding the Employer class:

❑ The Employer class uses a Hashtable to hold a collection of employees. Hashtable is a good choice when we use indexed properties, because it makes it easy to find items in the collection. However, there are other options. For example, you could implement an indexed property whose get property performs a database query to get a value from a database, and whose set property performs a database update to modify a value in a database.

❑ Employer has an indexed property named Employee. The property has an Integer argument to specify the ID of the employee you want to get or set in the Hashtable.

❑ The get property procedure uses the Integer argument to get the required item from the Hashtable (Hashtable has an Item property, which makes it easier to access the items). After you have retrieved the required item, it is converted into a Person object, and this object is returned from the get procedure.

If the Hashtable does not contain an item with the specified ID, the Hashtable's Item property returns Nothing. In this case, it also returns Nothing from our get procedure, to indicate that the requested item was not found.

❑ The set property procedure receives two pieces of information: the ID of the person you are trying to set, and the Person object you want to associate with this ID in the Hashtable. We use the Item property to set the appropriate item in the Hashtable. If there is already an item with this ID, the item will be reassigned to point to the new Person. If there is not already an item with this ID, a new item will be created in the Hashtable for the new Person.

Now let's look at some simple client code that uses the `Employee` property defined in the `Employer` class:

```
Module SingleIndexedProperty
   Sub Main()
      Dim Employer As New Employer()

      Employer.Employee(1) = New Person("Andy", 25000)
      Employer.Employee(2) = New Person("Jayne", 35000)
      Employer.Employee(3) = New Person("Thomas", 17000)
      Employer.Employee(4) = New Person("Emily", 16500)

      Console.Write("Enter an ID: ")
      Dim ID As Integer
      ID = Integer.Parse(Console.ReadLine())

      Dim Who As Person
      Who = Employer.Employee(ID)

      If Who Is Nothing Then
         Console.WriteLine("Unrecognized ID: {0}", ID)
      Else
         Console.WriteLine("Person details: {0}", Who)
      End If
   End Sub
End Module
```

Note the following about the `Main()` method:

❑   It creates several `Person` objects, and uses the `Employee` set property procedure to insert these objects into the `Employer`'s collection of employees.

❑   It asks the user to enter an ID for an employee. It uses the `Employee` get property function to find the `Person` object with this ID in the `Employer`'s collection of employees.

❑   It tests whether the `Employee` get property returns `Nothing`. This will happen if you specify an unrecognized ID.

❑   If the ID is found, it displays the details for that `Person` object.

If you run the program and enter a recognized ID, the application displays a message such as the following:

```
Enter an ID: 3
Person details: Thomas 17000
```

If you enter an unrecognized ID (an ID that isn't in the `Hashtable`), the application displays a message such as the following:

```
Enter an ID: 42
Unrecognized ID: 42
```

Defining a Default Indexed Property

In the previous example, you saw how to define and use a single indexed property in a class. In this situation, it is often more convenient (and safer) to define the property as the *default property* for the class. This means you can omit the property name when you access the property.

Using Default Properties in .NET Framework Classes

A good example of a default property is the Item property in the Hashtable class. Earlier you saw how to use the Item property explicitly:

```
Dim DialCodes As New Hashtable()
DialCodes.Item("UK") = 44
Console.WriteLine("Code: {0}", DialCodes.Item("UK"))
```

Item is the default property in Hashtable. This means we can simplify the client code as follows:

```
Dim DialCodes As New Hashtable()
DialCodes("UK") = 44
Console.WriteLine("Code: {0}", DialCodes("UK"))
```

Defining a Default Property in Our Own Classes

To define a default property in a class, prefix the property definition with the Default keyword as follows:

```
Default Property NameOfProperty(ArgumentList) As Type
    ...
End Property
```

Note that only an indexed property can be defined as a default property; we cannot define a scalar property as a default property. This is different from Visual Basic 6.0, which allows us to define scalar properties as default properties. For example, the Label control in Visual Basic 6.0 has a default property named Caption, which enables us to write code such as the following:

```
' Visual Basic 6.0
Dim MyLabel As Label
MyLabel = "Hello"          ' Implicitly set Caption property
MyLabel.Caption = "Hello"  ' Explicitly set Caption property
```

175

This notation can cause problems if you are assigning one object to be equal to another, as it would just set the default properties of each object to be equal to each other. In VB6, you would use the Set keyword to explicitly set an object to be equal to something else. However, Visual Basic .NET does not support the Set keyword in property assignments, so it has no way to differentiate between assigning default scalar properties and the objects themselves. The outcome of this is that VB.NET does not support default scalar properties. These problems do not arise with indexed properties. Indexed properties always take at least one extra parameter to identify the required item in the underlying collection.

There are two language restrictions when we define default indexed properties:

❑ The default property must not be defined as Private or Shared.

❑ There can only be one default property in a class. Otherwise, the compiler wouldn't know which property to use when the default property syntax is used on an object.

The following guidelines will help you decide whether to define an indexed property as the default property in a class:

❑ If the class contains a single indexed property, it is usually helpful to define the property as the default property. This simplifies usage of the property in client code.

❑ If the class contains several indexed properties, only define a default property if one of them is clearly dominant.

To emphasize these design guidelines, we'll show two examples of defining default properties: one good example, and one dubious example.

A Good Example of Default Properties

This example shows good usage of default properties. The code for this example is located in default_property.vb.

```
Class Employer
   Private MEmployees As Hashtable

   Public Sub New()
     MEmployees = New Hashtable()
   End Sub

   Public Default Property Employee(ByVal ID As Integer) As Person
      Get
         Dim TheObject As Object
         TheObject = MEmployees(ID)
         Return CType(TheObject, Person)
      End Get
```

```
        Set(ByVal Value As Person)
            MEmployees(ID) = Value
        End Set
    End Property
End Class
```

Note the following points for the `Employer` class:

❑   The `Employer` class has a single indexed property named `Employee`. This indexed property is defined as the default property for the class.

❑   The `get` and `set` property procedures implicitly use the default `Item` property in `Hashtable`, to retrieve or insert an item in the `Hashtable`.

Let's see how to use the improved `Employer` class in the client code. Notice how much easier it is to access `Person` objects in the `Employer`'s collection of employees:

```
Module DefaultProperty
    Sub Main()
        Dim Employer As New Employer()

        Employer(1) = New Person("Andy", 25000)
        Employer(2) = New Person("Jayne", 35000)
        Employer(3) = New Person("Thomas", 17000)
        Employer(4) = New Person("Emily", 16500)

        Console.Write("Enter an ID: ")
        Dim ID As Integer
        ID = Integer.Parse(Console.ReadLine())

        Dim Who As Person
        Who = Employer(ID)

        If Who Is Nothing Then
            Console.WriteLine("Unrecognized ID: {0}", ID)
        Else
            Console.WriteLine("Person details: {0}", Who)
        End If
    End Sub
End Module
```

If you run the program it behaves exactly like the `single_indexed_property` application shown previously.

A Dubious Example of Default Properties

This example shows dubious usage of default properties. The `Employer` class now has two indexed properties:

❑   `Employee` is an indexed collection of employees, and uses employee IDs as the key. This is the default property for the `Employer` class.

177

❑ HeadOffice is an indexed collection of head offices for the employer. The employer has a separate head office in each country that it operates in. This collection is indexed by country name, and gives the name of the city where the head office is located in that country.

The code for this example is located in dubious_default_property.vb.

```
Class Employer
  Private MEmployees As Hashtable
  Private MHeadOffices As Hashtable

  Public Sub New()
    MEmployees = New Hashtable()
    MHeadOffices = New Hashtable()
  End Sub

  Public Default Property Employee(ByVal ID As Integer) As Person
    Get
      Dim TheObject As Object
      TheObject = MEmployees(ID)
      Return CType(TheObject, Person)
    End Get

    Set(ByVal Value As Person)
      MEmployees(ID) = Value
    End Set
  End Property

  Public Property HeadOffice(ByVal Country As String) As String
    Get
      Dim TheObject As Object
      TheObject = MHeadOffices(Country)
      Return CType(TheObject, String)
    End Get

    Set(ByVal Value As String)
      MHeadOffices(Country) = Value
    End Set
  End Property
End Class
```

Note the following points regarding the Employer class:

❑ The Employer class has two Hashtable objects, namely MEmployees and MHeadOffices. MEmployees holds a collection of employees (indexed by ID), and MHeadOffices holds a collection of city names (indexed by country).

❑ The Employee indexed property gets and sets items in the MEmployees collection. This is the default property in the class.

❑ The HeadOffice indexed property gets and sets items in the MHeadOffices collection. This is a non-default property.

178

Let's see how to use the revised Employer class in the client code:

```
Sub Main()
    Dim Employer As New Employer()

    Employer(1) = New Person("Andy", 25000)
    Employer(2) = New Person("Jayne", 35000)
    Employer(3) = New Person ("Thomas", 17000)
    Employer(4) = New Person("Emily", 16500)

    Employer.HeadOffice("USA") = "Aspen"
    Employer.HeadOffice("Canada") = "Whistler"
    Employer.HeadOffice("France") = "Val d'Isère"
    Employer.HeadOffice("Austria") = "Zell am See"
    Employer.HeadOffice("Switzerland") = "Zermatt"
    Employer.HeadOffice("Italy") = "Livigno"

    Console.Write("Enter a country: ")
    Dim Country As String
    Country = Console.ReadLine()

    Dim City As String
    City = Employer.HeadOffice(Country)

    If City Is Nothing Then
        Console.WriteLine("No head office in {0}", Country)
    Else
        Console.WriteLine("Head office in {0}: {1}", Country, City)
    End If
End Sub
```

Note the following points in the client code:

❑ When we use the default property syntax, it isn't entirely clear to the human reader whether we are accessing the Employee property or the HeadOffice property.

❑ When we want to access the HeadOffice property, we must use the HeadOffice property name explicitly.

If we run the program and enter a recognized country, the application displays a message such as the following:

```
Enter a country: Austria
Head office in Austria: Zell am See
```

Defining Overloaded Indexed Properties

As you have seen, properties are implemented as methods in our class. Because of this fact, we can define overloaded indexed properties. That is, we can define several indexed properties with the same name, as long as each has a unique signature. This enables us to provide several different ways to index into the underlying collection for the indexed property. When we use an indexed property in the client code, the compiler uses the parameters we've supplied to decide which overloaded property to use.

Consider the `Employer` class. You've seen how to provide a single indexed property called `Employee`, to access employees by ID. We can provide an overloaded property, also called `Employee`, to get and set employees by name.

As will be shown shortly, we need to reconsider how we store `Employee` objects in the `Employer` object. To support this new arrangement, we're also going to modify `Employee` so that the employee's ID is stored as part of the `Employee` object (previously, it didn't store the employee's ID in the `Employee` object; the `Employer`'s `Hashtable` stored the ID for each employee).

The revised `Employee` class is written as follows. The source code for this example is located in `overloaded_properties.vb`:

```
Class Person
   Private MName As String
   Private MWage As Double
   Private MID As Integer

   Public Sub New(ByVal Name As String, ByVal Wage As Double, _
               ByVal ID As Integer )
         MName = Name
         MWage = Wage
         MID = ID
   End Sub

   Public Property Name() As String
     Get
        Return MName
     End Get

     Set(ByVal Value As String)
        MName = Value
     End Set
   End Property

   Public ReadOnly Property Wage() As Double
     Get
        Return MWage
     End Get
   End Property
```

```
Public Sub PayRaise(ByVal Amount As Double)
   MWage += Amount
End Sub

Public ReadOnly Property ID() As Integer
   Get
      Return MID
   End Get
End Property

Public Overrides Function ToString() As String
   Return "[" & MID & "]" & " " & MName & " " & MWage
End Function
End Class
```

Let's take a look at the complete definition of the Employer class, to see how to implement the overloaded Employee properties:

```
Class Employer
   Private MEmployees As ArrayList

   Public Sub New()
      MEmployees = New ArrayList()
   End Sub

   Public Property Employee(ByVal ID As Integer) As Person
      Get
         Dim CountValue As Integer
         Dim ReturnValue as Person = Nothing
         For CountValue = 0 To MEmployees.Count - 1
            Dim PersonInstance As Person
            PersonInstance = CType(MEmployees(CountValue), Person)
            If PersonInstance.ID = ID Then
               ReturnValue = PersonInstance
               Exit For
            End If
         Next
         Return ReturnValue
      End Get

      Set(ByVal Value As Person)
         Dim CountValue As Integer
         For CountValue = 0 To MEmployees.Count - 1
            Dim PersonInstance As Person
            PersonInstance = CType(MEmployees(CountValue), Person)
            If PersonInstance.ID = ID Then
               MEmployees(CountValue) = Value
               Return
            End If
         Next
         MEmployees.Add(Value)
      End Set
   End Property
```

```
Public Property Employee(ByVal Name As String) As Person
    Get
        Dim CountValue As Integer
        Dim ReturnValue As Person = Nothing
        For CountValue = 0 To MEmployees.Count - 1
            Dim PersonInstance As Person
            PersonInstance = CType(MEmployees(CountValue), Person)
            If PersonInstance.Name = Name Then
                ReturnValue=PersonInstance
                Exit For
            End If
        Next
        Return ReturnValue
    End Get

    Set(ByVal Value As Person)
        Dim CountValue As Integer
        For CountValue = 0 To MEmployees.Count - 1
            Dim PersonInstance As Person
            PersonInstance = CType(MEmployees(CountValue), Person)
            If PersonInstance.Name = Name Then
                MEmployees(CountValue) = Value
                Return
            End If
        Next
        MEmployees.Add(Value)
    End Set
End Property
End Class
```

Note the following points in the `Employer` class definition:

❑   The `Employer` class uses an `ArrayList` to hold the employee collection. Previously we used `Hashtable`, because we only needed to index into the employee collection by ID. Now that we have multiple ways of indexing into the collection (by ID or name), `Hashtable` is less attractive.

   `ArrayList` might not be such a good choice if the number of employees grows to be very large. For example, if there are a million employees, a linear search through the `ArrayList` will have very poor performance indeed. In this scenario, a better solution might be to keep the employee data on a database, and use the indexed properties as a wrapper for accessing the database.

❑   The first `Employee` property indexes into the employee collection by ID.

   The `get` property loops through the `ArrayList` searching for an employee with the specified ID. If there is no employee with this ID, it returns `Nothing`.

   The `set` property loops through the `ArrayList` searching for an employee with the specified ID. If the employee is found, it reassigns this item to point to the new `Person` and then return from the procedure. Otherwise, it adds an item to the `ArrayList` for the new `Person`.

182

❏ The second `Employee` property indexes into the employee collection by name. The get and set properties are similar to those just described, but they search for the employee by name not by ID.

We can use the overloaded `Employee` properties as follows in the client code:

```
Module OverloadedProperties
  Sub Main()
    Dim Employer As New Employer()

    Employer.Employee(100) = New Person("Andy", 25000, 100)
    Employer.Employee(200) = New Person("Jayne", 35000, 200)
    Employer.Employee(300) = New Person("Thomas", 17000, 300)
    Employer.Employee(400) = New Person("Emily", 16500, 400)

    Employer.Employee("Nigel") = New Person("Nigel", 50000, 500)
    Employer.Employee("Claire") = New Person("Claire", 60000, 600)

    Console.Write("Enter an ID: ")
    Dim ID As Integer
    ID = Integer.Parse(Console.ReadLine())

    Dim Who As Person
    Who = Employer.Employee(ID)

    If Who Is Nothing Then
      Console.WriteLine("Unrecognized ID: {0}", ID)
    Else
      Console.WriteLine("Person details: {0}", Who)
    End If

    Console.Write(Microsoft.VisualBasic.Constants.vbCrLf & _
      "Enter a name: ")
    Dim Name As String
    Name = Console.ReadLine()

    Who = Employer.Employee(Name)

    If Who Is Nothing Then
      Console.WriteLine("Unrecognized name: {0}", Name)
    Else
      Console.WriteLine("Person details: {0}", Who)
    End If
  End Sub
End Module
```

Note the following points regarding the `Main()` subroutine:

❏ The first four elements in the `ArrayList` are inserted by ID

❏ The next two elements in `ArrayList` are inserted by name

❏ We can retrieve any element by name or by ID, regardless of how we inserted it into the `ArrayList`

If you run the program and enter recognized employee IDs and names, the application displays messages such as the following:

```
Enter an ID: 500
Person details: [500] Nigel 5000
Enter a name: Andy
Person details: [100] Andy 25000
```

Defining Indexed Properties with Multiple Keys

The Common Language Specification supports the use of multi-dimensional arrays in .NET languages. This means we can define indexed properties that take multiple arguments, and use these arguments in combination to find an item in the underlying collection. This is similar to the use of composite primary keys in a database table, where several columns are required to uniquely identify each row.

To illustrate multi-key indexed properties, we'll extend the Person example we introduced earlier so that each person has a location as well as an ID. At each location, every person will have a unique ID. To identify a particular person, we will therefore need to specify the person's location and ID.

To implement this design, we'll create a new structure (value type) named PersonKey. This structure will act as a composite key to uniquely identify each person, using a combination of the person's location and ID.

We'll use PersonKey as the key type in the Employer's Hashtable. Whenever we get or set an item in the Hashtable, the Hashtable will call the GetHashCode() method on the keys to locate the required Person object. We must write GetHashCode() in our PersonKey structure, so that each Person's unique combination of location and ID yields a different hash code.

Here is the code for the PersonKey structure. The source code for this example is located in multi_key_properties.vb.

```
Structure PersonKey
    Private MLocation As String
    Private MID As Integer

    Public Sub New(ByVal Location As String, ByVal ID As Integer)
        MLocation = Location
        MID = ID
    End Sub

    Public ReadOnly Property Location() As String
        Get
```

```
            Return MLocation
        End Get
    End Property

    Public ReadOnly Property ID() As Integer
        Get
            Return MID
        End Get
    End Property

    Public Overrides Function GetHashCode() As Integer
        Return Location.GetHashCode() + ID
    End Function

    Public Overloads Overrides Function Equals(ByVal Obj As Object) _
                                              As Boolean
        If (Obj Is Nothing) Or Not (Me.GetType() Is Obj.GetType()) Then
            Return False
        Else
            Dim Other As PersonKey = CType(Obj, PersonKey)
            If Me.Location = Other.Location And Me.ID = Other.ID Then
                Return True
            Else
                Return False
            End If
        End If
    End Function
End Structure
```

Note the following points about the PersonKey strucure:

❏   PersonKey holds a person's location and ID. Every person will have a unique combination of location and ID.

❏   PersonKey provides read-only properties to get the Location and ID.

❏   PersonKey has a GetHashCode() method, which returns an Integer value based upon the person's location and ID. Every PersonKey will yield a different hash code, to achieve an even distribution of keys in the Employer's Hashtable.

❏   Whenever we override GetHashCode(), we must always override the Equals() method to indicate if this object is equal to another object. The Equals() method will be used by Hashtable, to compare keys for equality.

Now let's see how to write the Person class. As it happens, Person has no knowledge of PersonKey:

```
Class Person
  Private MName As String
  Private MWage As Double

  Public Sub New(ByVal Name As String, ByVal Wage As Double)
    MName = Name
    MWage = Wage
  End Sub

  Public Property Name() As String
    Get
      Return MName
    End Get

    Set(ByVal Value As String)
      MName = Value
    End Set
  End Property

  Public ReadOnly Property Wage() As Double
    Get
      Return MWage
    End Get
  End Property

  Public Sub PayRaise(ByVal Amount As Double)
    MWage += Amount
  End Sub

  Public Overrides Function ToString() As String
    Return MName & " " & MWage
  End Function
End Class
```

Finally, let's look at the `Employer` class. `Employer` has a `Hashtable` of employees;
`PersonKey` objects are used as keys, and `Person` objects are used as values:

```
Class Employer
  Private MEmployees As Hashtable

  Public Sub New()
    MEmployees = New Hashtable()
  End Sub

  Public Property Employee(ByVal Location As String, _
                      ByVal ID As Integer) As Person
    Get
      Dim Key As New PersonKey(Location, ID)
      Return MEmployees(Key)
    End Get

    Set(ByVal Value As Person)
```

```
            Dim Key As New PersonKey(Location, ID)
            MEmployees(Key) = Value
        End Set
    End Property
End Class
```

Note the following points for the `Employer` class:

❑ `Employer` has a `Hashtable`, which will hold `Person` objects indexed by `PersonKey` objects.

❑ The `Employee` property gets and sets items in the `Hashtable`. We create a `PersonKey` object using the specified location and ID, and use this to index into the `Hashtable`. The `Hashtable` implicitly calls the `GetHashCode` and `Equals` methods on the `PersonKey` objects in the `Hashtable`, to find this key in the `Hashtable`.

We can use the multi-key property as follows in client code:

```
Module MultiKeyProperties
    Sub Main()
        Dim Employer As New Employer()

        Employer.Employee("London", 100) = New Person("Andy", 25000)
        Employer.Employee("London", 200) = New Person("Jayne", 35000)
        Employer.Employee("Boston", 200) = New Person("Thomas", 17000)
        Employer.Employee("Geneva", 200) = New Person("Emily", 16500)

        Dim Who As Person
        Who = Employer.Employee("Boston", 200)
        Console.WriteLine("{0}", Who)

        Who = Employer.Employee("Geneva", 200)
        Console.WriteLine("{0}", Who)
    End Sub
End Module
```

Note the following in the `Main()` method:

❑ You must specify the person's location and ID when you insert items into the `Employee` property. In this example, four different people are inserted; each person has a unique combination of location and ID.

❑ You must also specify the person's location and ID when you get items from the `Employee` property. These two pieces of information uniquely specify a particular person.

The output of this application is as follows:

```
Thomas 17000
Emily 16500
```

Summary

In this chapter, we've seen how to make good use of properties in classes. Properties help to make our classes easier to use in client code, and can act as a convenient place to put validation logic to ensure fields in our class are assigned meaningful values.

Properties are a feature of the common language specification. This is another good reason for using properties in our classes: they provide a standard way to expose data in a controlled manner to classes written in any CLS-compliant language.

Here is a quick reminder of the ground we've covered in this chapter:

❑ Defining scalar properties, including the tradeoff between properties, fields, and methods

❑ Defining read/write properties, read-only properties, and write-only properties

❑ Using properties to achieve lazy initialization and to create derived attributes

❑ Defining shared properties to represent class-wide information

❑ Defining indexed properties, including default properties and overloaded properties

Properties are an important part of the CLS. Most of the classes you may write in Visual Basic .NET will benefit from thoughtful use of properties.

VB.NET

Class Design

Handbook

6

6

Events and Delegates

Event-based programming is a cornerstone of the .NET Framework – it is fundamental to all .NET user interface code, including Windows Forms and ASP.NET pages. Events can also be used effectively anywhere in applications, to decouple the functionality of an object from other objects that depend on it. By exposing and firing events from within an object, we enable other objects to respond to its activities in ways that we did not necessarily anticipate when we coded the class. Events can, therefore, be a powerful component in the interface of any VB.NET type we code.

The event mechanism in the .NET Framework makes use of ***delegates***. We introduced delegates briefly in Chapter 1, when we reviewed the .NET Framework common type system. A delegate encapsulates the signature of a function or subroutine. We define delegates to represent the signature of methods that we want to 'call back' in our application. We can then create an instance of a delegate, and bind it to a particular method. When we are ready, we can use the delegate to invoke our chosen method.

In this chapter, we'll investigate the delegate mechanism in some detail. We'll see how delegates are compiled into MSIL code, which will help you understand how delegates work internally. Then we'll look at some advanced delegate issues, such as multi-cast delegates and asynchronous delegates.

Once we've seen how to use delegates, we'll examine the .NET Framework event model. Visual Basic programmers will be familiar with events, but the event model in Visual Basic .NET is quite different from that of previous versions of Visual Basic. We'll describe how the event model makes use of delegates, and see how to use events in user-interface code. We'll also see how to use events as a general way of decoupling an event source object (which generates events) from event receiver objects (which receive event notifications).

Delegates

To understand how events work in Visual Basic .NET, we must first describe how to use delegates. The event model uses delegates to identify event handler methods in our application. Delegates are also useful in their own right, above and beyond their role in the event mechanism.

A delegate is like a pointer to a method in an object in our application. Unlike a simple function pointer, though, a delegate is type safe. We define a delegate to specify the signature of methods we would like to call through the delegate. We can then create a delegate object and bind it to any method whose signature matches that of the delegate.

Delegates are useful in the following scenarios:

❏ To register one of our object's methods as a call-back method with another object. When something important happens to that object, it can invoke our call-back method. The object that invokes the delegate doesn't need to know anything about our object or its methods; the delegate contains all the information about which method to invoke on which object. Therefore, the object that invokes the delegate will continue to work correctly in the future even if we define new types of object with new method names.

❏ To choose one of a series of methods (with the same signature) for use in an algorithm. For example, in Chapter 1 we saw how to define a delegate to represent mathematical functions such as `Math.Sin`, `Math.Cos`, and `Math.Tan`.

❏ To separate the selection of a method from its invocation. We can create a delegate to indicate which method we want to call, but delay its execution until we are ready. For example, we can create a delegate to represent a method to call every ten seconds in a real-time application. We can then create a separate thread, and use the delegate to invoke the required method every ten seconds.

Creating and Using Simple Delegates

To use delegates in our application, we perform the following three steps:

❏ Declare the delegate type

❏ Create a delegate object, bound to a particular method

❏ Invoke the method by using the delegate object

We'll show an example of how to declare a delegate to draw different types of shape on a Windows form. As a fully visual example, we won't show all the form code here in the book. The source code for this example is located in the download code folder `DelegatesEvents\UsingDelegates`.

The form will have the following appearance:

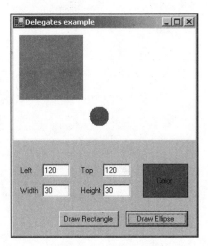

When the user clicks the **Draw Rectangle** button, the application displays a rectangle with the specified position, size, and color. Likewise, when the user clicks the **Draw Ellipse** button, the application displays an ellipse with the specified characteristics.

To achieve this functionality, we could write two completely separate button-click event handler methods to handle the **Draw Rectangle** and **Draw Ellipse** click events. However, this would result in a great deal of duplicate code: both methods would need to perform the following tasks:

❑ Make sure all the textboxes have been filled in, to specify the position and size of the shape

❑ Make sure the shape fits in the drawing area on the screen

❑ Create a brush with the specified color

❑ Draw the appropriate kind of shape (a rectangle or an ellipse)

To avoid duplication of code, we'll use a delegate to represent the drawing operation required. The delegate will either point to the `FillRectangle` method or the `FillEllipse` method, both of which are defined in the `Graphics` class in the .NET Framework class library. Then we'll write a generic method that takes this delegate as a parameter, and uses the delegate to invoke the appropriate drawing operation when we are ready.

Let's begin by looking at some of the supporting code for the application:

```
Public Class Form1
    Inherits System.Windows.Forms.Form

    ' Declare a Rectangle field, to indicate available drawing area
    Private mRect As Rectangle
```

```
' When the form loads, paint the available drawing area
Private Sub Form1_Load(ByVal sender As Object, _
                        ByVal e As PaintEventArgs) _
            Handles MyBase.Paint

    mRect = New Rectangle(0, 0, CInt(Width), CInt(Height / 2))
    e.Graphics.FillRectangle(New SolidBrush(Color.White), mRect)

End Sub

' Handle the Click event for the btnColor button
Private Sub btnColor_Click(ByVal sender As System.Object, _
                            ByVal e As System.EventArgs) _
            Handles btnColor.Click

    Dim dlgColor As New ColorDialog()
    dlgColor.ShowDialog(Me)
    btnColor.BackColor = dlgColor.Color

End Sub

' Delegate-related code (see later)...

End Class
```

Note the following points in this code:

❏   We declare a `Private` field named `mRect`, to represent the drawing area on the form.

❏   We initialize the `mRect` field when the form loads, and paint the rectangle white.

❏   We've provided a click-event handler method for the **Color** button on our form. The method displays the standard color dialog box, so the user can choose a color for the next shape. To indicate which color has been selected, we repaint the **Color** button using the selected color.

Now let's start looking at the delegate-specific code. First of all, this is how we declare a delegate to represent the required drawing method:

```
' Define a Delegate type, to indicate signature of method to call
Delegate Sub MyDelegate(ByVal aBrush As Brush, _
                         ByVal aRect As Rectangle)
```

This delegate represents subroutines that take two parameters:

❏   A `Brush` object, to specify the color of the shape

❏   A `Rectangle` object, to specify the position and size of the shape

As we'll see shortly, this delegate corresponds with the signatures of the `FillRectangle` and `FillEllipse` methods in the `Graphics` class.

It's also possible to define a delegate type to represent functions. Replace the `Sub` keyword with `Function`, and specify the return type at the end of the delegate definition. We'll see an example of how to define delegates for functions later in this chapter.

The next step is to create an instance of the `MyDelegate` type, and bind it to a specific method on a particular object. Here is a verbose example, showing how to create a `MyDelegate` instance and bind it to the `FillRectangle` method on a `Graphics` object:

```
' Handle the Click event for the btnRectangle button
Private Sub btnRectangle_Click(ByVal sender As System.Object, _
                          ByVal e As System.EventArgs) _
            Handles btnRectangle.Click

    ' Create a Graphics object (we need its FillRectangle method)
    Dim aGraphics As Graphics = CreateGraphics()

    ' Declare a MyDelegate variable
    Dim aDelegate As MyDelegate

    ' Create a delegate object, and bind to the FillRectangle method
    aDelegate = New MyDelegate(AddressOf aGraphics.FillRectangle)

    ' Call MyDrawShape, and pass the delegate as a parameter
    MyDrawShape(aDelegate)

End Sub
```

Note the following points in the `btnRectangle_Click` method above:

❑   We create a `Graphics` object, because the drawing methods (such as `FillRectangle` and `FillEllipse`) are defined as instance methods in this class. Therefore, we need an instance of the `Graphics` class to enable us to call these methods.

❑   We declare a local variable of type `MyDelegate`. This reinforces the fact that delegates are data types. Later in the chapter, we'll show the MSIL code for the `MyDelegate` data type.

❑   We create an instance of the `MyDelegate` type, and bind it to the `FillRectangle` method on the `Graphics` object. The `AddressOf` keyword gives us the address of this method on this object.

It's also possible to bind delegates to `Shared` methods. For example, in Chapter 1 we created delegates and bound them to the `Shared` methods `Math.Sin`, `Math.Cos`, and `Math.Tan`. To bind a delegate to a `Shared` method rather than an instance method, specify a class name before the method (for example, `Math.Sin`), rather than specifying an object name before the method (for example, `aGraphics.FillRectangle`).

❑ We pass the `MyDelegate` instance into another method named `MyDrawShape`. As we'll see shortly, `MyDrawShape` uses the delegate to invoke the specified drawing operation (`aGraphics.FillRectangle`) when it is ready.

Now that we've seen how to create delegates the hard way, let's see how to take some short cuts. The following code shows how to create a `MyDelegate` instance and bind it to the `FillEllipse` method on a `Graphics` object in a single step; notice how much simpler this code is than the previous example:

```
' Handle the Click event for the btnEllipse button
Private Sub btnEllipse_Click(ByVal sender As System.Object, _
                        ByVal e As System.EventArgs) _
                Handles btnEllipse.Click

    ' Call MyDrawShape, with delegate bound to FillEllipse
    Dim aGraphics As Graphics = CreateGraphics()
    MyDrawShape(AddressOf aGraphics.FillEllipse)

End Sub
```

In this example, note the following statement in particular:

```
MyDrawShape(AddressOf aGraphics.FillEllipse)
```

When the compiler sees this statement, it examines the `MyDrawShape` method and realizes it expects a `MyDelegate` parameter. Therefore, the compiler implicitly creates a new `MyDelegate` object, and binds it to the specified method address (`AddressOf aGraphics.FillEllipse`). In other words, the statement above has exactly the same effect as the following verbose syntax:

```
MyDrawShape( New MyDelegate(AddressOf aGraphics.FillEllipse) )
```

Given the fact the compiler can create the `MyDelegate` object implicitly from the `AddressOf` expression, most developers tend not to bother using the `New MyDelegate(...)` syntax. For this reason, delegates are rarely mentioned explicitly in Visual Basic .NET code; however, it's important you understand the role they play under the covers.

Our final task is to use the delegate in the `MyDrawShape` method, to invoke the required drawing operation. Here is the code for the `MyDrawShape` method:

```
' MyDrawShape uses a delegate to indicate which method to call
Public Sub MyDrawShape(ByVal theDelegate As MyDelegate)

    ' Are any text fields blank?
    If txtLeft.Text.Length = 0  Or txtTop.Text.Length = 0 Or _
        txtWidth.Text.Length = 0 Or txtHeight.Text.Length = 0 Then
```

```
                ' Display an error message, and return immediately
                MessageBox.Show("Please fill in all text boxes", _
                                "Error", _
                                MessageBoxButtons.OK, _
                                MessageBoxIcon.Error)
            Return

        End If

        ' Get the coordinate values entered in the text fields
        Dim aRect As New Rectangle(Integer.Parse(txtLeft.Text), _
                                   Integer.Parse(txtTop.Text), _
                                   Integer.Parse(txtWidth.Text), _
                                   Integer.Parse(txtHeight.Text))

        ' Make sure the coordinates are in range
        If mRect.Contains(aRect) Then

            ' Get the color of the btnColor button
            Dim aBrush As New SolidBrush(btnColor.BackColor)

            ' Invoke the delegate, to draw the specified shape
            theDelegate.Invoke(aBrush, aRect)

        Else

            ' Display error message, and return immediately
            MessageBox.Show("Coordinates are outside drawing area", _
                            "Error", _
                            MessageBoxButtons.OK, _
                            MessageBoxIcon.Error)

        End If

End Sub
```

Note the following points in the MyDrawShape method:

❑ MyDrawShape takes a delegate of type MyDelegate. The delegate object specifies the required drawing operation, and also specifies the Graphics object to use for the drawing operation. It's important to realize MyDrawShape has no idea what method is specified in the delegate. This makes it easier to extend the method in the future, for example if new kinds of drawing operation are introduced.

❑ MyDrawShape performs various administrative tasks, such as getting the size, position, and color information entered by the user.

❑ When ready, MyDrawShape uses the delegate to invoke the specified drawing method. Delegates have an Invoke method, with the same signature as the method they represent. For example, MyDelegate has an Invoke method that takes a Brush parameter and a Rectangle parameter.

197

To compile the application, open a .NET Framework command-prompt window, move to the folder that contains the example, and type the following command on one line:

```
> vbc  /r:System.dll /r:System.Windows.Forms.dll
          /r:System.Drawing.dll /t:winexe /m:Form1
          UsingDelegates.vb
```

We've used several compiler switches here:

❏ The /r compiler switch specifies a reference to another .NET Framework **assembly** (.dll or .exe file). These assemblies contain compile-time information, commonly known as **metadata**, about the types and methods used in our application. The compiler uses this metadata to verify we've used these types and methods correctly in our code. You'll learn more about assemblies and metadata in Chapter 8.

❏ The /t compiler switch specifies the type of target we want to build. /t:winexe indicates a Windows application, as you probably guessed.

❏ The /m compiler switch specifies the main class in our application. In the case of a Windows application, we must specify the class that represents the main form in the application. In the case of a console application, we must specify the class that contains the Main method.

To run the application, type the following command:

```
> UsingDelegates
```

The application runs, and we can then create rectangles and ellipses in any colors of our choosing.

Fun though this is, it's perhaps useful to see how our application is compiled into MSIL code. Close the application, and type the following command at the command prompt:

```
> ildasm UsingDelegates.exe
```

The MSIL Disassembler window displays the following information (we've expanded the nodes we're interested in in this screenshot, to show the details for each of our types):

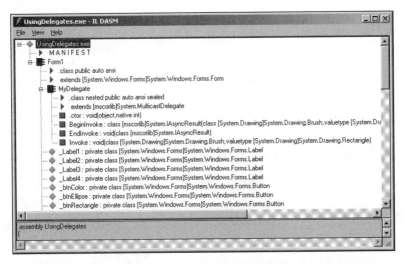

There's a great deal of information here, as you might expect in a Windows application. The important part as far as we are concerned is the MSIL code for MyDelegate. Note the following points about MyDelegate:

❑   MyDelegate is a class. Whenever we define a new delegate type in our application, the compiler generates a class to encapsulate the information in the delegate's signature.

❑   MyDelegate is a nested class within Form1, because this is the only place where our delegate is accessed. This is a good example of how to use nested classes (or to be more precise, nested delegates) to maximize the encapsulation of types in our application. If in the future we need to access MyDelegate in other parts of the application, we can move the definition of MyDelegate outside of Form1, to make it globally accessible in our application.

❑   The MSIL syntax extends [mscorlib]System.MulticastDelegate indicates that the generated class MyDelegate inherits from a standard .NET Framework class named MulticastDelegate. We'll describe what we mean by *multicast delegates* later in this chapter. MulticastDelegate is logically located in the System namespace, and is physically located in the mscorlib assembly. We'll discuss inheritance in more detail in Chapter 7, and we'll investigate namespaces and assemblies in Chapter 8.

❑   MyDelegate defines several methods in addition to those inherited from its superclass MulticastDelegate. First, it has methods named BeginInvoke and EndInvoke, which enable us to invoke methods asynchronously via the delegate, if required. In other words, we can use a delegate to invoke a method in a background thread; the main thread in the application can continue execution, without having to wait for the method to complete. We'll see an example of asynchronous delegates later in this chapter.

❑ MyDelegate has another method named `Invoke()`, which enables us to invoke methods synchronously via the delegate. The compiler generated the `Invoke` method from the signature we specified when we defined the `MyDelegate` type. In the client code, we use `Invoke` to invoke a method with the specified signature; for example, the sample application we introduced earlier used `Invoke` to call the `FillRectangle()` or `FillEllipse()` method.

Creating and Using Multicast Delegates

The .NET Framework supports two distinct kinds of delegate:

❑ **Single-cast** delegates, which enable us to call a single method on a single object. When we call `Invoke()` on a single-cast delegate, the delegate calls the specified method on the designated object.

❑ **Multicast** delegates, which enable us to call a series of methods on potentially different objects. Multicast delegates maintain an invocation list, to remember which method to call on which object. When we call `Invoke` on a multicast delegate, the delegate calls the specified methods on the designated objects, in sequence.

Multicast delegates are useful if we need to perform the same operation on a collection of objects, or if we need to perform a series of operations on the same object, or any combination of these two cases. We can use multicast delegates implicitly to keep a collection of all the methods that need to be executed, and the objects upon which these methods are to be executed.

Multicast delegates are created by combining instances of the same delegate type.

To create and use a multicast delegate, we must follow these steps:

❑ Define a delegate type, to represent the signature of the methods we want to call via the delegate. Multicast delegates can only be used to execute methods with the same signature, which is consistent with the general ethos of strong data typing with delegates.

❑ Write methods with the same signature as the delegate.

❑ Create a delegate object, and bind it to the first method we want to call via the delegate.

❑ Create another delegate object, and bind it to the next method we want to call.

❑ Call the `Combine` method in the `System.Delegate` class, to combine the two delegates into an integrated multicast delegate. The `Combine` method returns a new delegate, whose invocation list contains both delegates.

❑   Repeat the previous two steps, to create as many delegates as needed and combine them into an integrated multicast delegate.

❑   If we need to remove a delegate from a multicast delegate, call the Remove method defined in the System.Delegate class. The Remove method returns a new delegate, whose invocation list does not contain the removed delegate. If the delegate we just removed was the only delegate in the invocation list, the Remove method returns Nothing instead.

❑   When we are ready to invoke the methods specified by the multicast delegate, simply call Invoke as before. This invokes the methods in the order they appear in the invocation list, and returns the result of the last method in the invocation list.

To illustrate these concepts, and to show the Visual Basic .NET syntax for multicast delegates, we'll work through a complete example that uses multicast delegates to paint any number of child forms in a Windows Forms application. The application has a main form that allows the user to create new child forms, and to change the color of all these forms at any time. The main form uses a multicast delegate to invoke a Repaint method on each child form.

The source code for this example is located in the download folder DelegatesEvents\MulticastDelegates. Before we look at the code, let's see how the application will work. The main form in the application appears as follows:

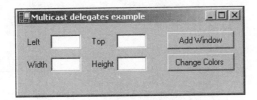

The user enters some screen coordinates, and then clicks **Add Window** to create the child form. At this stage in the application, we create a new delegate and bind it to the Repaint method on the new child form. We combine this delegate into a multicast delegate in the main form, to keep track of all the open child forms.

The main form displays a message in its status bar, to indicate the number of entries in the invocation list of the multicast delegate. This tells us how many child forms are currently open:

If the user clicks **Add Window** several times, we'll see several child forms on the screen. The multicast delegate keeps track of all these child forms. To be more precise, the invocation list in the multicast delegate holds the Repaint method for each of the child forms.

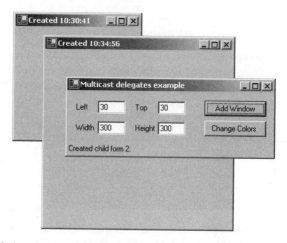

When the user clicks Change Color to select a new color, we invoke the multicast delegate to repaint all the child forms. In other words, we call Invoke on the multicast delegate, which invokes the Repaint method on each child form. Each form repaints itself in the specified color:

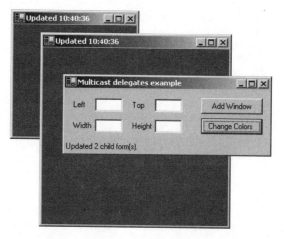

There is one more issue to consider. If the user closes a child form, we need to remove the corresponding delegate from the multicast delegate in the main form. To achieve this effect, the main form has a method named ChildFormClosing, which the child form can call just before it closes. In the ChildFormClosing method, we remove the child form's delegate from the multicast delegate, because we won't need to repaint the form in future.

Now that we've seen how the application works in principle, let's look at the code. We'll begin with the source code for the child form, because this is fairly straightforward. There is no delegate-related code in this class; child forms have no awareness of the other child forms in the application. The source code for the ChildForm class is provided in ChildForm.vb:

```vbnet
Imports System
Imports System.Windows.Forms
Imports System.ComponentModel
Imports System.Drawing

Public Class ChildForm
    Inherits System.Windows.Forms.Form

    #Region " Windows Form Designer generated code "
        ' Omitted for brevity...
    #End Region

    Private Sub ChildForm_Load(ByVal sender As System.Object, _
                        ByVal e As System.EventArgs) _
            Handles MyBase.Load

        ' Display the date-and-time of creation, in the caption bar
        Me.Text = "Created " & DateTime.Now.ToLongTimeString()

    End Sub

    Public Function Repaint(ByVal theColor As Color) As String

        ' Set the color for this form, and update the caption bar
        Me.BackColor = theColor
        Me.Text = "Updated " & DateTime.Now.ToLongTimeString()
        Return Me.Text

    End Function

    Protected Sub ChildForm_Cancel(ByVal sender As System.Object, _
                        ByVal e As CancelEventArgs) _
            Handles MyBase.Closing

        ' Tell the main form we are closing, so the main form can
        ' remove us from its multicast delegate
        Dim MyOwner As MainForm = CType(Me.Owner, MainForm)
        MyOwner.ChildFormClosing(Me)

    End Sub

End Class
```

Note the following points in the ChildForm class:

❑ The ChildForm_Load method displays the form's creation time on the caption bar.

❑ The Repaint method has a Color parameter, to tell the form which color to repaint itself. This method will be called by the main form's multicast delegate, whenever the user selects a new color.

❑ The ChildForm_Cancel method informs the main form that this child form is about to close. We use the Owner property to get a reference to the main form, and then call its ChildFormClosing method.

203

Now let's see the code for the main form in the application. This main form contains all the delegate-related processing, so unsurprisingly there are plenty of issues to consider. The first step is to define our delegate type, and to declare a field to refer to the multicast delegate object:

```
Imports System
Imports System.Windows.Forms
Imports System.Drawing

Public Class MainForm
    Inherits System.Windows.Forms.Form

    ' Define a Delegate type
    Delegate Function MyDelegate(ByVal aColor As Color) As String

    ' Declare a MyDelegate field, to refer to the multicast delegate
    Private mTheDelegate As MyDelegate

    ' Plus other methods (see later)...

End Class
```

Note the following points in the `MainForm` class definition above:

❑ `MyDelegate` defines the signature of the methods we want to call via this delegate type. As you'd expect, the delegate's signature matches that of the `Repaint` method in the `ChildForm` class.

Notice there is no difference in how we define single-cast delegate types and multicast delegate types in Visual Basic .NET. In fact, every delegate type in Visual Basic .NET is implicitly a multicast delegate. It's up to us whether we use the delegate to represent a single method or several methods.

❑ `mTheDelegate` is a field that will point to the multicast delegate. In other words, `mTheDelegate` will refer to a `MyDelegate` instance. Initially, `mTheDelegate` is `Nothing` because there are no child forms yet. When we create the first child form, we'll create a new `MyDelegate` instance and assign it to `mTheDelegate`.

Now let's see how to create a new child form, and combine its `Repaint` method into our multicast delegate:

```
' Handle the Click event for the btnAddWindow button
Private Sub btnAddWindow_Click(ByVal sender As System.Object, _
                     ByVal e As System.EventArgs) _
          Handles btnAddWindow.Click

    ' Are any text fields blank?
    If txtLeft.Text.Length = 0 Or txtTop.Text.Length = 0 Or _
       txtWidth.Text.Length = 0 Or txtHeight.Text.Length = 0 Then
```

```vb
                ' Display an error message, and return immediately
                MessageBox.Show("Please fill in all text boxes.", _
                            "Error adding window", _
                            MessageBoxButtons.OK, _
                            MessageBoxIcon.Error)
        Return

    End If

    ' Create a new child form with the specified location and size
    Dim aChildForm As New ChildForm()
    aChildForm.Owner = Me
    aChildForm.DesktopBounds = New Rectangle( _
                            Integer.Parse(txtLeft.Text), _
                            Integer.Parse(txtTop.Text), _
                            Integer.Parse(txtWidth.Text), _
                            Integer.Parse(txtHeight.Text))

    aChildForm.Show()

    ' Create a new delegate for the child form's Repaint method
    Dim newDelegate As MyDelegate = AddressOf aChildForm.Repaint

    ' If multicast delegate is Nothing, this is the first child form
    If mTheDelegate Is Nothing Then

        ' Use new delegate as the basis for the multicast delegate
        mTheDelegate = newDelegate
        sbStatus.Text = "Created first child form."

    Else

        ' Combine new delegate into the multicast delegate
        mTheDelegate = System.Delegate.Combine(mTheDelegate, _
                                        newDelegate)

        ' Use multicast delegate to count the child forms
        sbStatus.Text = "Created child form " & _
                    mTheDelegate.GetInvocationList().Length & _
                    "."

    End If

End Sub
```

Note the following points in the btnAddWindow_Click method shown above:

❑ We begin by verifying the user has entered numbers in all the text fields. If all is well, we create a new child form with the specified location and size, and display the form on the screen. We specify the main form as the Owner of the child form.

❑ We create a new MyDelegate instance, and bind it to the Repaint method on the new child form.

❑ If mTheDelegate is Nothing, there are no other child forms currently open. Therefore, we assign our delegate directly to the mTheDelegate field. The multicast delegate comprises a single entry, which represents the Repaint method on the new child form.

❑ If mTheDelegate is not Nothing, there are already some child forms currently open. Therefore, we combine our delegate into a new multicast delegate, and assign the new multicast delegate to mTheDelegate.

Delegates have a GetInvocationList method, which returns an array of delegate objects representing all the entries in the multicast delegate. We can use the Length property to find the size of this array. In our example, this tells us how many child forms are currently open.

Once the user has created some child forms, they can click **Change Color** to change the color of these forms. The following code achieves this:

```
' Handle the Click event for the btnColor button
Private Sub btnColors_Click(ByVal sender As System.Object, _
                            ByVal e As System.EventArgs) _
              Handles btnColors.Click

    ' If multicast delegate is Nothing, there are no child forms
    If mTheDelegate Is Nothing Then

        MessageBox.Show("There are no child forms to change.", _
                        "Error changing color", _
                        MessageBoxButtons.OK, _
                        MessageBoxIcon.Error)

    Else

        ' Ask user to choose a color
        Dim dlgColor As New ColorDialog()
        dlgColor.ShowDialog()

        ' Invoke multicast delegate, to repaint all the child forms
        mTheDelegate.Invoke(dlgColor.Color)

        ' Use multicast delegate to count the child forms
        sbStatus.Text = "Updated " & _
                        mTheDelegate.GetInvocationList().Length & _
                        " child form(s)."

    End If

End Sub
```

Note the following points in the btnColors_Click method shown above:

❑ If mTheDelegate is Nothing, there are no child forms open, so we display an error message and return immediately. Notice how easy it is to use the multicast delegate to keep track of the presence or absence of child forms.

❑ If mTheDelegate is not Nothing, we ask the user to choose a new color for the existing forms. We then call Invoke on our multicast delegate, to invoke the Repaint method on all the child forms. Again, notice how convenient it is to use the multicast delegate to iterate through the child forms and repaint each one.

❑ For aesthetic reasons, we display a message in the status bar of the main form, to indicate how many child forms have been repainted. As before, we get this information by calling GetInvocationList on the multicast delegate.

The final method we need to look at in the MainForm class is the ChildFormClosing method. Child forms call this method just before they close, to enable the main form to keep track of its child forms. The code for the ChildFormClosing method is shown below:

```
' Child forms call this method, to tell us they are closing
Public Sub ChildFormClosing(ByVal aChildForm As ChildForm)

    ' Create a delegate for the ChildForm that is closing
    Dim unneededDelegate As MyDelegate = _
            AddressOf aChildForm.Repaint

    ' Remove the delegate from the multicast delegate
    mTheDelegate = System.Delegate.Remove(mTheDelegate, _
                                    unneededDelegate)

    ' If multicast delegate is Nothing, there are no child forms
left
    If mTheDelegate Is Nothing Then

        sbStatus.Text = "Final child form has been closed."

    Else

        ' Use multicast delegate to count the child forms
        sbStatus.Text = "Child form closed, " & _
                mTheDelegate.GetInvocationList().Length & _
                " form(s) remaining."

    End If

End Sub
```

Note the following points in the ChildFormClosing method shown above:

❑ The ChildFormClosing method receives a ChildForm parameter, to indicate which child form is closing.

❑ We create a new delegate, and bind it to the `Repaint` method on the soon-to-be-defunct child form. We then call the `Remove` method in the `System.Delegate` class, to remove this delegate from the multicast delegate. The `Remove` method returns one of two possible values:

- If we've just removed the final delegate from the multicast delegate, the multicast delegate no longer exists. In this case, the `Remove` method returns `Nothing`.

- Otherwise, the `Remove` method returns a new multicast delegate that does not contain the removed delegate.

❑ Note that delegates exhibit value semantics; even though we have created a new delegate pointing to the method, we can use it to remove another delegate pointing to the same method. The two delegates are considered equivalent.

❑ We display an appropriate message in the status bar of the main form, to indicate how many child forms are left.

That concludes our journey through the source code for the sample application. To compile the application, open a .NET Framework command-prompt window, move to the folder that contains the example, and type the following command on one line:

```
> vbc /r:System.dll /r:System.Windows.Forms.dll
           /r:System.Drawing.dll /t:winexe /m:MainForm
           MainForm.vb   ChildForm.vb
```

To run the application, type the following command:

```
> MainForm.exe
```

The application appears as follows, and enables us to open child windows and set their colors as previously advertised:

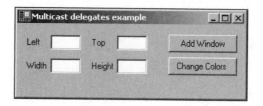

Multicast delegates make it easy to maintain a collection of objects that need to be notified in unison, when something important happens. When we invoke the multicast delegate, the multicast delegate implicitly iterates through all the entries in its invocation list, to call the specified method on each designated object.

Creating and Using Asynchronous Delegates

All of the examples we have seen so far have used delegates to invoke methods synchronously, using the Invoke method in the delegate. When we invoke a method synchronously, we have to wait for the method to return before we can continue processing.

We can also use delegates to invoke methods asynchronously. This means we can invoke the method in a background thread, and continue doing useful work in the main thread at the same time. This can be useful if we have a lengthy task to perform, and we don't want to hang around for the result.

To support asynchronous method calls via delegates, the Visual Basic .NET compiler generates the following two methods in our delegate class (in addition to the Invoke method, to support synchronous method calls):

❑   BeginInvoke

We call BeginInvoke to invoke the required method asynchronously, in a background thread.

❑   EndInvoke

After the specified method has completed execution, we can call EndInvoke to get the return value from the method. EndInvoke also allows us to access any output parameters from the method; for example, if the method takes parameters ByRef, and modifies these parameters during execution, we can use EndInvoke to get the modified values for these parameters.

There are several ways to use asynchronous delegates, depending on our needs. Here are the possibilities, in order of increasing complexity:

❑   Invoke a method that does not return a result

❑   Invoke a method that returns a result, and wait a finite time for the result

❑   Invoke a method that returns a result, and define a callback method to receive the result whenever it arrives

Events

In the first half of this chapter, we've seen how to use delegates to invoke methods on objects. We've seen how to use single-cast delegates to invoke single methods, and how to use multicast delegates to invoke multiple methods in sequence. We've also seen that we can use delegates to invoke methods asynchronously, if required.

In the second half of this chapter, we turn our attention to events. The .NET Framework event model relies on delegates to indicate which method(s) to call when a particular event is raised.

All Visual Basic programmers will be familiar with the use of events in graphical user interface (GUI) applications. When the user interacts with a control on the form, an event is raised and an event-handler method is called to deal with the event. However, events are not limited to GUI programming; we can use events as a general-purpose way of notifying interested objects whenever something important happens in our application.

We'll examine the following issues in this section:

❑   What is the event architecture in the .NET Framework?

❑   How do we publish events?

❑   How do we subscribe to events?

❑   How do we raise events?

Event Architecture

Here is a brief summary of the event architecture in the .NET Framework. We've also provided a formal definition for some of the key terms associated with event processing in .NET:

❑   An object that can raise events is known as an ***event source***. For example, a `Button` object is an event source because it raises events such as `Click` and `MouseEnter`. The event source ***publishes*** the events it can raise; in Visual Basic .NET, we use the `Event` keyword to publish an event in a class definition.

❑   Objects that define event handler methods are known as ***event receivers***. Event receivers ***subscribe*** to the events they wish to handle on the event source. An event receiver must provide an event-handler method with the correct signature for the event it is subscribing to. The event source uses a multicast delegate to keep track of these event-handler methods.

❑   The event source ***raises*** events when something important happens. For example, `Button` objects raise the `Click` event when the user clicks the button control on the screen. When an event is raised, the event source automatically uses its multicast delegate to call the specified event-handler method on each event receiver.

The following diagram illustrates the relationship between an event-source object and event-receiver object(s):

Figure 1

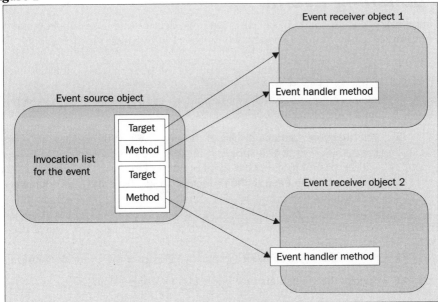

In this simple example, the event-source object only raises a single kind of event. The event-source object has an invocation list for this event, to keep track of the event-receiver objects that have subscribed to this event. Each entry in the invocation list stores two pieces of information:

❑   `Target` is a reference to an event-receiver object

❑   `Method` is a reference to the event-handler method on the event-receiver object

When the event source object raises an event, it uses the information in the invocation list to call each of the registered event-handler methods.

> *In Figure 1, we've only shown the event-handler methods in the event-receiver objects. In reality, the event-receiver objects will have additional methods, properties, fields, and so on.*

It should not come as a surprise that .NET uses a multicast delegate to provide the infrastructure for maintaining an invocation list of targets and methods.

So much for the theory, let's see how to use events in real Visual Basic .NET code. We'll begin by seeing how to define events in a class.

Publishing Events

To publish events in Visual Basic .NET, we must declare `Event` members in the event-source class. We must specify two pieces of information for each event:

❑ The name of the event. For example, the `Button` class publishes events named `Click`, `MouseOver`, and so on. We should declare `Event` members for things that can happen to instances of our class, which might interest other objects.

❑ The signature (parameter list) of the event. When the event-source object raises the event, it will supply values for these parameters. These values will be passed to the event-handler method in the event-receiver object. This implies the event-handler methods must have the same signature as the event.

There are two slightly different ways to publish an event in the event-source class:

❑ Specify the event signature explicitly, as part of the event declaration

❑ Specify the event signature implicitly, by using a delegate

We'll investigate both techniques in the next few pages. To help you understand the merits and disadvantages of each approach, we'll take a look at the MSIL code that gets generated in each case. Then we'll look at some related issues, such as defining shared events.

Specifying the Event Signature Explicitly

The simplest way, although not necessarily the best way, to publish an event is to specify the signature as part of the `Event` declaration. In the next few pages, we'll see two examples of how to define events using an explicit signature:

❑ Defining a single event using an explicit signature

❑ Defining several events that have the same signature

Defining a Single Event using an Explicit Signature

The following example shows how to define a single event using an explicit signature. The example uses a class named `BankAccount`, and defines an event named `Overdrawn`. We've only shown the event definition in this class at the moment, but we'll build on this functionality as we proceed through the chapter.

The source code for this example is located in the download folder `DelegatesEvents\PublishSingleEventBySignature`:

```
Imports System

Public Class BankAccount

    Public Event Overdrawn(ByVal AccountHolder As String, _
                           ByVal HowMuchOverdrawn As Double, _
                           ByVal WhenOverdrawn As DateTime)

    ' Plus other members...

End Class
```

Note the following points in this example:

❑ In Visual Basic .NET, we use the `Event` keyword to publish an event in a class.

❑ Events are members of the class, and can therefore have an access modifier. The default accessibility is `Public`, because the nature of events is to broadcast information to other objects in the application. However, it is also possible to restrict event accessibility if appropriate:

   • We can declare events as `Private`, which means only methods in our own class can register as event-handler methods. We can use this technique to trigger behavior in our own class. For example, we might have a background thread that triggers a `Tick` event every second, and define event-handler methods in our class to perform tasks on each timer tick. Such a pattern is rare, but can lead to quite elegant code.

   • We can declare events as `Friend`, which means only methods in the same assembly can register as event-handler methods. We can use this technique in large applications that are spread over several assemblies. To reduce dependencies between assemblies, we can define class members with `Friend` accessibility so that they cannot be accessed in other assemblies. This makes it easier to change the code inside one assembly, without adversely affecting the code in any other assembly. We investigate assemblies in detail in Chapter 8.

   • We can declare events as `Protected`, which means only methods in this class, or classes that inherit from this class, can register as event-handler methods.

❑ The name of the event in this example is `Overdrawn`. Later in the chapter, we'll see how to raise this event when the customer tries to withdraw too much money from the account.

❑ The `Overdrawn` event has three parameters: the name of the account holder, the amount the account is overdrawn, and the date and time at which the account became overdrawn. We'll need to supply these parameters when we raise the event. The parameters will then be passed into each event-handler method, so event receiver objects get some context about whose account is overdrawn, by how much, and when it happened.

❑ Events cannot have a return type. Events constitute a one-way flow of information from the event-source object to the event-receiver objects. It is an error to specify a return type in an event definition. As such, while events make use of delegates, it's clear there are ways we can use delegates that are not exposed by events. Ignoring the other capabilities of delegates and just using the event infrastructure would be a mistake.

Let's see how our sample is compiled into MSIL code. Type the following command at the command prompt:

```
> ildasm PublishSingleEventBySignature.dll
```

The MSIL Disassembler window displays the following information (we've expanded the nodes in this screenshot, to show the details for each entry):

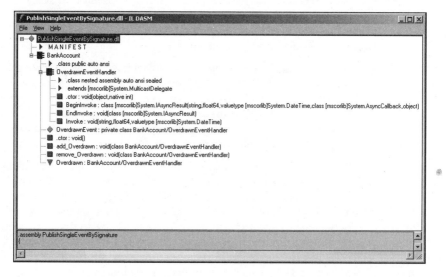

The MSIL code provides a great deal of insight into how the .NET event mechanism works internally. Let's describe some of the members of the BankAccount class:

❑ OverdrawnEventHandler

This is a multicast delegate type. The compiler generated this delegate type from our Overdrawn event definition. When we define events with an explicit signature, the compiler takes the name of the event, appends EventHandler, and creates a multicast delegate type with this name.

The OverdrawnEventHandler delegate type has all the members we might expect, given our discussion of delegates in the first part of the chapter. The Invoke method is the most important member of the delegate; when we raise the event, the event mechanism uses Invoke to invoke the event-handler methods in the event-receiver objects.

❑ OverdrawnEvent

This field will hold an instance of the OverdrawnEventHandler delegate type. The invocation list for this delegate instance contains all the information about the event-receiver objects and event-handler methods for this event.

Notice that OverdrawnEvent is private. The client code does not interact directly with this delegate instance; all the code to manage the delegate instance is encapsulated within the BankAccount class itself.

The MSIL syntax BankAccount/OverdrawnEventHandler indicates OverdrawnEventHandler is a nested type defined inside the BankAccount class.

❑ add_Overdrawn

The compiler generated this method, to add a new event handler for the Overdrawn event. This method is called whenever another event-receiver subscribes to this event. Notice the add_Overdrawn method receives a parameter of type class BankAccount/OverdrawnEventHandler. This parameter is an instance of the OverdrawnEventHandler delegate type, and specifies a new event-receiver object and event-handler method for the Overdrawn event.

If you open up the IL, take a look at statements IL_0002, IL_0007, and IL_0008. These statements combine the new delegate instance into the OverdrawnEvent multicast delegate member in our BankAccount object. Notice the MSIL call to the method System.Delegate::Combine, to combine the new delegate into the multicast delegate.

❑ remove_Overdrawn

The compiler generated this method, to remove an existing event handler for the Overdrawn event. This method is called whenever an event receiver unsubscribes from this event. Looking at the IL, you'll fnd remove_Overdrawn is similar to add_Overdrawn, except that we now call the System.Delegate::Remove method to remove the specified delegate.

❑ Overdrawn

This member is used for internal purposes within the class, to identify the names of the methods for adding and removing event handlers for the Overdrawn event. It's similar in form to the property members we saw in Chapter 5, which pointed to the getter and setter methods. The MSIL code for this member is shown below:

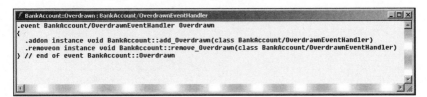

```
BankAccount::Overdrawn : BankAccount/OverdrawnEventHandler          _ □ x
.event BankAccount/OverdrawnEventHandler Overdrawn
{
    .addon instance void BankAccount::add_Overdrawn(class BankAccount/OverdrawnEventHandler)
    .removeon instance void BankAccount::remove_Overdrawn(class BankAccount/OverdrawnEventHandler)
} // end of event BankAccount::Overdrawn
```

That concludes our journey into MSIL, for the time being at least. It's a worthwhile exercise examining the MSIL code for events, because it helps us understand how the .NET event mechanism works internally. To summarize our findings, if we define an event named Xxxx with an explicit signature, the compiler generates the following members in our class:

- ❑ A multicast delegate type named XxxxEventHandler

- ❑ A private field named XxxxEvent, to hold an instance of this delegate type

- ❑ A helper method named add_Xxxx, to add event receivers to the invocation list of the delegate instance

- ❑ A helper method named remove_Xxxx, to remove event receivers from the invocation list of the delegate instance

- ❑ An internal member named Xxxx, which identifies the helper methods for adding and removing event receivers

Defining Several Events that have the Same Signtaure

It's not unusual for a class to publish several events, to indicate all the important things that can happen in the class. It's quite common for these events to have the same signature, to make it easier for event-receiver objects to anticipate the parameter list they need to specify in their event-handler methods, or even to use the same method to handle multiple events.

Many of the standard events in the .NET Framework adopt the same pattern for event signatures. Specifically, the events define the following two parameters:

- ❑ The source object that raised the event.

- ❑ Data for the event. The data is usually represented by a class that inherits from System.EventArgs.

For consistency with the .NET Framework, we recommend you adopt this pattern when you define events in your own class.

The following example shows how to define events using this pattern. The code for this example is located in the folder DelegatesEvents\PublishSeveralEventBySignature. Let's begin by looking at the BankAccount class:

```
Public Class BankAccount

    ' Define events, using recommended pattern for event signatures
    Public Event Overdrawn(ByVal Source As BankAccount, _
                           ByVal e As BankAccountEventArgs)

    Public Event LargeDeposit(ByVal Source As BankAccount, _
                              ByVal e As BankAccountEventArgs)

    ' Plus other members...

End Class
```

The BankAccount class defines two events. The signature for these events follows the recommended pattern in the .NET Framework:

❏   The first parameter for each event is the event-source object. We've specified BankAccount as the type for this parameter. This means event-handler methods will receive a strongly-typed reference to the BankAccount object that raised the event, so they can find out information about that bank account.

Many standard events in the .NET Framework use System.Object for the first parameter, for maximum genericity and uniformity across all events. However, we've avoided this approach in our example, because it requires the event-handler method to downcast the parameter into the required type (BankAccount) if it wants to find out information about the bank account that raised the event.

❏   The second parameter for each event is a BankAccountEventArgs object. We'll show the source code for the BankAccountEventArgs class next.

The BankAccountEventArgs class provides contextual information about bank account events. Here is the definition of the BankAccountEventArgs class:

```
Public Class BankAccountEventArgs
    Inherits EventArgs

    ' Private fields
    Private mAccountHolder As String
    Private mAmount As Double
    Private mTimeStamp As DateTime

    ' Constructor, to initialize private fields
    Public Sub New(ByVal AccountHolder As String, _
                   ByVal Amount As Double, _
                   ByVal TimeStamp As DateTime)

        mAccountHolder = AccountHolder
        mAmount = Amount
        mTimeStamp = TimeStamp
```

217

```
    End Sub

    ' Properties, to get the values held in the private fields
    Public ReadOnly Property AccountHolder() As String
        Get
            Return mAccountHolder
        End Get
    End Property

    Public ReadOnly Property Amount() As Double
        Get
            Return mAmount
        End Get
    End Property

    Public ReadOnly Property TimeStamp() As DateTime
        Get
            Return mTimeStamp
        End Get
    End Property

End Class
```

Note the following points in the `BankAccountEventArgs` class:

❑   `BankAccountEventArgs` inherits from `System.EventArgs`, as recommended in the .NET Framework event model.

❑   `BankAccountEventArgs` provides properties that can be used by event-handler methods, to find out more information about the event. We resisted the temptation to simply declare `Public` fields, because this violates the overall goal of encapsulation for all data types.

To examine the MSIL code for this sample, compile it into a DLL, and open it up in `ildasm`.

The MSIL Disassembler window displays the following information (we've expanded the nodes in this screenshot, to show the details for the relevant entries):

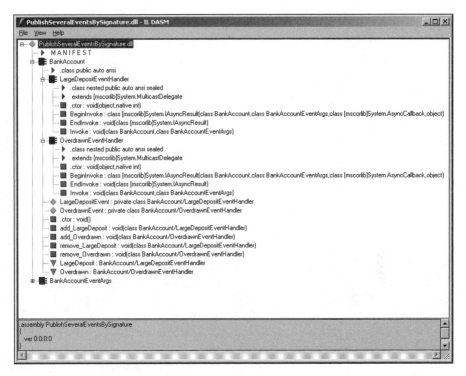

Notice that the compiler has generated two separate delegate types within the BankAccount class:

❑ LargeDepositEventHandler

The compiler generated this delegate type from our definition of the LargeDeposit event. The Invoke method in this delegate type will invoke event-handler methods with the signature specified by the LargeDeposit event.

❑ OverdrawnEventHandler

The compiler generated this delegate type from our definition of the Overdrawn event. The Invoke method in this delegate type will invoke event-handler methods with the signature specified by the Overdrawn event.

Do you notice any similarities between LargeDepositEventHandler and OverdrawnEventHandler? In fact, these delegate types are identical, because they were generated from events with identical signatures. But they are separate types, and each type will take up separate memory in our application. The compiler always generates a separate delegate type for each event, even if the events have the same signature. If we define many events in our class, we're going to get a lot of redundancy.

Is there a better way of doing it? Well, yes. We can base our events on an existing delegate type. This enables the compiler to reuse the same delegate type for each event. We'll do just that in the next section.

Specifying the Event Signature Implicitly by Using a Delegate

If we define several events with the same signature in a class, the preferred way to define the events is by using an existing delegate.

The following example shows how to define a delegate to represent the signature for events in the `BankAccount` class. The source code for this example is located in the download folder `DelegatesEvents\PublishSingleEventByDelegate`:

```
Imports System

Public Delegate Sub BankAcountEventHandler( _
                    ByVal Source As BankAccount, _
                    ByVal e As BankAccountEventArgs)

Public Class BankAccount

    ' Define events, using our delegate type to denote the
signatures
    Public Event Overdrawn As BankAccountEventHandler
    Public Event LargeDeposit As BankAccountEventHandler

    ' Plus other members...

End Class

Public Class BankAccountEventArgs
    Inherits EventArgs

    ' Same as before...

End Class
```

Note the following points in this example:

- ❏ `BankAcountEventHandler` is a delegate type, and defines the common signature used by events in the `BankAccount` class. We've followed the naming convention `XxxxEventHandler` for our delegate type, which is consistent with the naming convention used by the compiler when it generates delegate types from events with explicit signatures.

- ❏ In the `BankAccount` class, we use the `BankAccountEventHandler` delegate to implicitly specify the signature of the `Overdrawn` and `LargeDeposit` events. This makes it easier for developers to see that the `Overdrawn` and `LargeDeposit` events have the same signature. It also makes it easier for us to change the signature for these events in future; we can change the signature in the delegate, rather than having to modify the signature in each individual event declaration.

220

The MSIL Disassembler window for the compiled DLL of this code displays the following information (we've expanded the nodes in this screenshot, to show the details for the relevant entries):

Notice the following points in the MSIL code:

❑   There is a single delegate type named `BankAccountEventHandler`.

❑   The `BankAccount` class has fields named `LargeDepositEvent` and `OverdrawnEvent`, which are defined with the `BankAccountEventHandler` delegate type. This delegate type specifies the common signature for these events.

❑   The `BankAccount` class has a pair of methods named `add_LargeDeposit` and `remove_LargeDeposit`, to add and remove subscribers for the `LargeDeposit` event. These methods combine and remove entries in the invocation list of the `LargeDepositEvent` delegate instance.

❑   The `BankAccount` class also has a pair of methods named `add_Overdrawn` and `remove_Overdrawn`, to add and remove subscribers for the `Overdrawn` event. These methods combine and remove entries in the invocation list of the `OverdrawnEvent` delegate instance.

As you can see, using a predefined delegate for events considerably simplifies the MSIL code that gets generated by the compiler. In a large class, containing many events, the savings can be considerable

Defining Shared Events

To conclude our discussions on how to publish events, we'll show how to publish Shared events in a class. Shared events are much less common than instance events, for reasons that will become apparent when we look at how to subscribe to events in the next section.

The following example shows how to define a Shared event, to indicate that the interest rate for all bank accounts has changed. The source code for this example is located in the download folder DelegatesEvents\PublishSharedEvents:

```
Imports System

Public Delegate Sub InterestRateEventHandler(ByVal NewValue As
Double)

Public Class BankAccount

    Public Shared Event RateChanged As InterestRateEventHandler
    Public Shared Event ThresholdChanged As InterestRateEventHandler

    ' Plus other members...

End Class
```

Note the following points in this example:

❑   InterestRateEventHandler is a delegate type, and defines the common signature used by interest-rate-related events in the BankAccount class. Notice the signature does not contain a 'source' parameter, because the event will be raised by the BankAccount class rather than a particular BankAccount instance. If you want to follow the conventional signature when publishing an event like this, you'll have to pass Nothing as the parameter representing the originating object.

❑   In the BankAcount class, we use the InterestRateEventHandler delegate to specify two Shared events, named RateChanged and ThresholdChanged.

Again, compile a DLL and view the assembly with ildasm.

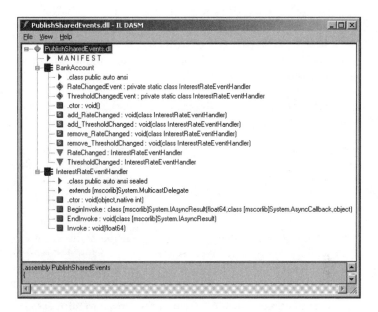

Notice the following points in the MSIL code:

❑ The `InterestRateEventHandler` delegate type appears as a normal delegate type. There is no indication that the delegate type applies to instance events or Shared events.

❑ The `BankAccount` class has fields named `RateChangedEvent` and `ThresholdChangedEvent`. These fields are declared as `static` (which is MSIL-speak for Shared).

❑ The `BankAccount` class has a pair of methods named `add_RateChanged` and `remove_RateChanged`, to add and remove subscribers for the `RateChanged` event. These methods are declared as `static` (Shared).

❑ The `BankAccount` class also has a pair of methods named `add_ThresholdChanged` and `remove_ThresholdChanged`, to add and remove subscribers for the `ThresholdChanged` event. These methods are also declared as `static` (Shared).

We'll see how to subscribe to Shared events, and how to raise Shared events, later in the chapter.

Subscribing to Events

In the previous section, we saw how to publish events in the event-source object. In this section, we'll see how event-receiver objects can subscribe to these events. There are two different ways to subscribe to an event:

❑ Define event handlers statically, by using the `WithEvents` and `Handles` keywords

❑ Define event handlers dynamically, by using the `AddHandler` and `RemoveHandler` keywords

We'll investigate both techniques in the next few pages, and describe when to use one approach or the other.

When a method has been subscribed to an event, it will be called whenever the event is raised. An event is raised by an object that published it using the `RaiseEvent` keyword.

Note the following points about the `RaiseEvent` statement:

❑ The `RaiseEvent` statement requires the name of the event we want to raise, followed by a list of parameter values enclosed in parentheses. These values will be passed into the event-handler methods for this event. If the event does not take any parameters, we must omit the parentheses.

❑ The `RaiseEvent` statement can only be used to raise events defined in the class in which it is used. We cannot raise events defined in other classes. This is a built-in defense mechanism in Visual Basic .NET, to prevent external objects from accidentally (or maliciously) raising our events without our permission.

If we do want to allow external objects to raise one of our events, we can provide a `Public` method that can be called externally to raise the event on demand.

❑ The `RaiseEvent` statement triggers all the event-handler methods for this event. `RaiseEvent` implicitly uses the `Invoke` method on the multicast delegate for this event, to invoke all the event-handler methods in its invocation list.

The event-handler methods are invoked in the order they were added to the invocation list. If the event-handler methods were registered statically, using the `WithEvents` and `Handles` keywords, we cannot control the order in which the event-handler methods are registered. Therefore, the event-handler methods should not make any assumptions about the sequence they are invoked.

❑ We can use `RaiseEvent` to raise `Shared` events. Use the syntax `RaiseEvent SharedEventName(ParameterList)` to raise a `Shared` event.

Defining Event Handlers Statically

In this section, we'll see how to use the `WithEvents` and `Handles` keywords to define event handlers statically. In other words, we'll see how to define fixed event-handler methods at compile time. This approach is suitable if we know what objects we are dealing with, and we know for sure which methods will handle these events. We'll look at two examples:

- ❑ Defining event handlers for GUI controls
- ❑ Defining event handlers for general kinds of objects

Defining Event Handlers for GUI Controls

When we create a form in Visual Studio .NET, we can add controls to the form and define event handlers for these controls. This is an everyday task for most Visual Basic developers, and we rarely stop to think about what is actually happening under the hood. The time has come to look at the code that gets generated by Visual Studio .NET, and see how it fits in with our understanding of the .NET Framework event model.

We'll use the following Windows Form to help us with our enquiries. The code for this example is located in the download folder `DelegatesEvents\SubscribeGUIStatically`. We used Visual Studio .NET to create this code, but we could have written it all manually; there is no magic here.

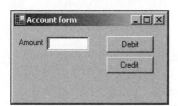

When we add controls to the form, Visual Studio .NET adds field declarations such as the following to our form class:

```
Friend WithEvents txtAmount As System.Windows.Forms.TextBox
Friend WithEvents btnDebit As System.Windows.Forms.Button
Friend WithEvents btnCredit As System.Windows.Forms.Button
```

The `WithEvents` keyword indicates we might want to handle some of the events raised by the object contained in the specified field. There is no obligation to handle any of these events.

The following restrictions apply on where we can use the `WithEvents` keyword:

❑ We can only use WithEvents on fields within a class definition. We cannot use WithEvents within a Structure definition.

❑ We can only use WithEvents for class-level fields in our class. We cannot use WithEvents for local variables.

The following restrictions apply on how we use the WithEvents keyword:

❑ We can only use WithEvents for types that raise events. This makes sense; there is no point gearing up to handle events from an object that will never generate an event!

❑ We can only use WithEvents to handle events from a Class type or an Interface type. We cannot use WithEvents to handle events from a Structure type.

❑ We can only use WithEvents to handle instance events. We cannot use WithEvents to handle Shared events, because the WithEvents mechanism requires an instance of a type. The only way to handle Shared events is by using the AddHandler and RemoveHandler keywords, which we discuss in the section *Defining Event Handlers Dynamically* later in this chapter.

When we add event handlers for controls on our form, Visual Studio .NET generates methods such as the following (we've written some simple code in each event-handler method, for added excitement):

```
Private Sub btnDebit_Click(ByVal sender As System.Object, _
                ByVal e As System.EventArgs) _
            Handles btnDebit.Click

    MessageBox.Show("Debit $" & CInt(txtAmount.Text), _
                "Click event handler for btnDebit")

End Sub

' Handle the Click event on btnCredit
Private Sub btnCredit_Click(ByVal sender As System.Object, _
                ByVal e As System.EventArgs) _
            Handles btnCredit.Click

    MessageBox.Show("Credit $" & CInt(txtAmount.Text), _
                "Click event handler for btnCredit")

End Sub
```

Note the following points in these event-handler methods:

❑ The event-handler methods adhere to the standard .NET Framework pattern for event signatures:

- The first parameter is the sender of the event, such as a button. For genericity, the predefined events in the .NET Framework use `System.Object` as the declared type for this parameter. At run time, the event source object will be a specific kind of control, such as a `Button` in this example.

- The second parameter is a `System.EventArgs` object (or an object of a class that inherits from `System.EventArgs`). Note that the `System.EventArgs` class itself is an empty class; it is just a placeholder in the inheritance hierarchy, from which we can inherit our own 'event arguments' classes.

❑ The `Handles` keyword specifies a particular instance event on a specific object (this explains why we can't use the `WithEvents/Handles` mechanism to handle `Shared` events):

- The `btnDebit_Click` method handles the `Click` event from the `btnDebit` object

- The `btnCredit_Click` method handles the `Click` event from the `btnCredit` object

All of the event-related syntax in the previous code sample was generated by Visual Studio .NET. It's also possible to write event-handler methods manually. Consider the following event-handler method:

```
Private Sub btnAny_Click(ByVal sender As System.Object, _
                         ByVal e As System.EventArgs) _
              Handles btnDebit.Click, btnCredit.Click

    If TypeOf sender Is Button Then

        Dim theButton As Button = CType(sender, Button)

        sbStatus.Text = "Clicked " & theButton.Text & _
                        ", amount $" & txtAmount.Text

    End If

End Sub
```

Note the following points in this event-handler method:

❑ The `Handles` keyword allows us to handle any number of events in the same method. For example, the `btnAny_Click` method handles two different events:

- The `Click` event from the `btnDebit` object

- The `Click` event from the `btnCredit` object

❑ In the btnAny_Click method, we display a message in the status bar to indicate which button was clicked. To obtain this information, we need to get the Text property from the button that raised the event. The sender parameter identifies the event-source object, but sender is typed as Object (not Button). We must therefore downcast (convert) the sender parameter into the Button type, by using the expression CType(sender, Button).

Downcasting is an inherently dangerous operation, because it assumes we categorically know the run-time type of the object we are dealing with. We could argue the event-source object is definitely a Button, because the event-handler method only handles events from btnDebit and btnCredit. However, in future we might add another event to this list, for a different type of control. Therefore, before we downcast sender into a Button object, we use the following test:

```
If TypeOf sender Is Button Then ...
```

This test confirms the sender parameter really does refer to a Button object at run time. We recommend you always perform type checking before you carry out a downcast operation.

To compile the application, open a .NET Framework command-prompt window, move to the folder that contains the example, and type the following command on one line:

```
> vbc /r:System.dll /r:System.Windows.Forms.dll
        /r:System.Drawing.dll /t:winexe /m:Form1
        SubscribeGUIStatically.vb
```

To run the application, type the following command:

```
> SubscribeGUIStatically.exe
```

The main form in the application appears, and allows us to enter a number in the text field as follows:

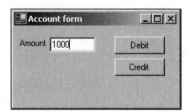

When we click the **Debit** button (for example), the Button object raises the Click event. The invocation list for this event executes all the event-handler methods for this event. There are two event-handler methods for the Click event on the btn_Debit button:

228

❑   The `btnDebit_Click` method displays the following message box:

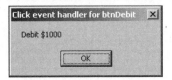

❑   The `btnAny_Click` method displays a message in the status bar of the main form:

It's useful to see how our application is compiled into MSIL code. Type the following command at the command prompt:

```
> ildasm SubscribeGUIStatically.exe
```

The MSIL Disassembler window displays the following information (we've expanded the nodes in this screenshot, to show the details for each entry):

This MSIL code helps us understand how the compiler generates event-handler code when it sees the WithEvents/Handles keywords. For each field we declared with the WithEvents keyword, the compiler generates the following MSIL code:

❑   The compiler generates a private field with a leading underscore. For example:

  •   The btnCredit field has been renamed to _btnCredit

  •   The btnDebit field has been renamed to _btnDebit

  •   The txtAmount field has been renamed to _txtAmount

❑   The compiler generates a 'get' property procedure to get each control. For example:

  •   The get_btnCredit procedure gets the Button control referenced by the _btnCredit field

  •   The get_btnDebit procedure gets the Button control referenced by the _btnDebit field

  •   The get_txtAmount procedure gets the TextBox control referenced by the _txtAmount field

- ❑ The compiler generates a 'set' property procedure for each control. Each 'set' procedure takes any methods in the class that were declared as 'handling' an event from the relevant field, and adds them as event handlers. For example:

  - The set_btnCredit procedure adds btnCredit_Click and btnAny_Click as event-handler methods for the Click event on the _btnCredit button

  - The set_btnDebit procedure adds btnDebit_Click and btnAny_Click as event-handler methods for the Click event on the _btnDebit button

  - The set_txtAmount procedure does not add any event-handler methods, because we don't handle any events from the _txtAmount text field

- ❑ Visual Studio .NET generates code in the InitializeComponent method, to create the components and put them into the member fields. Since the fields get turned into properties, this will call the 'set' property procedures. This hooks up our event-handler methods to the events they need to handle.

Defining Event Handlers for General Kinds of Objects

The previous example showed how to use the WithEvents and Handles keywords to define static event handlers for GUI events. We can use this technique to handle non-GUI events too, such as the Overdrawn and LargeDeposit events raised by BankAccount objects.

In the next few pages, we'll extend the 'account form' we introduced in the previous section, so that it is associated with a BankAccount object. The account form will handle the Overdrawn and LargeDeposit events that are raised by the BankAccount object, and will display a message box when either event occurs. This example illustrates how to use events to decouple business object (such as BankAccount) from the GUI code that displays these objects.

The source code for this example is located in the download folder DelegatesEvents\SubscribeGeneralStatically. Let's begin by looking at the complete implementation for the BankAccount class, to remind ourselves of the events in this class and to see how they occur:

```
Imports System

Public Delegate Sub BankAccountEventHandler( _
                    ByVal Source As BankAccount, _
                    ByVal e As BankAccountEventArgs)

Public Class BankAccount
```

```
    ' Define events, using our delegate type
    ' to denote the signatures
    Public Event Overdrawn As BankAccountEventHandler
    Public Event LargeDeposit As BankAccountEventHandler

    ' Private fields for this BankAccount instance
    Private mHolder As String
    Private mBalance As Double

    ' Constructor
    Public Sub New(ByVal Holder As String, ByVal Balance As Double)
        mHolder = Holder
        mBalance = Balance
    End Sub

    ' Debit money from account
    Public Sub Debit(ByVal Amount As Double)

        mBalance -= Amount

        ' Raise event if account is overdrawn (discussed later...)
        If (mBalance < 0) Then
            Dim Args As New BankAccountEventArgs(mHolder, _
                                                 Amount, _
                                                 DateTime.Now)
            RaiseEvent Overdrawn(Me, Args)
        End If

    End Sub


    ' Credit money into account
    Public Sub Credit(ByVal Amount As Double)

        mBalance += Amount

        ' Raise event if the amount deposited is suspiciously large!
        If Amount >= 1000000 Then
            Dim Args As New BankAccountEventArgs(mHolder, _
                                                 Amount, _
                                                 DateTime.Now)
            RaiseEvent LargeDeposit(Me, Args)
        End If

    End Sub


    ' Property to get the current balance
    Public ReadOnly Property Balance() As Double
        Get
            Return mBalance
        End Get
    End Property
```

```
      ' Displayable representation of account
      Public Overrides Function ToString() As String
         Return mHolder
      End Function

   End Class

   Public Class BankAccountEventArgs
      Inherits EventArgs

      ' Same as before...

   End Class
```

Note the following points in this code listing:

❑ The BankAccountEventHandler delegate defines the signature for all events raised by BankAccount instances.

❑ The BankAccount class defines two events, named Overdrawn and LargeDeposit, using the signature defined in the BankAccountEventHandler delegate.

❑ The Debit method raises an Overdrawn event if the balance is negative after the debit.

❑ The Credit method raises a LargeDeposit event if the amount being deposited is $1,000,000 or more.

❑ The BankAccount class also contains a constructor, a property to get the current balance, and a ToString method to return a textual representation of the BankAccount object. You'll see why we need these members shortly.

Now let's see how to define the BankAccountForm class, so that it handles the Overdrawn and LargeDeposit events from a BankAccount object. We can declare a BankAccount field and qualify it with the WithEvents keyword, as follows:

```
   Public Class BankAccountForm
      Inherits System.Windows.Forms.Form

      ' The BankAccountForm is associated with a BankAccount object
      Private WithEvents mTheAccount As New BankAccount("Smith", 0)

      ' Plus other code (see below...)

   End Class
```

We need to extend our form class, so that it calls the Debit and Credit operations on the BankAccount object when the user clicks the Debit or Credit buttons on the form:

```
' Handle the Click event on btnDebit
Private Sub btnDebit_Click(ByVal sender As System.Object, _
                      ByVal e As System.EventArgs) _
            Handles btnDebit.Click

   ' Debit money, and display new balance in caption bar
   mTheAccount.Debit(CInt(txtAmount.Text))
   Text = mTheAccount.ToString() & _
          ", balance: " & mTheAccount.Balance

End Sub

' Handle the Click event on btnCredit
Private Sub btnCredit_Click(ByVal sender As System.Object, _
                      ByVal e As System.EventArgs) _
            Handles btnCredit.Click

   ' Credit money, and display new balance in caption bar
   mTheAccount.Credit(CInt(txtAmount.Text))
   Text = mTheAccount.ToString() & _
          ", balance: " & mTheAccount.Balance

End Sub
```

The BankAccount object generates Overdrawn and LargeDeposit events under certain conditions during a debit or credit operation. We can use the Handles keyword to handle these events in the form class, as follows:

```
' Handle the Overdrawn event on mTheAccount
Private Sub mTheAccount_Overdrawn(ByVal Source As BankAccount, _
                      ByVal e As BankAccountEventArgs) _
            Handles mTheAccount.Overdrawn

   MessageBox.Show("Account holder: " & _
              e.AccountHolder & vbCrLf & _
              "Amount of transaction: " & _
              e.Amount & vbCrLf & _
              "Current balance: " & Source.Balance, _
              "Overdrawn event at " & e.TimeStamp, _
              MessageBoxButtons.OK, _
              MessageBoxIcon.Exclamation)
End Sub

' Handle the LargeDeposit event on mTheAccount
Private Sub mTheAccount_LargeDeposit(ByVal Source As BankAccount, _
                      ByVal e As BankAccountEventArgs)_
            Handles mTheAccount.LargeDeposit

   MessageBox.Show("Account holder: " & _
              e.AccountHolder & vbCrLf & _
              "Amount of transaction: " & _
              e.Amount & vbCrLf & _
              "Current balance: " & Source.Balance, _
              "LargeDeposit event at " & e.TimeStamp, _
              MessageBoxButtons.OK, _
              MessageBoxIcon.Exclamation)
End Sub
```

234

In the code fragment shown, the mTheAccount_Overdrawn method handles the Overdrawn event on the mTheAccount object. The mTheAccount_LargeDeposit method handles the LargeDeposit event on the mTheAccount object. The event-handler methods use the information provided in the BankAccount and BankAccountEventArgs parameters, to display a message box containing information about the event.

To compile the application, open a .NET Framework command-prompt window, move to the folder that contains the example, and type the following command:

```
> vbc /r:System.dll /r:System.Windows.Forms.dll
        /r:System.Drawing.dll /t:winexe /m:BankAccountForm
        BankAccountForm.vb BankAccount.vb
```

To run the application, type the following command:

```
> BankAccountForm.exe
```

The main form in the application appears, and allows us to make debits and credits with the associated BankAccount object. If the account becomes overdrawn, it raises an Overdrawn event. The BankAccountForm handles this event, and displays a message box such as the following:

If the user tries to deposit a suspiciously large amount of money, the BankAccount object raises a LargeDeposit event. The BankAccountForm handles this event, and displays a message box such as the following:

This example has shown how to use events to decouple business objects from GUI objects. We can raise events in the business object, and handle the events in the GUI object. However, there are some restrictions when we use the WithEvents and Handles keywords in this scenario:

- ❑ The event-handler methods are hard-coded to handle specific events (Overdrawn and LargeDeposit) on a specific event-source object (mTheAccount).

- ❑ The event source object must be defined as an instance variable in the event receiver class (BankAccountForm). We cannot define event handlers for local variables, or for a collection of objects.

- ❑ We cannot turn event handling on or off. For example, the BankAccountForm will always receive events from mTheAccount; there is no way to disable events if we want to stop receiving event notifications.

- ❑ We can only handle instance events. We cannot handle Shared events.

We'll see how to overcome these limitations in the following section.

Defining Event Handlers Dynamically

In this section, we see how to use the AddHandler and RemoveHandler keywords to handle events dynamically in the event-receiver object. This approach offers the flexibility that is lacking when we handle events statically. Using the AddHandler and RemoveHandler keywords, we can subscribe to and unsubscribe from any event on any object at any time. This provides a much more adaptable arrangement than is possible with static events, and is usually the preferred approach for business object events.

To illustrate this technique, we'll work through a complete example that turns event handling on and off dynamically for a collection of BankAccount objects. The source code for this example is located in the download folder DelegatesEvents\SubscribeDynamically. The example has a main form with the following appearance:

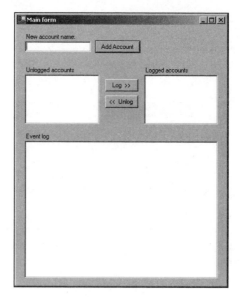

When the user clicks **Add Account**, the application creates a new `BankAccount` object and displays its name in the 'unlogged' listbox on the left of the form. We also create a `BankAccountForm`, to allow the user to debit and credit money with this account:

We saw this form in the previous section of this chapter. In that example, the account form defined static event handlers for the `Overdrawn` and `LargeDeposit` events raised by the bank account. We're going to rearrange the logic now, so that account form does not handle any bank account events. Instead, the user will be able to turn event handling on or off, in the main form in the application:

❏   To enable event logging for a particular account, the user selects an account from the 'unlogged' list box, and then clicks the **Log** button. The application moves the account to the 'logged' list box, and uses `AddHandler` to add event-handler methods for the events from this `BankAccount` object.

❏   To disable event logging for a particular account, the user selects an account from the 'logged' list box, and then clicks the **Unlog** button. The application moves the account to the 'unlogged' list box, and uses `RemoveHandler` to remove event-handler methods for the events from this `BankAccount` object.

When the main form receives an event from a logged `BankAccount` object, the main form displays the event information in the event log textbox as follows:

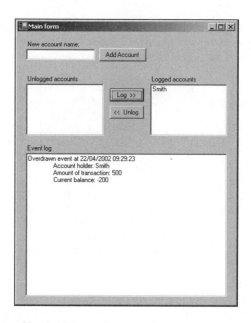

There are three source files in this application:

❑ BankAccount.vb

This file contains the BankAccount class, which provides all the business rules for bank accounts. BankAccount objects raise events according to the required business logic for bank accounts. The signature for these events is defined by the BankAccountEventHandler delegate, and makes use of the BankAccountEventArgs class.

The code in this file is unchanged from the previous example, and does not contain any user-interface code whatsoever.

❑ BankAccountForm.vb

This file contains the BankAccountForm class, which provides a user interface for BankAccount objects. There will be one BankAccountForm object for each BankAccount object.

The code in this file is modified slightly from the previous example, because BankAccountForm does not handle BankAccount events any more. We'll see the revised source code for this class shortly.

❑ MainForm.vb

This file contains the MainForm class, which unsurprisingly represents the main form in the application. This form creates BankAccount objects on demand, and associates them with BankAccountForm objects. The main form contains all the code to add and remove event handlers dynamically, and to handle these events when they occur.

238

Before we look at the event-related code in the `MainForm` class, let's quickly see how the `BankAccountForm` differs from before. The first difference comes in the declaration of the `mTheAccount` field:

```
Public Class BankAccountForm
    Inherits System.Windows.Forms.Form

    ' Every BankAccountForm is associated with a BankAccount
    Private mTheAccount As BankAccount
```

Notice that `mTheAccount` is no longer qualified with the `WithEvents` keyword, because the account form doesn't handle `BankAccount` events any more. `BankAccount` events are now handled dynamically by the main form, as we'll see shortly. By implication, this means we can delete the `mTheAccount_Overdrawn` and `mTheAccount_LargeDeposit` event-handler methods in the account form class.

You may have noticed the declaration of `mTheAccount` doesn't actually create a `BankAccount` object. Instead, the `BankAccount` object will be created in the main form, and passed into the account form shortly thereafter. To enable the account form to become associated with the `BankAccount` object, we provide a write-only property as follows:

```
' Property to set the BankAccount for this form
Public WriteOnly Property Account() As BankAccount
    Set(ByVal Value As BankAccount)
        mTheAccount = Value
        Text = mTheAccount.ToString() & _
               ", balance: " & mTheAccount.Balance
    End Set
End Property
```

Now let's see how the main form brings everything together. We'll begin by showing how the main form creates a new account, and associates the new account with an account form:

```
Public Class MainForm
    Inherits System.Windows.Forms.Form

    ' Create a new BankAccount, and display it in a BankAccountForm
    Private Sub btnAddAccount_Click(ByVal sender As System.Object, _
                                    ByVal e As System.EventArgs) _
                Handles btnAddAccount.Click

        ' Create a new BankAccount object
        Dim anAccount As New BankAccount(txtNewAccountName.Text, _
                                         0.0)
        ' Display BankAccount object in the "unlogged" list box
        lstUnlogged.Items.Add(anAccount)
```

```
              ' Reset focus to text box,
              ' and clear it ready for next account
              txtNewAccountName.Text = ""
              txtNewAccountName.Focus()

              ' Create new BankAccountForm, to display BankAccount object
              Dim aBankAccountForm As New BankAccountForm()
              aBankAccountForm.Account = anAccount
              aBankAccountForm.Show()

          End Sub

          ' Plus other code...

      End Class
```

Note the following points in the `btnAddAccount_Click` method:

❏ We create a new `BankAccount` object, with the specified account holder name and an initial balance of 0.

❏ We add the new `BankAccount` object to the 'unlogged' listbox. In our application, all bank accounts will be unlogged initially, so we don't expect to receive any events to start off with. Note that the listbox implicitly uses the `BankAccount`'s `ToString` method to display the bank account details.

❏ We create a new `BankAccountForm` object, and use its `Account` property to associate it with the new `BankAccount` object.

Each time the user creates a new account, a separate `BankAccountForm` appears on the screen. This enables the user to debit and credit money into individual accounts, as required. This might cause the `BankAccount` objects to generate events, but we have not yet added any event handlers for these events.

To enable event logging on a particular account, the user selects an account from the 'unlogged' list box and then clicks the **Log** button. The **Log** button dynamically adds event handlers for the selected account, as follows:

```
Public Class MainForm
    Inherits System.Windows.Forms.Form

    ' Dynamically add event handlers for the selected account
    Private Sub btnLog_Click(ByVal sender As System.Object, _
                             ByVal e As System.EventArgs) _
             Handles btnLog.Click

        ' Get selected item in 'unlogged' list box
        Dim Selected As Object = lstUnlogged.SelectedItem

        ' Make sure the user has selected an item!
        If Selected Is Nothing Then
```

```
        MessageBox.Show( _
                "Please select an account to log.", _
                "Error logging account", _
                MessageBoxButtons.OK, _
                MessageBoxIcon.Error)
    Else

            ' Downcast selected item to the BankAccount type
            Dim Acc As BankAccount = _
                CType(Selected, BankAccount)

            ' Add handlers for all events on
            ' this BankAccount object
            AddHandler Acc.Overdrawn, _
                    AddressOf Me.BankAccount_Overdrawn

            AddHandler Acc.LargeDeposit, _
                    AddressOf Me.BankAccount_LargeDeposit

            ' Move account to the 'logged' list box
            lstLogged.Items.Add(Selected)
            lstUnlogged.Items.Remove(Selected)

        End If

    End Sub

    ' Plus other code...

End Class
```

Note the following points in the btnLog_Click method:

- ❑ We use the SelectedItem property in the 'unlogged' listbox, to get the selected item.

- ❑ If the user has selected an item, we downcast this object into the BankAccount data type. This enables us to access the members defined in the BankAccount class.

- ❑ We use the AddHandler statement to dynamically add an event-handler method for the Overdrawn event on the selected BankAccount object. The AddHandler statement requires two arguments:

  - The first argument specifies the event-source object (the selected BankAccount object), and the event we want to handle (Overdrawn).

  - The second argument specifies the event-handler method. We've specified an event-handler method named BankAccount_Overdrawn in the main form.

AddHandler gives us the flexibility to dynamically add event-handler methods for any event from any object. We can even use AddHandler to add event-handler methods for Shared events; use the syntax ClassName.SharedEventName for the first argument to AddHandler.

❑ We use the AddHandler statement again, to dynamically add an event-handler method for the LargeDeposit event on the selected BankAccount object.

To disable event logging on a particular account, the user selects an account from the 'logged' listbox and then clicks the **Unlog** button. The **Unlog** button dynamically removes event handlers for the selected account, as follows:

```
Public Class MainForm
    Inherits System.Windows.Forms.Form

    ' Dynamically remove event handlers for the selected account
    Private Sub btnUnlog_Click(ByVal sender As System.Object, _
                        ByVal e As System.EventArgs) _
                Handles btnUnlog.Click

        ' Get selected item in 'logged' list box
        Dim Selected As Object = lstLogged.SelectedItem

        ' Make sure the user has selected an item!
        If Selected Is Nothing Then

            MessageBox.Show("Please select an account to unlog.", _
                        "Error unlogging account", _
                        MessageBoxButtons.OK, _
                        MessageBoxIcon.Error)
        Else
            ' Downcast selected item to the BankAccount type
            Dim Acc As BankAccount = CType(Selected, BankAccount)

            ' Remove handlers for all events on this BankAccount
            RemoveHandler Acc.Overdrawn, _
                        AddressOf Me.BankAccount_Overdrawn

            RemoveHandler Acc.LargeDeposit, _
                        AddressOf Me.BankAccount_LargeDeposit

            ' Move account to the 'unlogged' list box
            lstUnlogged.Items.Add(Selected)
            lstLogged.Items.Remove(Selected)

        End If

    End Sub

    ' Plus other code...

End Class
```

As you can see, the btnUnog_Click method is essentially the inverse of the btnLog_Click method. The only salient difference is that we use RemoveHandler to remove the specified event-handler method on the designated event. Like the AddHandler statement, RemoveHandler requires two arguments:

❑   The first argument specifies the event source object, and the event for which we want to remove an event-handler method.

❑   The second argument specifies the event-handler method we want to remove. Note that we remove event-handler methods individually; this enables us to remove some event-handler methods, while retaining others. We can be choosy.

All that remains is to show the event-handler methods in the main form:

```
Public Class MainForm
    Inherits System.Windows.Forms.Form

    ' Handle Overdrawn event from any BankAccount
    Public Sub BankAccount_Overdrawn( _
                            ByVal sender As BankAccount, _
                            ByVal args As BankAccountEventArgs)

        Me.txtEventLog.AppendText( _
            "Overdrawn event at " & args.TimeStamp & vbCrLf & _
            vbTab & "Account holder: " & _
            args.AccountHolder & vbCrLf & _
            vbTab & "Amount of transaction: " & _
            args.Amount & vbCrLf & _
            vbTab & "Current balance: " & sender.Balance & _
            vbCrLf & vbCrLf)
    End Sub

    ' Handle LargeDeposit event from any BankAccount
    Public Sub BankAccount_LargeDeposit( _
                            ByVal sender As BankAccount, _
                            ByVal args As BankAccountEventArgs)

        Me.txtEventLog.AppendText( _
            "LargeDeposit event at " & args.TimeStamp & vbCrLf & _
            vbTab & "Account holder: " & _
            args.AccountHolder & vbCrLf & _
            vbTab & "Amount of transaction: " & _
            args.Amount & vbCrLf & _
            vbTab & "Current balance: " & sender.Balance & _
            vbCrLf & vbCrLf)

    End Sub

    ' Plus other code...

End Class
```

Note the following points in these event-handler methods:

❑ There is no `Handles` keyword at the end of the event-handler methods. The `Handles` keyword is only required if we are using static event handling via the `WithEvents` keyword, to help the compiler hook up event-handler methods at compile time. If we are using dynamic event binding, the `AddHandler` and `RemoveHandler` statements take care of hooking up event-handler methods at run time.

❑ The event-handler methods have the correct signature to handle the `Overdrawn` event and the `LargeDeposit` event, respectively. Otherwise, we'd get a compiler error when we use `AddHandler` and `RemoveHandler` with these methods.

❑ The event-handler methods use the information supplied in the `BankAccount` and `BankAccountEventArgs` parameters, to obtain contextual information about the event. We display this information in the event-log textbox at the bottom of the main form.

To compile the application, open a .NET Framework command-prompt window, move to the folder that contains the example, and type the following command on one line:

```
> vbc /r:System.dll /r:System.Windows.Forms.dll
        /r:System.Drawing.dll /t:winexe /m:MainForm
        MainForm.vb BankAccountForm.vb BankAccount.vb
```

To run the application, type the following command:

```
> MainForm.exe
```

To illustrate the dynamic event handling in this application, the following screenshot shows what happens when we perform these tasks:

❑ Create an account named Emily, and add it to the 'logged' list.

❑ Create another account named Thomas, but do not add it to the 'logged' list.

❑ Credit $300 in each account, and then debit $500 from each account.

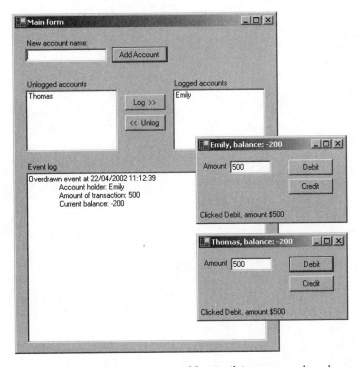

Notice the event log shows events generated by Emily's account, but does not show the events generated by Thomas's account. Thomas's account does generate events, but we choose not to handle them.

Summary

This has been a long chapter, but we've covered a lot of important ground. Events have been a fundamental part of Visual Basic since its inception in the early 1990s, and a good understanding of how events work in Visual Basic .NET is essential.

As we've seen, events in the .NET Framework make use of multicast delegates. We can define delegate types to specify the method signatures for our event-handler methods. The event mechanism implicitly creates delegate objects, and uses these delegate objects to keep track of the event handlers for each event.

Delegates can be used with or without the event mechanism. We've seen how to use delegates in general programming tasks, such as specifying which method to invoke but delaying its execution until we are ready.

We've seen many examples in this chapter, to illustrate recommended best practices for events and delegates in Visual Basic .NET. We've also spent some time looking at MSIL code, to see how events and delegates work internally. This will help you decide how to use events and delegates effectively in your own applications.

VB.NET

Class Design

Handbook

7

7

Inheritance and Polymorphism

Inheritance and polymorphism are extremely important object-oriented concepts. Visual Basic .NET is the first version of Visual Basic to provide full support for these features.

Inheritance allows us to define a base class that contains the common data and operations for a group of related classes. We define these common members once, in the base class. For example, we might define a base class named Animal that contains the data and operations that pertain to any kind of animal.

We can then define derived classes that inherit these members automatically. All we need to define in the derived class are the additional data and operations for that particular class. For example, we might define a class named Cat that inherits all the members from Animal, and defines additional cat-related data and operations. This illustrates two important benefits of inheritance: the ability to reuse code from the base class (without needing to copy-and-paste code in the editor); and the ability to define a hierarchy of inherited classes to reflect the relationship between entities in our business model.

Derived classes can also override operations defined in the base class. This is what we mean by *polymorphism*. For example, if the Animal class has a general-purpose method named Eat, we might decide to override this method in the Cat class to provide a cat-specific version of the Eat method. This highlights another important benefit of inheritance: the ability to extend existing classes (such as Animal) with new classes (such as Cat), without having to modify any of the code in the existing class. This is known as type extension, and it helps to make our code more future-proof; we can seamlessly add new derived classes in the future as our business needs evolve.

As you can see from this brief introduction, there are several tasks we need to embrace in this chapter. First of all, we need to describe the object-oriented concepts of inheritance and polymorphism, and provide a formal definition for terms such as ***base class***, ***derived class***, ***superclass***, ***subclass***, ***overriding***, ***polymorphism***, ***abstract class***, ***abstract method***, ***interface***, and so on. Then we need to consider how these concepts map to Visual Basic .NET keywords such as `Overridable`, `NotOverridable`, `Inherits`, `Overrides`, `MustInherit`, `NotInheritable`, `Interface`, `Implements`, and so on. Along the way, we'll discuss important design issues and offer advice and examples to show how to use these features effectively in your Visual Basic .NET code.

Inheritance and Polymorphism Concepts

We begin our journey by discussing the object-oriented concepts, terminology, and design issues for inheritance and polymorphism. At the end of this section, we'll also introduce the idea of interfaces. Newcomers to object-oriented development are sometimes unconvinced (or even skeptical) when they hear OO evangelists enthuse about the importance of interfaces, but it's all true! Hopefully you'll be convinced by the time you finish this section.

Throughout this section, we'll use the ***Unified Modeling Language*** (***UML***) to illustrate the relationships between base classes and derived classes. UML defines a formal graphical notation for all aspects of inheritance and polymorphism, which makes it easier to visualize how the concepts translate to actual classes. We realize this isn't a book about UML, so we'll keep this section relatively short, but it is important you understand these issues before delving into the details of inheritance in Visual Basic .NET.

Designing Inheritance Hierarchies

Inheritance allows us to define new classes, based directly on existing classes in our system. The inherited class is called the ***base class***, ***parent class***, or ***superclass***, depending on which terminology you prefer. The classes that inherit from the superclass are called the ***derived classes***, ***child classes***, or ***subclasses***. For the remainder of this chapter, we'll refer to the inherited class as the ***superclass***, and we'll refer to the inheriting classes as the ***subclasses***.

Inheritance describes an ***is a*** (or ***is a kind of***) relationship between subclasses and superclasses. For example, a cat is a kind of animal, so we might chose to define the `Cat` class as a subclass of `Animal`. We say that the `Cat` class ***inherits from*** the `Animal` class; in other words, the `Cat` class ***extends*** the `Animal` class by providing additional cat-specific data and operations. Some developers, especially in the C++ community, prefer to say that the `Cat` class is ***derived from*** the `Animal` class.

The following diagram shows the UML notation for inheritance. In this simple example, the superclass is BankAccount. There are three subclasses named SavingsAccount, CheckingAccount, and StudentAccount, which represent the different types of bank account in our application. The triangle in the diagram is the UML notation for inheritance:

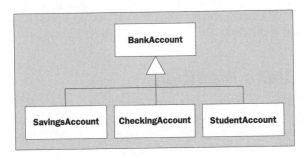

The example above shows a single level of inheritance. It is also possible to define inheritance hierarchies that are several levels deep, if our business model indicates this is appropriate. For example, we might decide there are a number of types of savings account, offering different interest rates and conditions for withdrawing money from the account:

❑   InstantAccessSavingsAccount is a kind of SavingsAccount that allows instant access to available funds, but consequently offers only mediocre returns on the invested funds.

❑   NinetyDaysSavingsAccount is a kind of SavingsAccount that requires customers to give 90 days notice before each withdrawal, and therefore offers better returns on the invested funds.

The UML diagram for this example is shown below:

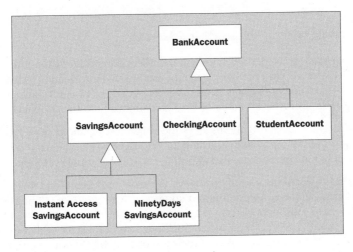

There are no hard-and-fast rules for the ideal depth of an inheritance hierarchy. Typically, most inheritance hierarchies tend to be relatively shallow (two or three levels) and broad (many subclasses inheriting from each superclass). However, there are exceptions to this rule of thumb; for example, if we are developing a zoological application to classify all types of creature in the animal kingdom, we might need more than a dozen levels of inheritance. As with most design decisions, it all depends on the requirements of the application.

Defining Class Members

The superclass defines the common data and operations required by all its subclasses. The subclasses inherit all the members from the superclass, and can define additional members if required. The following UML diagram shows some data and operations for the simple `BankAccount` hierarchy:

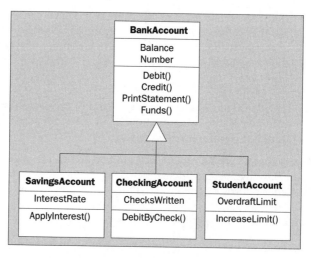

Note the following points in this inheritance hierarchy:

❑   `BankAccount` defines two data members named `Balance` and `Number`, because all kinds of bank account require this information. `BankAccount` also defines operations named `Debit`, `Credit`, `PrintStatement`, and `Funds`, because all kinds of bank account require these operations.

❑   `SavingsAccount` inherits all of the data and operations from `BankAccount`, and defines an additional data member (`InterestRate`) and an additional operation (`ApplyInterest`) because savings accounts offer interest.

❑   `CheckingAccount` inherits all of the data and operations from `BankAccount`, and defines an additional data member (`ChecksWritten`) to store information about all the checks that have been written for this account. The `CheckingAccount` class also defines an additional operation (`DebitByCheck`) to allow the customer to debit money by writing a check.

❑ StudentAccount inherits all of the data and operations from BankAccount, and defines an additional data member (OverdraftLimit) to offer students an overdraft facility. The StudentAccount class also defines an additional operation (IncreaseLimit) so students can increase their overdraft limit if times get tough.

When we create objects of the class types shown in the UML diagram above, the objects will contain the following data and operations.

pe of object	Data in object	Operations available on object
ankAccount	Balance, Number	Debit, Credit, PrintStatement, Funds
avingsAccount	Balance, Number, InterestRate	Debit, Credit, PrintStatement, Funds, ApplyInterest
heckingAccount	Balance, Number, ChecksWritten	Debit, Credit, PrintStatement, Funds, DebitByCheck
tudentAccount	Balance, Number, OverdraftLimit	Debit, Credit, PrintStatement, Funds, IncreaseLimit

As this table shows, subclasses inherit all of the data and operations from their superclass. This enables us to develop subclasses more quickly than would be the case in the absence of inheritance; when we write a subclass, all we need to specify is how the subclass differs from the superclass. Because we have fewer new lines of code to write, there should be fewer new bugs and less testing overhead too. The only downside is that the subclasses are dependent on the superclass; if we modify the superclass, we may need to modify the subclasses so that they remain consistent with the superclass. In an ideal world, we would always design the superclass so that it never needs to be modified in the future.

Single Inheritance vs. Multiple Inheritance

The .NET Framework (and therefore Visual Basic .NET) only allows a class to inherit implementation from a single superclass; this is known as *single inheritance of implementation*. Some programming languages, such as C++, allow classes to inherit directly from multiple superclasses; unsurprisingly, this is known as *multiple inheritance of implementation*.

There are several reasons why multiple inheritance of implementation is disallowed in the .NET Framework:

❑ If our class could inherit directly from several superclasses, and the superclasses defined operations with the same name and signature, our class would inherit all of these operations. If the client code tried to invoke an operation with this name, the compiler wouldn't know which inherited operation to call; the compiler would therefore have to generate a compiler error, to highlight the ambiguity.

❏   If our class could inherit from several superclasses, and the superclasses themselves inherited from a common 'grandparent' superclass, the data in the common grandparent class would be inherited multiple times by our class. This duplication of data would cause problems in our class, because our object should only inherit one copy of the data from its superclasses.

Overriding and Polymorphism

A subclass can *override* operations from its superclass. This allows us to introduce new types that customize the behavior of existing types in the application. The superclass indicates which methods might need to be overridden, and the subclass can override these methods if it needs to provide customized behavior. Note the following points:

❏   When we design the superclass, we must make a conscious decision about which operations are overridable and which operations are not overridable. Typically, the superclass will contain a mixture of overridable and non-overridable operations. It's not always obvious whether a particular operation should be declared as overridable or non-overridable; if in doubt, it's best to err on the side of caution and declare the operation as non-overridable. We'll show the Visual Basic .NET syntax for doing this later in the chapter.

❏   The subclass is not obliged to override the overridable operations. It can inherit the existing operations from the superclass as-is, if they are adequate for the needs of the subclass.

❏   If the subclass does decide to override an overridable operation, the subclass must define an operation with exactly the same name and signature as the operation in the superclass.

UML does not provide any specific notation to indicate that an operation is overridable; we infer an operation is overridable if it is overridden in any of its subclasses.

In the following UML diagram, CheckingAccount and StudentAccount override the PrintStatement operation, to print additional information about the account. StudentAccount also overrides the Funds operation, because the available funds for a student account depend on the overdraft facility:

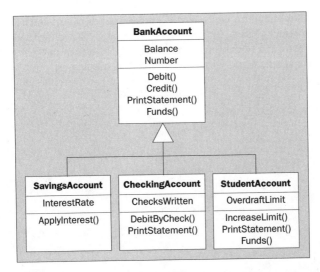

The ability for the same operation to be defined in many different classes is known as *polymorphism*. The implementation of the operation is specific to each class.

Polymorphism is an extremely important aspect of inheritance; it allows us to write generic code that invokes operations on an object, without needing to know the exact type of the object. For example, we can write a generic method that takes any kind of BankAccount object, and calls the Funds operation on the object. Automatically, the correct Funds operation will be called, depending on the actual type of bank account object passed into the method. This frees the client code from having to interrogate the object to find out what type of bank account it is. Furthermore, the client code will continue to work correctly even if a new kind of bank account is added to the application in the future; when we call the Funds operation, the correct version of the operation will always be called.

Abstract Classes and Abstract Operations

An **abstract class** is a class that cannot be instantiated. In other words, the client code cannot create objects of an abstract class type. Superclasses are often declared as abstract classes, because they do not contain enough information to represent tangible objects in our system; the superclasses just act as a repository for the common data and operations required by their subclasses.

> *The opposite of an abstract class is a concrete class. The client code can create objects of a concrete class type.*

An **abstract operation** is an operation that must be overridden in the subclasses. By definition, we can only define abstract operations in an abstract class. Abstract operations are useful because they enable the superclass to specify a common set of operations that must be supported by all the subclasses. Client code can rely on the fact that all subclasses support the operations defined in the superclass.

In the following UML diagram, we've made BankAccount an abstract class (UML uses italics to denote abstract classes and abstract operations). We've defined two abstract operations (PrintSpecialComments and MaxSingleDebit) in BankAccount, and implemented these abstract operations in each of the subclasses:

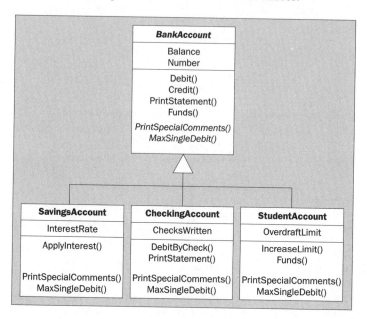

Inheritance of Interface

So far in this chapter, we've seen how a subclass can inherit data and functionality from a superclass. The subclass inherits the implementation of the superclass, and provides additional data and functionality as appropriate. This form of inheritance is known as *inheritance of implementation*, and is used primarily to reduce duplication between common subclasses; common data and behavior is promoted to the superclass, so that it can be inherited by all the subclasses.

We now turn our attention to a different type of inheritance altogether: *inheritance of interface*. With inheritance of interface, we define an *interface* that specifies a set of related methods, properties, and events required in our application. The interface defines the names and signatures of these methods, properties, and events, but it does not provide any implementation. The implementation must be provided by other classes or structures in the application; we say these classes or structures *implement* the interface.

> *Notice the difference in terminology between inheritance of implementation and inheritance of interface. With inheritance of implementation, a superclass is inherited by subclasses. With inheritance of interfaces, an interface is implemented by implementing classes or structures.*

Interfaces are a difficult concept to grasp initially. More to the point, the benefits of interfaces are not always easy to appreciate at the outset. What is the point of defining interfaces, if they don't actually *do* anything? Let's discuss some of the reasons for defining interfaces.

❑ Interfaces allow us to specify required capabilities in our system, without needing to worry about how these capabilities will be implemented. This enables us to design our system in terms of the services it must deliver, rather than forcing us to consider implementation details too early in our design.

❑ We can implement an interface in several different ways. That is, we can define many different classes and structures that implement the same interface. If in the future our business logic requires a new way to implement the interface, we can simply define new classes and structures that implement the interface accordingly.

❑ We can write generic methods that take interface typed parameters, rather than specific class or structure types. In other words, we can write methods that are interested in the capabilities of an object, not its exact type. This makes it easier for us to slot new types into our application in the future, because we haven't restricted our methods to take specific object types; our methods are quite happy taking any object that implements the required interface. We'll see an example of this concept later in the chapter, when we look at the Visual Basic .NET syntax for interfaces.

Let's see a conceptual example of inheritance of interface. The following UML diagram shows an abstract class, two interfaces, and a concrete class:

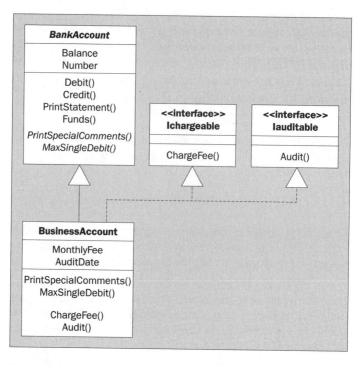

Note the following points in this UML diagram:

- ❏ BankAccount is an abstract class, and is the superclass for all different kinds of bank account.

- ❏ IChargeable is an interface, and defines the operations that must be implemented by all classes that want to exhibit 'chargeable' behavior. Notice the <<interface>> UML notation; this notation is known as a *stereotype*, and indicates IChargeable is an interface rather than a class.

- ❏ IAuditable is another interface, and defines the operations that must be implemented by all classes that want to exhibit 'auditable' behavior.

- ❏ BusinessAccount is a concrete class. BusinessAccount is a kind of bank account, so it inherits from BankAccount. BusinessAccount also implements the IChargeable and IAuditable interfaces. Notice the dotted-line notation in UML, to indicate inheritance of interface rather than inheritance of implementation.

As you might have noticed in this example, BusinessAccount inherits from more than one interface (two, to be precise). This is an example of *multiple inheritance of interface*, and is perfectly acceptable in an object-oriented design. Interfaces do not contain any implementation code or data, so we avoid all of the problems that can arise with multiple inheritance of implementation.

That concludes our brief introduction to object-oriented concepts, terminology, and design issues. In the next section, we'll see how to apply these concepts in Visual Basic .NET.

Visual Basic .NET and Inheritance

Visual Basic .NET provides full support for all the concepts and techniques introduced in the previous section. We'll begin by showing that all types in Visual Basic .NET form part of a unified inheritance hierarchy, inherited ultimately from the System.Object class. We'll discuss the design implications of the unified inheritance hierarchy, and see how this affects the code that we write and the types that we use in the .NET Framework class library.

Then we'll turn our attention to defining our own classes in the inheritance hierarchy. We'll review the syntax for defining superclasses and subclasses, and consider the important design decisions that influence the organization and contents of these classes in Visual Basic .NET. We'll also see how and when to define abstract classes and abstract methods, to reinforce the design decisions in our object model.

Finally, we'll take a careful look at interfaces. Interfaces are an essential feature in all .NET Framework languages, which emphasizes the prominent role interfaces play in most object oriented designs. We'll show how to define new interfaces, implement the interfaces in classes and structures, and consume the interfaces in client code.

The .NET Unified Inheritance Hierarchy

All types in the .NET Framework inherit ultimately from a common class named Object, which is defined in the System namespace. Many observers have commented on the fact that Object is a spectacularly bad name for a class; a better name might have been TheClassAtTheTopOfTheInheritanceHierarchy, but maybe that's a bit too verbose. However, in the spirit of naming types after the things that a variable of that type can contain, it works; a variable of type Object can contain any object.

Microsoft's decision to enforce a unified inheritance hierarchy for the .NET Framework is in keeping with most other object oriented programming systems, most notably Java, although similar schemes have been used in class libraries from SmallTalk onwards. Just about the only object oriented language that does not enforce the idea of a unified inheritance hierarchy is C++, and even that has changed in Managed Extensions for C++.

> *Managed Extensions for C++ is a set of language extensions defined by Microsoft, which enables C++ developers to create **managed classes** (and other managed types) for use in the .NET Framework. All managed types ultimately must inherit from Object.*

We'll discuss the design implications of the unified inheritance hierarchy shortly. Before we do that, let's see a simple example to prove that all types in Visual Basic .NET inherit ultimately from `System.Object`. The example also shows how inheritance relationships are compiled into MSIL code, which can help you understand what's going on under the covers.

The source code for this example is located in the download folder `Inheritance\InheritanceFromObject`:

```
' Import the System namespace, where Object and Type are defined
Imports System

' Define a class (implicitly inherits from System.Object)
Public Class MyClass1
    ' No new members in this simple class
End Class

' Define a class that explicitly inherits from System.Object
Public Class MyClass2
    Inherits Object
    ' No new members in this class, either
End Class

' Define a structure (implicitly inherits from System.ValueType)
Public Structure MyStructure
    Private Data As Integer    ' Structures need at least one member
End Structure

' Structures cannot explicitly specify a superclass
' Public Structure MyBadStructure
'       Inherits ValueType
'     Private Data As Integer
' End Structure

' Define a class that contains the Main subroutine for this
application
Public Class MyApp

    Shared Sub Main()

        ' Create a MyClass1 object, and examine its type and base type
        Dim obj1 As New MyClass1()
        Dim type As Type = obj1.GetType()
        Console.WriteLine("obj1 is an instance of type {0}",_
                        type.Name)
        Console.WriteLine("Base type is {0}", type.BaseType)
        Console.WriteLine("-------------------------------------------")
```

```
' Create a MyClass2 object, and examine its type and base type
Dim obj2 As New MyClass2()
type = obj2.GetType()
Console.WriteLine("obj2 is an instance of type {0}",
                  type.Name)
Console.WriteLine("Base type is {0}", type.BaseType)
Console.WriteLine("-------------------------------------------")

' Create a MyStructure object, and examine its type and base
' type
Dim val As New MyStructure()
type = val.GetType()
Console.WriteLine("val is an instance of type {0}", type.Name)
Console.WriteLine("Base type is {0}", type.BaseType)
Console.WriteLine("Base-base type is {0}",_
                  type.BaseType.BaseType)
Console.WriteLine("-------------------------------------------")

    End Sub

End Class
```

In this example, we define three new types to illustrate the default inheritance rules in Visual Basic .NET:

❑ MyClass1. This class does not explicitly specify a superclass, so it implicitly inherits directly from System.Object. Note that the Inherits statement must appear on a new line; it cannot appear on the same line as the Class statement.

❑ MyClass2. This class explicitly inherits directly from System.Object, by using the Inherits statement. The Inherits statement must be on its own line in the code; we cannot place the Inherits statement on the same line as the Class statement. In practice, there is no reason to inherit explicitly from System.Object; we only use the Inherits statement when we want to inherit directly from a different superclass in the hierarchy.

❑ MyStructure. This structure implicitly inherits from System.ValueType (which itself inherits from System.Object). All structures in Visual Basic .NET must inherit from System.ValueType; we cannot use an Inherits statement to specify a different superclass for a structure. For example, the commented-out structure named MyBadStructure would cause a compiler error if we removed the comments.

The .NET Framework defines simplified inheritance rules for value types (structures in Visual Basic .NET). All value types must inherit from `System.ValueType`. Furthermore, we cannot inherit from a value type, which means there is no way to override an operation defined in a value type. Therefore, the compiler can decide (at compile time) which version of the method will be called, rather than having to resolve the method call at run time (which can happen when we invoke a method on a reference-type object). Compile-time method resolution is faster and more efficient than run-time method resolution, because it avoids run-time method lookups to determine which method to invoke.

In the `Main` subroutine, we create an object of each of these three types. We then use the `GetType` method to obtain type information for each object. The `GetType` method returns a `Type` object, which provides full information about the object's type, its members, and its location in the inheritance hierarchy. In this example, we use the `BaseType` property to obtain information about the object's base type (or superclass type).

To compile this application, open a .NET Framework command prompt window, move to the folder that contains the example, and type the following command:

> vbc InheritanceFromObject.vb

To run the application, type the following command:

> InheritanceFromObject.exe

The application displays the following output on the console window. Notice that the base type for objects `obj1` and `obj2` is `System.Object`. The base type for `val` is `System.Value`, and its grand-parent type is `System.Object`:

```
obj1 is an instance of type MyClass1
Base type is System.Object

obj2 is an instance of type MyClass2
Base type is System.Object

val is an instance of type MyStructure
Base type is System.ValueType
Base-base type is System.Object
```

It's useful to see how these classes are compiled into MSIL code. To run the MSIL Disassembler tool, type the following command:

> ildasm InheritanceFromObject.exe

The MSIL Disassembler window displays the following information (we've expanded the nodes in this screenshot, to show the details for each of our types):

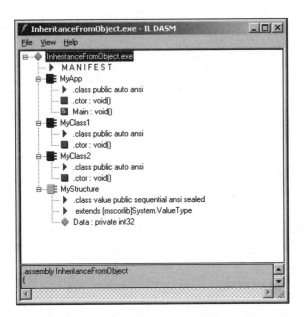

Note the following points in the MSIL Disassembler window:

❑ MyClass1 and MyClass2 do not have any explicit superclass information.

❑ MyStructure extends (inherits from) System.ValueType. The [mscorlib] notation indicates System.ValueType is defined in an assembly named mscorlib; this is a standard .NET assembly, which contains the majority of the predefined types in the .NET Framework. We'll learn more about assemblies in the next chapter.

If we double-click the .class entry for these types, another window opens showing the MSIL definition for that type. Here is the MSIL code for MyClass1; the MSIL code clearly shows that MyClass1 inherits from System.Object:

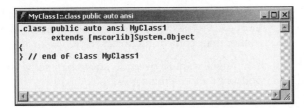

The following screenshot shows the MSIL code for MyStructure. The MSIL code confirms that MyStructure inherits from System.ValueType. Also notice MyStructure is qualified with the sealed keyword. sealed is a MSIL keyword that means 'not inheritable'; this substantiates our earlier observation that value types are not inheritable in the .NET Framework:

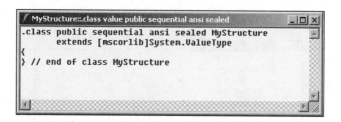

Benefits and Implications of a Unified Inheritance Hierarchy

The unified inheritance hierarchy in the .NET Framework has several important consequences:

❑ All types in the .NET Framework are related to each other, because they all inherit from `System.Object`. `System.Object` provides basic methods that are inherited by all .NET types. We can override these methods in our types, if necessary.

❑ We can write generic methods that work with any type of object, by specifying `System.Object` as the parameter type or return type. A good example of this genericity is provided by the .NET Framework collection classes, such as `Stack`, `Queue`, and `Hashtable`. The methods in these classes have `System.Object` parameters and return types, which means we can store any type of object in these collections.

The following table lists all the methods defined in `System.Object`. Every type in the .NET Framework inherits these methods, and some types choose to override selective methods We looked at overriding these methods back in Chapter 2. The table describes which methods are typically overridden, and why.

Method	Description
Equals	Equals indicates whether two objects are equivalent. By default, Equals compares object references, and returns True if they refer to the same object. Equals is overridden by System.ValueType, to compare the values of two objects (rather than comparing object references).
	You might want to override Equals in some structures, to perform a more efficient value comparison than that performed in System.ValueType.
	You might also want to override Equals in some classes, where it makes sense to compare objects for equality. For example, the String class overrides Equals to see if two String objects contain the same text. In contrast, the File class does not override Equals, because it's unclear what it means for two files to be 'equal'.

Method	Description
Finalize	Finalize is overridden in classes that require finalization code to be executed before an object is garbage collected. The garbage collection process calls the Finalize method just before the object's memory is reclaimed. Only override the Finalize method in classes that have something substantive to do at garbage collection time. Don't be tempted to write empty Finalize methods in all your classes, just for the sake of tidiness and completeness; the presence of a Finalize method can significantly delay the disposal of objects by the garbage collection process, and places an unnecessary strain on the garbage collector.
GetHashCode	GetHashCode computes and returns an integer hash code for instances of a type. This method is overridden by structures and classes that are used as keys in a hash table. The hash table calls GetHashCode to compute the hash code for an object, and uses the hash code to locate objects in the hash table.
GetType	GetType returns a Type object, to describe the type of any object at run time. We used GetType earlier in this section, to investigate the location of classes in the .NET Framework inheritance hierarchy. You should not override GetType in your own classes (although for some reason, Microsoft have not explicitly disallowed overriding of GetType). The implementation of GetType in System.Object should be sufficient for all your needs.
MemberwiseClone	MemberwiseClone creates a shallow copy of an object. A shallow copy is one where object references are copied, but copies of the objects are not created. This method cannot be overridden. If you want to suppress shallow copying for a class, as we saw in Chapter 4, we can implement the ICloneable interface and write a Clone method that provides the appropriate copy semantics for the class.
ReferenceEquals	ReferenceEquals is a Shared method, which determines whether two object references point to the same object. As you'll see later in this chapter, we do not inherit Shared methods, so this method is only available through the Object class.

Table continued on following page

263

Method	Description
ToString	ToString returns a textual representation of the data in an object.
	This method is overridden extensively in the .NET Framework. In fact, we recommend you override this method in all your classes and structures, to return meaningful information about the state of your objects. This can be useful for diagnostic purposes, to help pinpoint potential problems in your application.

Inheritance of Implementation

Now that we've seen how to inherit from System.Object, we'll consider how to define our own superclasses and subclasses within this unified inheritance hierarchy. In this section, we'll review the syntax for defining superclasses and subclasses in Visual Basic .NET, and discuss the design heuristics that will influence the design of these classes.

Defining the Superclass

Traditionally, Visual Basic has encouraged a *rapid application development* (*RAD*) style of programming. It's easy to drag-and-drop controls from the toolbox, and to write event handlers as-and-when they might be needed.

When we use inheritance in Visual Basic .NET, we must put more effort into up-front design. We need to plan how the superclass might be inherited by subclasses now and in the future; otherwise, we may find it difficult to define these subclasses. Worse still, we may find it necessary to modify the superclass to accommodate the requirements of these subclasses. Modifying the superclass is bad news, because it can cause ripple-effect changes to all the subclasses that depend on it. For example, if we modify the signature of an overridable method in the superclass, we'll need to modify the signature of that method wherever it is overridden by subclasses. We'll also need to modify any client code that calls the method.

There are several issues we need to consider when we design the superclass:

❑ Should the class be abstract or concrete?

❑ What fields and constructors are required?

❑ Which members should be overridable?

❑ Should any of the operations be abstract?

We'll consider each of these issues separately in the next few pages. To illustrate our discussions, we'll show how to define the BankAccount class introduced earlier in the chapter. The code for this example is located in the download folder Inheritance\DefiningSuperclasses.

Should the Class be Abstract or Concrete?

Abstract classes contain only a partial implementation, and rely on subclasses to complete the implementation. Generally, most classes designed to be used as superclasses tend to be abstract classes. To designate a class as abstract in Visual Basic NET, we use the `MustInherit` keyword as follows:

```
' Define an abstract class
Public MustInherit Class BankAccount

    ' Define members for BankAccount (see later...)

End Class
```

It is also possible to declare a class as `NotInheritable`. This prevents the class from being inherited by any subclasses. Use `NotInheritable` for classes that are not suited for inheritance, or which could be abused by being extended, or if you are sure there are no reasons for extending the class in the future.

What Fields and Constructors are Required?

All classes can define fields and constructors. When we design a class that will be inherited by subclasses, there are a couple of extra issues to consider. Firstly, what accessibility should we use for the fields in our class?

❑ If we define the fields as `Public`, they will be accessible to the entire application. This is not recommended, because it violates the goals of encapsulation.

❑ If we define the fields as `Private`, they will only be accessible by our class. Subclasses will not inherit the fields; methods in the subclass will not be allowed to access the fields. `Private` means private *to our class*.

❑ If we want to allow subclasses to access the fields in our class, we can define the fields as `Protected`. The `Protected` access modifier allows members to be accessed in our class, and in any of our subclasses.

The `Protected` access modifier might seem like an ideal solution, but there is a price to pay. By exposing our fields to the subclasses, we increase the dependency between our class and the subclasses. If we change the definition of the field in our class, we'll probably have to modify all of the subclasses that use it. For example, if we define a `Protected ArrayList` field in our class, and we later change our mind and use a `Hashtable` instead, we'll have to rewrite all the methods in all the subclasses that use this field. In a large application, this could require a significant programming effort.

Therefore, the preferred accessibility for fields is `Private`. If we want to allow subclasses to access a field, consider providing a `Protected` property to get or set the field. Subclasses can use the property when they need to access the data in the field. If we change how this field is implemented in our class, all we need to do is rewrite the property procedures in our class; we do not need to modify the code in the subclasses.

We also need to consider which constructors to define in our class. Constructors are not inherited by subclasses; each subclass will need to define its own constructors, and chain to the appropriate constructor in the superclass. Therefore, when we define constructors in the superclass, we need to ensure we offer enough flexibility for subclasses to call these constructors. A particular technique that is often used in abstract superclasses is to declare the constructors as `Protected`, so that they can be called from subclasses but not from the client code.

The following code fragment shows how to define fields and constructors in the `BankAccount` class:

```
Public MustInherit Class BankAccount

    ' Define private fields
    Private mBalance As Double
    Private mNumber As Integer
    Private Shared mNextNumber As Integer

    ' Define a protected constructor for this abstract class
    Protected Sub New(ByVal Balance As Double)
        mBalance = Balance
        mNumber = mNextNumber
        mNextNumber += 1
    End Sub

    ' Define other members (see later)...

End Class
```

Which Members should be Overridable?

If the superclass contains members that might need to be overridden in the subclasses, we declare these members as `Overridable` in Visual Basic .NET. We can define the following kinds of member as `Overridable`:

- ❑ Functions and subroutines (but not constructors or `Shared` methods)

- ❑ Instance properties (but not `Shared` properties)

`Shared` members are not overridable, because the runtime system needs access to a specific object when it tries to resolve which version of an overridable member to call. `Shared` members are accessed through the class name, not a specific object, so the runtime would not be able to resolve `Shared` overridable members.

The following code fragment shows how to define overridable and non-overridable methods and properties in the `BankAccount` class:

```
Public MustInherit Class BankAccount

    ' Fields and constructor, as before...

    ' Define a non-overridable instance method
    Public Function Debit(ByVal Amount As Double) As Boolean
        If Amount <= MaxSingleDebit And Amount <= Funds Then
            mBalance -= Amount
            Return True
        Else
            Return False
        End If
    End Function

    ' Define another non-overridable instance method
    Public Sub Credit(ByVal Amount As Double)
        mBalance += Amount
    End Sub

    ' Define a shared property
    Public Shared ReadOnly Property NextNumber() As Integer
        Get
            Return mNextNumber
        End Get
    End Property

    ' Define an overridable instance method
    Public Overridable Sub PrintStatement()
        Console.WriteLine("Account number: {0}", mNumber)
        Console.WriteLine("Balance: ${0}", mBalance)
    End Sub

    ' Define an overridable instance property
    Protected Overridable ReadOnly Property Funds() As Double
        Get
            Return mBalance
        End Get
    End Property

    ' Define other members (see later)...

End Class
```

Note the following points in this example:

❑   The Debit and Credit methods are not overridable. We've made the
    conscious decision that these methods will not need to be overridden in
    any subclasses. We don't want it to be possible for people to create bank
    account classes that don't handle credits and debits in this manner, so we
    rule out the possibility of such abuse by explicitly marking the methods
    NotOverridable. Notice that the Debit method uses the
    MaxSingleDebit property (discussed later), to make sure the customer
    isn't trying to debit too much money in one go. The Debit method also
    checks the Funds property (discussed below), to ascertain whether there
    are sufficient funds to allow the debit to proceed.

❑ The `NextNumber` property is not overridable. `Shared` members are not inherited, so are never overridable; in VB.NET, it is an error to use the `Overridable` keyword on a `Shared` member.

❑ The `PrintStatement` method is overridable. We've provided a default implementation for this method in our class, but the `Overridable` keyword allows subclasses to provide their own implementation for this method if they choose to do so.

❑ The `Funds` property is overridable. We've provided a default implementation for this property in our class, but the `Overridable` keyword allows subclasses to provide their own implementation if necessary.

This raises an interesting point. When we use `Funds` in the `Debit` method, the runtime system will polymorphically call the correct version of the `Funds` property procedure, depending on which type of bank account object is being debited.

Should any of the Operations be Abstract?

If we've defined our class as an abstract (`MustInherit`) class, we can specify some of the operations as abstract if necessary. Abstract operations must be overridden in subclasses before they can be used. To designate an operation as abstract in Visual Basic .NET, we use the `MustOverride` keyword. We can define the following kinds of member as `MustOverride`:

❑ Functions and subroutines (but not constructors or `Shared` methods)

❑ Instance properties (but not `Shared` properties)

The following code fragment shows how to define an abstract method and an abstract property in the `BankAccount` class:

```
Public MustInherit Class BankAccount

    ' Fields, constructor, and other methods, as before...

    ' Define an abstract instance method
    Public MustOverride Sub PrintSpecialComments()

    ' Define an abstract instance property
    Public MustOverride ReadOnly Property MaxSingleDebit() As Double

End Class
```

That concludes our definition of the `BankAccount` class. To compile this class, open a .NET Framework command prompt window, move to the folder that contains the example, and type the following command:

```
> vbc /target:library DefiningSuperclasses.vb
```

The /target:library compiler option creates a class library (that is, a DLL file) containing the BankAccount class. We created a class library, rather than an application, because the DefiningSuperclasses.vb file doesn't have a Main method.

It's useful to see how the BankAccount class looks in MSIL code. To run the MSIL Disassembler tool, type the following command:

```
> ildasm DefiningSuperclasses.dll
```

The MSIL Disassembler window displays the following information (we've expanded the nodes in this screenshot, to show the details for each of our types):

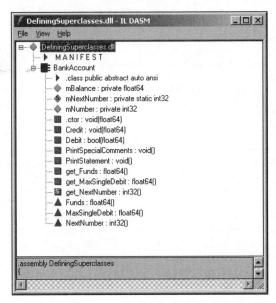

Note the following points in the MSIL Disassembler window:

❑ The BankAccount class is qualified with the abstract MSIL keyword, because we declared BankAccount as a MustInherit class in our Visual Basic .NET source code.

❑ The BankAccount class has the fields, constructor, methods, and properties that we defined in our Visual Basic .NET source code.

❑ The BankAccount class also has methods named get_Funds, get_MaxSingleDebit, and get_NextNumber. These are the 'get' property procedures for the Funds, MaxSingleDebit, and NextNumber properties.

To see the MSIL code for the methods and properties in the BankAccount class, we can double-click the appropriate entry in the MSIL Disassembler window. Of particular interest are the Overridable and MustOverride members. For example, here is the MSIL code for the PrintStatement method (this method was declared as an Overridable method in our Visual Basic .NET source code):

```
BankAccount::PrintStatement : void()                              _ □ ×
.method public newslot virtual instance void
        PrintStatement() cil managed
{
    // Code size        43 (0x2b)
    .maxstack  8
    IL_0000:  ldstr      "Account number: {0}"
    IL_0005:  ldarg.0
    IL_0006:  ldfld      int32 BankAccount::mNumber
    IL_000b:  box        [mscorlib]System.Int32
    IL_0010:  call       void [mscorlib]System.Console::WriteLine(string,
                                                                  object)
    IL_0015:  ldstr      "Balance: ${0}"
    IL_001a:  ldarg.0
    IL_001b:  ldfld      float64 BankAccount::mBalance
    IL_0020:  box        [mscorlib]System.Double
    IL_0025:  call       void [mscorlib]System.Console::WriteLine(string,
                                                                  object)
    IL_002a:  ret
} // end of method BankAccount::PrintStatement
```

Notice the following points in the MSIL code for the PrintStatement method shown above:

❑ The newslot MSIL keyword indicates this method will require a new slot in the *vtable* for this class. The vtable is a compiler-generated list of pointers to methods and properties; each entry in the vtable points to a specific overridable method or property in our class.

The compiler generates a separate vtable for each class. The runtime uses the vtable to decide which version of an overridable method or property to invoke. For example, if a subclass overrides a method from the superclass, the subclass's vtable entry for this method will point to the subclass's version of the method. The runtime uses this information to ensure the correct version of the method is always called. In other words, the vtable mechanism is the .NET Framework's way of achieving polymorphism.

❑ The virtual MSIL keyword indicates this method is overridable in subclasses (Visual C# uses the virtual keyword to indicate a method in a superclass is overridable, whereas Visual Basic .NET uses the Overridable keyword).

❑ The instance MSIL keyword indicates this is an instance method, not a class (Shared) method.

Here is the MSIL code for the PrintSpecialComments method (this method was declared as a MustOverride method in our Visual Basic .NET source code):

```
BankAccount::PrintSpecialComments : void()                        _ □ ×
.method public newslot virtual abstract instance void
        PrintSpecialComments() cil managed
{
} // end of method BankAccount::PrintSpecialComments
```

270

Notice the following points in the MSIL code for the PrintSpecialComments method shown above:

- ❏ PrintSpecialComments is qualified with the newslot, virtual, and instance MSIL keywords, just like the PrintStatement method we discussed earlier.

- ❏ PrintSpecialComments is also qualified with the abstract MSIL keyword. The abstract MSIL keyword indicates this method is abstract, which means it must be overridden in subclasses (Visual C# uses the abstract keyword to denote an abstract method, whereas Visual Basic .NET uses the MustOverride keyword).

Defining Subclasses

Let's now talk about how to define our subclasses. Subclasses inherit all the members from the superclass (except for the constructors), and can define additional members as required. Subclasses can also override selective members from the superclass, and are obliged to override abstract members from the superclass.

We'll consider the following issues in this section:

- ❏ What additional fields are required, and how do we perform initialization?

- ❏ What additional operations are required?

- ❏ What overridable members and abstract members do we need to override?

- ❏ Are there any members we need to shadow? We haven't mentioned shadowing yet, so don't think you missed it! We'll look at what it is and why you might need it in a moment.

- ❏ How do we use our inheritance hierarchy in client code?

We'll tackle each of these issues separately in the coming pages. To illustrate our discussions, we'll show how to define the StudentAccount class introduced earlier in the chapter. The code for this example is located in the download folder Inheritance\DefiningSubclasses. This folder contains the source code for the superclass (BankAccount.vb), the subclass (StudentAccount.vb), and a Main subroutine for a console application (MainApp.vb).

What Additional Fields are Required, and how do we Perform Initialization?

Subclasses inherit all the fields defined in the superclass, and are not obliged to add any extra fields unless they want to. But private fields will be needed to store any state pertaining to the subclass's extensions. However, superclass constructors are not inherited; the subclass must define its own constructors, and chain to the appropriate constructor in the superclass, as we saw in Chapter 4.

The following code fragment shows how to define the fields and constructor for the StudentAccount class:

```
Public Class StudentAccount
    Inherits BankAccount

    ' Define private field
    Private mOverdraftLimit As Double        ' Overdraft limit

    ' Define a public constructor for this concrete class
    Public Sub New(ByVal Balance As Double,_
                ByVal OverdraftLimit As Double)
        MyBase.New(Balance)
        mOverdraftLimit = OverdraftLimit
    End Sub

    ' Define other members (see later)...

End Class
```

Note the following points:

- ❑   StudentAccount inherits from BankAccount, by using the Inherits statement.

- ❑   StudentAccount automatically inherits all the fields from BankAccount, and defines an additional field to represent the overdraft limit.

- ❑   StudentAccount defines a Public constructor. The constructor calls the superclass constructor by using MyBase.New, to initialize the members defined in the superclass.

    MyBase.New must be the first statement in our constructor, to initialize the superclass members before initializing the members in our class. If we omit the MyBase.New statement, the compiler will try to call MyBase.New without any arguments; this will only work if the superclass has a no-argument constructor.

What Additional Operations are Required?

Subclasses inherit all the operations (methods and properties) defined in the superclass, and are not obliged to add any extra operations unless they want to. Typically, however, subclasses do tend to provide additional operations to support the extra functionality required in the subclass.

The additional operations can access all of the members in our class, plus all the Public and Protected members in our superclass.

If our class might be extended by further subclasses, we must decide whether our new operations should be declared Overridable (so they can be overridden by these subclasses). Indeed, we can even declare our new operations as MustOverride, to force subclasses to override the operations; if we do this, we must also declare our class as MustInherit.

The following code fragment shows how to define an additional method named IncreaseLimit in the StudentAccount class. This method will not need to be overridden by any further subclasses, so we have not declared the method as Overridable:

```
Public Class StudentAccount
    Inherits BankAccount

    ' Fields and constructor, as before...

    ' Define an additional method
    Public Sub IncreaseLimit(ByVal Amount As Double)
        mOverdraftLimit += Amount
    End Sub

    ' Define other members (see later)...

End Class
```

What Overridable Members and Abstract Members do we need to Override?

If the superclass defines Overridable operations, we can choose to override these operations in our class. If the superclass defines MustOverride operations, we are obliged to override these operations; otherwise, we must declare our class as MustInherit because it is missing part of its implementation. It's perfectly acceptable to do this; we can spread the implementation of MustOverride methods over several levels in the inheritance hierarchy if appropriate.

We use the Overrides keyword to indicate we are overriding an operation from the superclass; our operation must have exactly the same name and signature as the operation we are overriding. If we want to leverage the existing functionality in the superclass, we can use MyBase to invoke the superclass version of the operation.

There is one more issue to consider when we override a method. If we want to prevent the operation from being further overridden by subsequent subclasses, we can declare the method as NotOverridable. This is a big decision to make, because it assumes the current implementation of the operation satisfies all current and future requirements. Therefore, we recommend you use the NotOverridable keyword sparingly.

The following code fragment shows how the StudentAccount class can override methods from the BankAccount class:

```
Public Class StudentAccount
    Inherits BankAccount

    ' Field, constructor, and methods, as before...

    ' Override an Overridable method from the superclass
    Public Overrides Sub PrintStatement()
        MyBase.PrintStatement()
        Console.WriteLine("Overdraft limit: ${0}", mOverdraftLimit)
    End Sub

    ' Override an Overridable property from the superclass
    Protected Overrides ReadOnly Property Funds() As Double
        Get
```

273

```
            Return MyBase.Funds + mOverdraftLimit
        End Get
    End Property

    ' Override a MustOverride method from the superclass
    Public Overrides Sub PrintSpecialComments()
        Console.WriteLine("Student overdraft limit: ${0}", _
                          mOverdraftLimit)
    End Sub

    ' Override a MustOverride property from the superclass
    Public Overrides ReadOnly Property MaxSingleDebit() As Double
        Get
            Return 50
        End Get
    End Property

End Class
```

Note the following points:

❑   We have chosen to override the `PrintStatement` method from the superclass. In our implementation of `PrintStatement`, we call the superclass's `PrintStatement` method to print the balance and account number. We then print the student account's overdraft limit.

❑   We have also chosen to override the `Funds` property from the superclass. In our implementation of `Funds`, we use the `Funds` property from the superclass to get the current balance in the account. We then add `mOverdraftLimit` to this value, because student accounts are allowed to go overdrawn by this amount.

❑   We are required to override the `PrintSpecialComments` method. In this method, we print information about the student account's overdraft limit.

❑   We are also required to override the `MaxSingleDebit` property. In this property, we return a fixed value to indicate that all student accounts have a maximum single debit of $50.

Are there any Members we need to Shadow?

As we have seen in the previous examples, a class can override members from its superclass, and can also introduce entirely new members that were not mentioned at all in the superclass. For example, the `StudentAccount` class overrides the `PrintStatement` method from the superclass, and also introduces a new method named `IncreaseLimit`. There is a fundamental difference between these two methods:

❑   With `PrintStatement`, the superclass anticipated the likelihood that the method might need to be overridden. The superclass therefore declared the method as `Overridable`.

❑ With `IncreaseLimit`, the superclass had no idea whatsoever that this method would be needed in the subclass. There is therefore no mention of the `IncreaseLimit` method in the superclass.

The point we are making is that we can only override operations that have been explicitly declared as `Overridable` (or `MustOverride`) in the superclass. We cannot override operations that are not declared in this way.

Shadowing occurs when we define a member with the same name as an existing member in the superclass. Unlike overriding, shadowing works on any kind of member; is not limited to methods and properties. For example, we might define a function that shadows a field with the same name in the superclass. As another example, we might define a property that shadows a method with the same name in the superclass.

Shadowing occurs implicitly every time we define a member that is not qualified with the `Overrides` keyword. In other words, every member in our class either overrides a member in the superclass, or (potentially) hides a member with the same name in the superclass. To make shadowing more explicit, we can use the `Shadows` keyword as follows in our class:

```
Public Class StudentAccount
    Inherits BankAccount

    Private Shadows mOverdraftLimit As Double        ' Overdraft limit

    Public Shadows Sub IncreaseLimit(ByVal Amount As Double)
        mOverdraftLimit += Amount
    End Sub

End Class
```

There are two main reasons for using shadowing:

❑ Shadowing protects us against the chance that future modifications to the superclass will introduce new members that we have already defined in our class. The `Shadows` keyword makes it clear the member in our class has nothing to do with the member in the superclass.

❑ Shadowing causes our members to hide members with the same name in our superclass. If another class inherits from our class, it cannot see the members defined in our superclass.

How do we use our Inheritance Hierarchy in Client Code?

We've spent the last few pages discussing how to define superclasses and subclasses, and considered numerous decisions that influence the design of these classes. Now it's time to see how to use these classes in client code.

275

Essentially, there are two distinct scenarios to consider:

❑ The client code knows precisely what kind of object it is dealing with. For example, we might write a function that takes a parameter whose declared type is StudentAccount. In this scenario, we can use all of the Public members defined in StudentAccount and its superclasses.

❑ The client code doesn't know the exact data type of the object it is dealing with. For example, we might write a function that takes a parameter whose declared type is BankAccount.

When we call this function, we can pass any kind of bank account as a parameter (for example, StudentAccount, SavingsAccount, CheckingAccount, and so on). This is known as the **principle of substitutability**. However, when the compiler compiles our function, all it sees is the declared type of the parameter (BankAccount). Therefore, the compiler only lets us access the members in the BankAccount class. All is not lost, however; if we invoke any Overridable (or MustOverride) operations, the runtime system will invoke the correct version of the operation depending on what kind of object we are really dealing with. This is what we call **polymorphism**.

The following code fragment illustrates both these scenarios. You can find this source code in the file MainApp.vb in the download folder Inheritance\DefiningSubclasses:

```
Public Class MyApp

    ' Entry point for this application
    Shared Sub Main()

        ' Create a StudentAccount object, and pass it a subroutine
        ' that expects a StudentAccount
        Dim studentAccount0 As New StudentAccount(3000, 300)
        UseStudentAccount(studentAccount0)

        ' Create another StudentAccount object, and pass it to a
        ' subroutine that takes "any kind of" BankAccount object
        Dim studentAccount1 As New StudentAccount(5000, 500)
        UseAnyKindOfAccount(studentAccount1)

    End Sub

    ' This method specifically takes a StudentAccount object
    Shared Sub UseStudentAccount(ByVal aStudentAccount
                                 As StudentAccount)

        Console.WriteLine("Using a StudentAccount object")
```

```
        ' Use members originally defined in BankAccount
        aStudentAccount.Debit(50)
        aStudentAccount.Credit(100)
        aStudentAccount.PrintStatement()
        aStudentAccount.PrintSpecialComments()
        Console.WriteLine("Maximum single withdrawal: ${0}", _
                          aStudentAccount.MaxSingleDebit)


        ' Use new members introduced in SavingsAccount
        aStudentAccount.IncreaseLimit(200)
        aStudentAccount.PrintSpecialComments()   ' Verify limit is_
          updated

    End Sub

    ' This method takes "any kind of" BankAccount object
    Shared Sub UseAnyKindOfAccount(ByVal anAccount As BankAccount)

        Console.WriteLine(vbCrLf & "Using a kind of BankAccount_
                          object")

        ' Use members originally defined in BankAccount
        anAccount.Debit(50)
        anAccount.Credit(100)
        anAccount.PrintStatement()
        anAccount.PrintSpecialComments()
        Console.WriteLine("Maximum single withdrawal: ${0}", _
                          anAccount.MaxSingleDebit)

    End Sub

End Class
```

Note the following points in the client code:

- In Main, we create two StudentAccount objects and pass them into subroutines named UseStudentAccount and UseAnyKindOfAccount.

- The UseStudentAccount() subroutine has a parameter whose compile-time type is StudentAccount. The compiler knows the object passed into this subroutine is definitely a StudentAccount object (or an object of a class inherited from StudentAccount). The compiler therefore allows us to access all the Public members defined in SavingsAccount, plus any of its superclasses (BankAccount and System.Object).

- The UseAnyKindOfAccount subroutine has a parameter whose compile-time type is BankAccount. The compiler cannot predict the exact type of object that will be passed into this subroutine; all the compiler knows for sure is that the object will be some kind of bank account. The compiler therefore only allows us to access the Public members defined in BankAccount (and System.Object).

To compile all the classes in this example, open a .NET Framework command prompt window, move to the folder that contains the example, and type the following command

```
> vbc MainApp.vb BankAccount.vb StudentAccount.vb
```

This produces an executable file named `MainApp.exe`, which contains the compiled code for all the classes. To run the application, type the following command:

```
> MainApp.exe
```

The application displays the following output on the console window. If you work through the details, you'll find the application has called the correct `StudentAccount` and `BankAccount` members in each case:

```
Using a StudentAccount object
Account number: 0
Balance: $3050
Overdraft limit: $300
Student overdraft limit: $300
Maximum single withdrawal: $50
Student overdraft limit: $500

Using a kind of BankAccount object
Account number: 1
Balance: $5050
Overdraft limit: $500
Student overdraft limit: $500
Maximum single withdrawal: $50
```

Inheritance of Interface

As we mentioned earlier in the chapter, the .NET Framework supports two distinct forms of inheritance:

❑   Inheritance of implementation, where subclasses inherit data and functionality from a superclass. We've just explored inheritance of implementation thoroughly in the previous section.

❑   Inheritance of interface, where classes and structures implement the members specified in an interface. We'll see how to achieve inheritance of interface in this section.

Interfaces do not contain any implementation code. Rather, they define a contract that must be fulfilled in implementing classes or structures. This enables us to design our system in terms of the services it must deliver, rather than enforcing a particular implementation strategy.

Earlier versions of Visual Basic enabled us to implement interfaces, but did not allow us to define new interfaces of our own. With Visual Basic .NET, interfaces are a fully-fledged part of the language. We can use Visual Basic .NET to define interfaces for consumption in any .NET language. We can also implement and use interfaces written in any .NET language.

Interfaces are useful in situations where we cannot inherit from a superclass. For example, structures can implement interfaces, but they cannot inherit from a superclass (all structures inherit implicitly from `System.ValueType`). Likewise, a class can only inherit from one superclass, but it can implement any number of interfaces.

One of the main benefits of inheritance of interface is that it enables us to express monolithic classes and structures in terms of the interfaces they support. For example, imagine we have a class named `InsuranceContract` with fifty methods to define the business rules for an insurance contract. Imagine we have another (seemingly unrelated) class named `Trade`, which contains another fifty methods representing a trade in an investment bank. Although these classes are unrelated, there might be some aspect of the classes' capabilities that is common; for example, maybe both classes define a `Print` method to print details on the printer. How can we express this common capability?

One approach might be to define a superclass named `Printable`, with a single method named `Print`. The `InsuranceContract` and `Trade` classes could then inherit from this superclass. This would be convenient, but it's a misuse of inheritance of implementation. There are several problems with using inheritance of implementation in this scenario:

- ❑ Inheritance of implementation should only be used when we have an 'is a kind of' relationship between the subclass and its superclass. It's not right to say that `InsuranceContract` and `Trade` are 'kinds of' `Printable`. A more accurate description of the relationship would be to say `InsuranceContract` and `Trade` support the `Printable` behavior. This is a sure sign that we need inheritance of interface (capability), rather than inheritance of implementation (code reuse).

- ❑ How would we implement the `Print` method in the `Printable` class? The information to be printed depends on the data in each of the subclasses.

- ❑ The .NET Framework only allows us to inherit from one direct superclass. If `InsuranceContract` and `Trade` inherit from the `Printable` superclass, they will not be able to inherit from any other class.

To summarize our findings, inheritance of implementation purely for convenient reuse of methods is nearly always a mistake. Only use inheritance of implementation when there really is an 'is a kind of' relationship between the classes. If you want a slogan, 'think strategically, not tactically'.

The scenario we've described above should be resolved by using interfaces. We can define an interface named `IPrintable`, which specifies the set of services required for an object to be printable; in this simple example, `IPrintable` requires a single method named `Print`. We can then define classes and structures that implement the `IPrintable` interface; each class or structure must provide its own `Print` method, with the same signature as the `Print` method in the `IPrintable` interface.

279

By convention, all interface names in the .NET Framework start with the letter I. This makes it easier to differentiate interfaces from other types in the .NET Framework. Many interface names end with able, such as our IPrintable interface, and ICloneable and IDisposable in the .NET Framework class library; this highlights the fact that interfaces represent a capability, rather than containing implementation logic.

Let's see how to write the `IPrintable` interface and the `InsuranceContract` and Trade classes in Visual Basic .NET. You can find the full source code for this example in the folder `Inheritance\SimpleInterface`. We'll begin with the `IPrintable` interface:

```
Public Interface IPrintable
    Sub Print()
End Interface
```

Note the following points in the `IPrintable` interface:

❑ `IPrintable` is qualified with the `Public` accessibility modifier, which means the interface can be used in any assembly. For example, any assembly can define classes or structures to implement the interface. Likewise, any assembly can define methods that use this interface as the parameter type or return type.

If we want to restrict the accessibility of an interface, we can use the `Friend` qualifier rather than `Public`. The `Friend` qualifier means the interface can only be accessed within the assembly in which it is defined. `Friend` is the default accessibility for interfaces.

Sometimes it isn't obvious whether an interface should be declared `Public` or `Friend`. Our general advice is to err on the side of caution; if in doubt, declare the interface as `Friend`. It's always possible to increase the accessibility from `Friend` to `Public`, if we need to access the interface in a different assembly sometime in the future. However, it's usually impossible to restrict the accessibility from `Public` to `Friend`, because this will break any code that has come to rely on the public accessibility of the interface.

❑ `IPrintable` has a single method named `Print`. The method has no implementation, of course, because interfaces don't provide implementation details. Also notice that the method has no accessibility qualifiers; all members in an interface are implicitly `Public`, by definition.

❑ It's fairly common for interfaces to be quite small. Each interface specifies a particular slice of functionality in our application, and should only contain the members required to achieve this functionality. If we find ourselves defining interfaces that contain dozens of unrelated members, we should probably divide the interface into several smaller, coherent interfaces instead.

Now let's see how to implement the `IPrintable` interface in the `InsuranceContract` class:

```
Public Class InsuranceContract
    Implements IPrintable

    Private mName As String          ' Name of insured person
    Private mAmount As Double         ' Amount insured for
    Private mPremium As Double        ' Annual insurance premium

    ' Constructor
    Public Sub New(ByVal Name As String, _
                   ByVal Amount As Double, _
                   ByVal Premium As Double)
        mName = Name
        mAmount = Amount
        mPremium = Premium
    End Sub

    ' Implement the Print method (from IPrintable)
    Public Sub Print() Implements IPrintable.Print
        Console.WriteLine("Printing an Insurance Contract")
        Console.WriteLine("{0} insured for ${1}, premium ${2}" & _
            vbCrLf, mName, mAmount, mPremium)
    End Sub

    ' Additional methods etc. as required
    Public Sub AdjustPremium(ByVal PremiumDelta As Double)
        mPremium += PremiumDelta
    End Sub

End Class
```

Note the following points in the `InsuranceContract` class:

❑   `InsuranceContract` implements the `IPrintable` interface. Note that the `Implements` statement must appear on a new line; it cannot appear on the same line as the `Class` statement.

This is a simple example of inheritance of interface. Later in this chapter, we'll see how a class can implement several interfaces, and also inherit from a superclass at the same time.

❑   `InsuranceContract` implements the `Print` method defined in `IPrintable`. The `Implements IPrintable.Print` notation indicates which method we are implementing. This notation is required, because the name of the implementing method doesn't have to match the original method name in the interface. For example, we could have named our method `PrintAnInsuranceContract` (or anything else, for that matter); as long as our method includes the `Implements IPrintable.Print` notation, the compiler can figure out this method implements `Print` in the `IPrintable` interface.

The reason for this apparent laxity is that it allows a class to implement several different interfaces, even if these interfaces contain methods with the same name. In the implementing class, we can define differently-named methods and use the `Implements InterfaceName.MethodName` notation to indicate which interface methods they implement. We'll see an example of this technique later in this chapter.

❑ `InsuranceContract` defines additional fields, constructors, methods and so on, to represent an insurance contract. There is no limit on the additional members we can define in a class that implements an interface. `InsuranceContract` is just a regular class that happens to implement the `IPrintable` interface.

For the sake of completeness, here is the source code for the `Trade` class. The `Trade` class implements the `IPrintable` interface, but in a different way than the `InsuranceContract` class:

```
Public Class Trade
    Implements IPrintable

    Public Enum BuyOrSell
        Buy
        Sell
    End Enum

    Private mTypeOfTrade As BuyOrSell
    Private mTicker As String
    Private mUnitPrice As Double
    Private mQuantity As Integer

    ' Constructor
    Public Sub New(ByVal TypeOfTrade As BuyOrSell, _
                   ByVal Ticker As String, _
                   ByVal UnitPrice As Double, _
                   ByVal Quantity As Integer)
        mTypeOfTrade = TypeOfTrade
        mTicker = Ticker
        mUnitPrice = UnitPrice
        mQuantity = Quantity
    End Sub

    ' Implement the Print method (from IPrintable)
    Public Sub Print() Implements IPrintable.Print
        Console.WriteLine("Printing a Trade")
        Console.WriteLine("{0} {1} stocks of {2}, value ${3}" & _
            vbCrLf, mTypeOfTrade, mQuantity, mTicker, TotalValue())
    End Sub
```

```
' Additional methods etc. as required
Private Function TotalValue() As Double
    Return mUnitPrice * mQuantity
End Function

End Class
```

Note the following points in the `Trade` class:

❑   `Trade` implements the `IPrintable` interface.

❑   `Trade` implements the `Print` method defined in `IPrintable`. The `Implements IPrintable.Print` indicates which method we are implementing.

❑   `Trade` defines additional fields, constructors, methods and so on, to represent a trade.

Now let's see how to use the `IPrintable` interface in client code:

```
Public Class MyApp

    Shared Sub Main()

        ' Create an InsuranceContract object and a Trade object
        Dim aContract As New InsuranceContract("Tom Evans", 250000, _
                                                450)
        Dim aTrade As New Trade(Trade.BuyOrSell.Buy, "WROX", 9.5, _
                                100000)

        ' Pass objects into a generic method, which accepts any object
        ' that implements the IPrintable interface
        MyGenericMethod(aContract)
        MyGenericMethod(aTrade)

    End Sub

    Shared Sub MyGenericMethod(ByVal aPrintableObject As IPrintable)

        ' We know the aPrintableObject parameter has a Print method
        aPrintableObject.Print()

    End Sub

End Class
```

Note the following points in the client code:

❑   The `Main` subroutine creates an `InsuranceContract` object and a `Trade` object, and passes these objects into a generic method named `MyGenericMethod`. This is possible because `MyGenericMethod` takes an `IPrintable` parameter, which means we can pass any object that implements the `IPrintable` interface.

❏ MyGenericMethod doesn't know anything about the type of the object it receives as a parameter. All the method knows is that the object implements the IPrintable interface. In other words, the object supports the Print method. MyGenericMethod doesn't know (or care) about the other capabilities of the object; all it cares about is that the object can be printed.

This example corroborate our earlier assertion that interfaces help us write code based upon capabilities ('what can an object do') rather than types ('what is the type of the object'). This is often referred to as *programming by contract*; an interface defines a contract between types that implement an interface, and client code that uses the interface for parameter and return types.

To compile this application, open a .NET Framework command prompt window, move to the folder that contains the example, and type the following command:

```
> vbc SimpleInterface.vb
```

To run the application, type the following command:

```
> SimpleInterface.exe
```

The application displays the following output on the console window. Notice that the InsuranceContract object and the Trade object are printed correctly:

```
Printing an Insurance Contract
Tom Evans insured for $250000, premium $450

Printing a Trade
Buy 100000 stocks of WROX, value $950000
```

It's useful to see how the interface and classes are compiled into MSIL code. To run the MSIL Disassembler tool, type the following command:

```
> ildasm SimpleInterface.exe
```

The MSIL Disassembler window displays the following information (we've expanded the nodes in this screenshot, to show the details for each of our types):

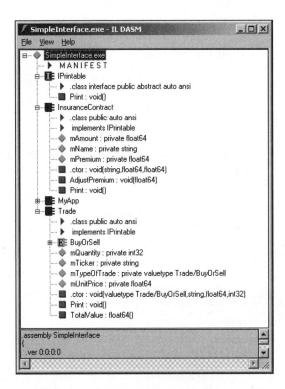

Note the following points in the MSIL Disassembler window:

❑ The IPrintable interface is qualified with the interface and public MSIL keywords, to indicate that IPrintable is a public interface type.

❑ The InsuranceContract class has an implements IPrintable statement, to indicate InsuranceContract implements the IPrintable interface.

❑ The Trade class also has an implements IPrintable statement, to indicate Trade implements the IPrintable interface.

The MSIL Disassembler window also reveals interesting information about the methods in our interface and implementing classes. Double-click the Print method in IPrintable, to view the MSIL code for this method:

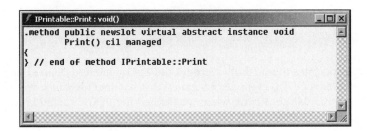

Note the following points in IPrintable's Print method:

❑ The method is public. All members in an interface are public.

❑ The newslot MSIL keyword indicates this method will require a new slot in the vtable for each implementing class.

❑ The virtual MSIL keyword indicates this method is overridable in subclasses. All members in an interface are overridable.

❑ The abstract MSIL keyword indicates this method is abstract, which means it must be overridden in subclasses. All members in an interface must be overridden.

❑ The instance MSIL keyword indicates this is an instance method, not a class method. All members in an interface are instance members, not class members.

Now double-click the Print method in InsuranceContract, to see the MSIL code for the Print method in this class:

```
InsuranceContract::Print : void()                                          _ □ ×
.method public newslot final virtual instance void
        Print() cil managed
{
  .override IPrintable::Print
  // Code size       49 (0x31)
  .maxstack  8
  IL_0000:  ldstr        "Printing an Insurance Contract"
  IL_0005:  call         void [mscorlib]System.Console::WriteLine(string)
  IL_000a:  ldstr        "{0} insured for ${1}, premium ${2}\r\n"
  IL_000f:  ldarg.0
  IL_0010:  ldfld        string InsuranceContract::mName
  IL_0015:  ldarg.0
  IL_0016:  ldfld        float64 InsuranceContract::mAmount
  IL_001b:  box          [mscorlib]System.Double
  IL_0020:  ldarg.0
  IL_0021:  ldfld        float64 InsuranceContract::mPremium
  IL_0026:  box          [mscorlib]System.Double
  IL_002b:  call         void [mscorlib]System.Console::WriteLine(string,
                                                                 object,
                                                                 object,
                                                                 object)
  IL_0030:  ret
} // end of method InsuranceContract::Print
```

Notice the following statement, which appears immediately after the opening brace of the method:

```
.override IPrintable::Print
```

This statement indicates the method overrides the Print method defined in the IPrintable interface. This compiler generated this statement because we specified Implements IPrintable.Print when we defined the Print method in the InsuranceContract class.

What Can We Define In An Interface?

In the previous example, the `IPrintable` interface defined a single method named `Print`. This was a simple example. In fact, an interface can contain the signatures for any of the following kinds of member:

❑   Instance methods

An interface can define the functions and subroutines that must be implemented by all implementing classes. Note that an interface cannot define constructors or `Shared` methods.

❑   Properties

An interface can define properties to represent data that must be supported by all implementing classes. The rules for defining properties in an interface are the same as for defining properties in a class (except that an interface does not provide any implementation for the properties, of course). An interface can define read-write properties, read-only properties, and write-only properties. Likewise, an interface can define indexed properties if required, and designate one of these indexed properties as the default property for the interface. However, the implementing class can only have one property designated as the default property; if a class implements several interfaces, each with its own default property, we'll get an error when we try to compile that class. Because you will impose a limitation on implementing classes, it is best not to describe a default property in an interface.

❑   Events

An interface can define events that implementing classes might fire. Each implementing class must implement these events. Events offer implementing classes a published mechanism for reporting important occurrences to the rest of the application. It also allows the client code to register handler methods for particular events on an interface, without needing to know the actual type of the object that raises the event. This reduces the dependencies between the event source (the implementing class that raises the event) and the event receiver (the client code that registers handler methods to receive event notifications). By reducing the dependencies between different parts of our application, it makes it easier for us to modify isolated parts of the application without breaking existing code. This increases the stability and robustness of our software, which is clearly a beneficial by-product of our design.

To illustrate these rules, we'll show an example of how to define and implement an interface that contains methods, properties, and events. You can find the full source code for this example in the folder `Inheritance\InterfaceMembers`. The interface in this example is named `ICalculable`, and represents an interface implemented by classes that perform a lengthy calculation that can be performed in a background thread. The `ICalculable` interface allows multiple results from the calculation:

```
Public Interface ICalculable

    ' A method, to perform a calculation
    Sub PerformCalculation()

    ' An event, to indicate the calculation is complete
    Event CalculationComplete(ByVal Src As ICalculable)

    ' A scalar property, to indicate how many results were calculated
    ReadOnly Property Count() As Integer

    ' An indexed property, to get the results of the calculation
    Default ReadOnly Property Results(ByVal Index As Integer) As Object

End Interface
```

Note the following points in the ICalculable interface:

❑   The PerformCalculation subroutine represents a method that performs a
       (potentially lengthy) calculation. The method doesn't take any parameters, and
       does not return a value either. This highlights one of the aims of interface
       design: to minimize the restrictions on how the interface can be implemented
       by the implementing classes. In this example, the ICalculable interface
       avoids being prescriptive about the information required to perform the
       calculation; each implementing class is free to use its own mechanism for
       providing this information. We'll show how to do this shortly.

❑   The CalculationComplete event indicates that the calculation has been
       completed, and the results are ready for inspection. The idea is that
       implementing classes raise this event when they have finished performing
       the calculation. Client code can register handler methods for this event. The
       handler methods must take a parameter of type ICalculable, so they can
       query the ICalculable object for the results of the calculation.

❑   The Count property indicates how many results were obtained during the
       calculation. This property is declared ReadOnly, so client code can query
       (but not modify) the number of results obtained during the calculation.

❑   The Results property enables client code to query the results of the
       calculation. This is an indexed property, and is declared as the Default
       property for the interface. Note the return type of the property is declared
       as Object, rather than a specific type such as Integer or Double. We
       chose Object because it offers maximum genericity; in other words, it
       allows implementing classes to return whatever types of result they like.
       This is an example of the .NET Framework unified inheritance hierarchy at
       work; we can use Object as a generic data type for method parameters
       and return types.

Now let's see how to implement the `ICalculable` interface. The following code fragment shows a class named `PrimeNumberFinder`, which finds the first *n* prime numbers. The class implements all the members defined in `ICalculable`, and also contains additional methods and fields as required to perform the prime number calculations:

```
Public Class PrimeNumberFinder
    Implements ICalculable

    Private mPrimesRequired As Integer   ' How many primes required?
    Private mResults As ArrayList        ' Prime numbers

    ' Constructor
    Public Sub New(ByVal PrimesRequired As Double)
        mPrimesRequired = PrimesRequired
        mResults = New ArrayList()
    End Sub

    ' Implement the PerformCalculation method, to find 'n' primes
    Public Sub PerformCalculation() _
        Implements ICalculable.PerformCalculation

        ' How many prime numbers found so far
        Dim PrimeCount As Integer = 0

        ' Loop through all numbers, to see if they are prime
        Dim Number As Integer
        For Number = 2 To Integer.MaxValue

            ' Does this number have a factor?
            Dim I As Integer
            For I = 2 To Number - 1
                If Number Mod I = 0 Then
                    ' I is factor of Number, so Number is not prime
                    Exit For
                End If
            Next

            ' Did we reach the end of the loop without finding a factor?
            If I = Number Then

                ' Number is prime, so add it to the ArrayList
                mResults.Add(Number)
                PrimeCount += 1

                ' Have we found all the prime numbers we need?
                If PrimeCount = mPrimesRequired Then

                    ' Raise event, to indicate the calculation is complete
                    RaiseEvent CalculationComplete(Me)
                    Exit Sub
```

```
                End If
             End If
        Next

    End Sub

    ' Implement the CalculationComplete event
    Public Event CalculationComplete(ByVal Src As ICalculable) _
        Implements ICalculable.CalculationComplete

    ' Implement the Count scalar property, to get number of primes
    ReadOnly Property Count() As Integer Implements ICalculable.Count
        Get
            Return mResults.Count
        End Get
    End Property

    ' Implement the Results indexed property
    Default ReadOnly Property Results(ByVal Index As Integer) As _
        Object Implements ICalculable.Results

        Get
            Return mResults(Index)
        End Get

    End Property

End Class
```

Note the following points in the `PrimeNumberFinder` class:

❑   The `PrimeNumberFinder` class has a field named `mPrimesRequired`, to
    remember how many prime numbers are required. The prime numbers will
    be stored in the `mResults` field, which is an `ArrayList`. `ArrayList` is
    one of the .NET Framework collection classes in the
    `System.Collections` namespace, and represents a resizable array.

❑   The `PrimeNumberFinder` constructor initializes the `mPrimesRequired`
    and `mResults` fields.

❑   The `PerformCalculation` method implements `PerformCalculation`
    from the `ICalculable` interface. The method finds the required number of
    prime numbers, and appends each prime number to the `mResults`
    collection. The details of this algorithm aren't really important (unless you
    are an author writing an example about prime numbers!).

When the `PerformCalculation` method has found the required number of prime numbers, it raises the `CalculationComplete` event. This event is defined in the `ICalculable` interface, and is implemented by the `PrimeNumberFinder` class (see the next bullet point). According to the definition of the `CalculationComplete` event in `ICalculable`, the event requires a parameter of type `ICalculable`. In other words, we must supply an object that implements the `ICalculable` interface. We've passed `Me`, which means 'the current object'. The current object in this context is a `PrimeNumberFinder` object, which is fine because `PrimeNumberFinder` implements the `ICalculable` interface.

❏ The `PrimeNumberFinder` class implements the `CalculationComplete` event, as mentioned above.

❏ The `PrimeNumberFinder` class implements the `Count` scalar property, to return the number of elements in the `mResults` collection.

❏ The `PrimeNumberFinder` class implements the `Results` indexed property, to return a specified result from the `mResults` collection.

Now that we've defined the `PrimeNumberFinder` class, let's see how to use the class in client code. In the following code fragment, we create two `PrimeNumberFinder` objects:

❏ `prime5` finds the first 5 prime numbers. We execute the `PerformCalculation` method in a separate thread, so that the main thread in the application can continue unhindered.

❏ `prime20` finds the first 20 prime numbers. The `PerformCalculation` method is executed in its own separate thread.

```
Public Class MainApp

    ' Entry point for this application
    Shared Sub Main()

        ' Find the first 5 prime numbers
        Dim prime5 As New PrimeNumberFinder(5)
        AddHandler prime5.CalculationComplete, AddressOf MyHandler
        Dim t As New Thread(AddressOf prime5.PerformCalculation)
        t.Start()

        ' Find the first 20 prime numbers
        Dim prime20 As New PrimeNumberFinder(20)
        AddHandler prime20.CalculationComplete, AddressOf MyHandler
        t = New Thread(AddressOf prime20.PerformCalculation)
        t.Start()

    End Sub

    ' Event handler method, for events from ICalculable objects
    Shared Sub MyHandler(ByVal Src As ICalculable)

        ' Lock the Console.Out object to prevent synchronization problems
```

```
        Monitor.Enter(Console.Out)

        ' Display the results from the ICalculable object
        Console.WriteLine("First {0} prime numbers", Src.Count)
        Dim I As Integer
        For I = 0 To Src.Count - 1
            Console.Write("{0} ", Src.Results(I))
        Next
        Console.WriteLine()

        ' Unlock the Console.Out object
        Monitor.Exit(Console.Out)

    End Sub

End Class
```

Note the following points in the client code:

❑ The constructor for the prime5 object receives the number 5, to indicate we want the first 5 prime numbers.

❑ The AddHandler keyword registers an event handler method for the CalculationComplete event on the prime5 object. When this event occurs, the MyHandler method will be called to handle the event.

❑ We create a new Thread object, to enable the prime number calculation to be performed in a separate thread (the Thread class is defined in the System.Threading namespace). The Thread constructor requires the address of the method to be executed in the new thread; we specify the PerformCalculation method on the prime5 object.

❑ We call the Start method on the Thread object, to create an operating system thread and execute the specified method (PerformCalculation) on the specified object (prime5).

❑ We repeat the above four steps to create an object named prime20, to find the first 20 prime numbers.

❑ The AddHandler method handles events from ICalculable objects. This method must have the same signature as the CalculationComplete event in the ICalculable interface. The AddHandler method receives an ICalculable parameter, and uses the Count and Results properties to display the results of the calculation. AddHandler doesn't know or care about the actual type of object that raised the event; all that matters is that the object implements ICalculable.

The Monitor. Enter (Console. Out) *and*
Monitor. Exit (Console. Out) *statements prevent synchronization problems when the* MyHandler *method displays results for prime number calculations. The* Monitor. Enter (Console. Out) *method acquires an exclusive lock on the* Console. Out *object, which prevents the object from being used by any other thread until the lock is released via* Monitor. Exit (Console. Out). *This is an important requirement in our example, because* prime5 *and* prime20 *perform their prime number calculations in separate threads. If one of these calculations is completed while* MyHandler *is already displaying the results of a previous calculation (in a separate thread), we must ensure the two sets of results do not get interleaved on the console output.* Monitor. Enter (Console. Out) *and* Monitor. Exit (Console. Out) *guarantee each set of results is displayed completely before the next set of results is displayed.*

To compile this application, open a .NET Framework command prompt window, move to the folder that contains the example, and type the following command:

```
> vbc InterfaceMembers.vb
```

To run the application, type the following command:

```
> InterfaceMembers.exe
```

The application displays the following output on the console window:

```
First 5 prime numbers
2 3 5 7 11
First 20 prime numbers
2 3 5 7 11 13 17 19 23 29 31 37 41 43 47 53 59 61 67 71
```

Implementing Multiple Interfaces

Earlier in this chapter, we observed that the .NET Framework only supports *single inheritance of implementation*; this means a class can only directly inherit from one superclass. However, the .NET Framework supports *multiple inheritance of interface*; this means a class can implement any number of interfaces. Multiple inheritance of interfaces is a familiar feature in many .NET Framework applications.

To implement multiple interfaces in a Visual Basic .NET class, we use the Implements statement for each interface we want to implement. In the following example, we define a class named MyImplementingClass that implements two interfaces:

❑ IDisposable

This is a standard .NET Framework interface that defines a single method named Dispose. The purpose of the Dispose method is to perform clean-up operations on objects when they are no longer required.

293

❑ IComparable

This is a standard .NET Framework interface that defines a single method named CompareTo. The purpose of the CompareTo method is to compare the current object with another object of the same type.

```
Public Class MyImplementingClass
    Implements IDisposable
    Implements IComparable

    ' Implement the Dispose method (from IDisposable)
    Public Sub Dispose() Implements IDisposable.Dispose
        ' Implementation code for IDisposable.Dispose...
    End Sub

    ' Implement the CompareTo method (from IComparable)
    Public Function CompareTo(ByVal Other As Object) As Integer _
                Implements IComparable.CompareTo
        ' Implementation code for IComparable.CompareTo...
    End Function

    ' Plus other members in MyImplementingClass, as appropriate...

End Class
```

When a class implements multiple interfaces, the class must implement all of the members from all of the interfaces. MyImplementingClass satisfies this requirement, because it implements all of the members defined in IDisposable and IComparable. This is a fairly simple example, because the members in IDisposable and IComparable have different names and signatures. Matters get more complicated if the interfaces contain methods with the same names and signatures. There are two possible scenarios for us to consider:

❑ The interfaces define members with the same name but different signatures.

❑ The interfaces define members with the same name and signature.

Interfaces Define Members with the Same Name but Different Signatures

If we implement interfaces that have members with the same name but different signatures, we must implement each member separately in the implementing class.

For example, imagine we have an interface named Interface1 with a method named TheMethod. Imagine we have another interface named Interface2, which also has a method named TheMethod but with a different signature:

```
Public Interface Interface1
    Sub TheMethod()
End Interface

Public Interface Interface2
    Sub TheMethod(ByVal Param As Integer)
End Interface
```

The implementing class must implement both versions of TheMethod separately, because the method signatures are different. The implementing class can use different names for each method, as shown in the following example. The Implements InterfaceName.MethodName notation at the end of each method indicates which method we are implementing in each case:

```
Public Class MyImplementingClass
    Implements Interface1
    Implements Interface2

    Public Sub Method1() Implements Interface1.TheMethod
        ' Implementation code for Interface1.TheMethod...
    End Sub

    Public Sub Method2(ByVal Param As Integer) _
                    Implements Interface2.TheMethod
        ' Implementation code for Interface2.TheMethod...
    End Sub

End Class
```

Alternatively, the implementing class can use the same name for each method, as shown in the following example. This approach offers greater consistency and readability:

```
Public Class MyImplementingClass
    Implements Interface1
    Implements Interface2

    Public Sub TheMethod() Implements Interface1.TheMethod
        ' Implementation code for Interface1.TheMethod...
    End Sub

    Public Sub TheMethod(ByVal Param As Integer) _
                    Implements Interface2.TheMethod
        ' Implementation code for Interface2.TheMethod...
    End Sub

    End Sub

End Class
```

Interfaces Define Members with the Same Name and Signature

If we implement interfaces that have members with the same name and signature, we can either implement the members separately, or provide a single implementation of the member that satisfies both interfaces simultaneously.

Imagine Interface1 and Interface2 define methods named TheMethod with exactly the same signature, as follows:

```
Public Interface Interface1
    Sub TheMethod(ByVal Param1 As Integer, ByVal Param2 As Double)
End Interface

Public Interface Interface2
    Sub TheMethod(ByVal Param1 As Integer, ByVal Param2 As Double)
End Interface
```

295

The implementing class can implement both versions of `TheMethod` separately, if it needs to provide a different implementation for `Interface1.TheMethod` and `Interface2.TheMethod`. The implementing class must use different names for the implementation methods, to avoid a name clash between the two methods in the implementing class:

```
Public Class MyImplementingClass
    Implements Interface1
    Implements Interface2

    Public Sub Method1(ByVal Param1 As Integer, ByVal Param2 As _
                Double) Implements Interface1.TheMethod
        ' Implementation code for Interface1.TheMethod...
    End Sub

    Public Sub Method2(ByVal Param1 As Integer, ByVal Param2 As
    Double) _
                Implements Interface2.TheMethod
        ' Implementation code for Interface2.TheMethod...
    End Sub

End Class
```

Alternatively, the implementing class can provide a single method that implements `Interface1.TheMethod` and `Interface2.TheMethod` simultaneously. This approach is suitable if a single implementation of `TheMethod` suffices for both interfaces. To achieve this affect, provide a comma-separated list of method names for the `Implements` keyword at the end of the implementation method:

```
Public Class MyImplementingClass
    Implements Interface1
    Implements Interface2

    Public Sub TheMethod(ByVal Param1 As Integer, ByVal Param2 As _
                Double) Implements Interface1.TheMethod, _
                Interface2.TheMethod
        ' Implement Interface1.TheMethod and Interface2.TheMethod...
    End Sub

End Class
```

Example of Implementing Multiple Interfaces

Let's look at a complete example, to illustrate the rules for implementing multiple interfaces in a class. You can download the full source code for this example from the folder `Inheritance\MultipleInterfaces`.

There are two interfaces in this example, named `ISwitchable` and `ITimeable`:

```
Public Interface ISwitchable
    Sub SwitchOn()
    Sub SwitchOff()
    ReadOnly Property IsOn() As Boolean
End Interface

Public Interface ITimeable
    Sub SwitchOn(ByVal HourOn As Integer)
    Sub SwitchOff(ByVal HourOff As Integer)
    ReadOnly Property IsOn() As Boolean
End Interface
```

Note the following points in these interfaces:

❑   The ISwitchable interface represents a device that can be switched on or off immediately, such as a light bulb.

❑   The ITimeable interface represents a device that can be set to come on and go off at specific hours of the day, such as a central heating system in a house.

❑   Both interfaces define methods named SwitchOn and SwitchOff, although the signatures of these methods are different in each interface.

❑   Both interfaces define a property named IsOn. The signature of this property is identical in each interface.

The following class shows how to implement both these interfaces. The class is named TimerSwitch, and represents a device that can be switched on or off immediately, or set to come on and go off at specific hours of the day. We'll show the full code listing for TimerSwitch first, and then discuss the design and coding issues afterwards:

```
Public Class TimerSwitch
    Implements ISwitchable
    Implements ITimeable

    Private mAlwaysOn As Boolean          ' Is the device on constantly?
    Private mHourOn, mHourOff As Integer      ' Time to go on/off

    ' Implement the SwitchOn method from ISwitchable
    Public Sub SwitchOnConstant() Implements ISwitchable.SwitchOn
        mAlwaysOn = True
        Console.WriteLine("Device is always on")
    End Sub

    ' Implement the SwitchOff method from ISwitchable
    Public Sub SwitchOffConstant() Implements ISwitchable.SwitchOff
        mAlwaysOn = False
        Console.WriteLine("Device is not always on")
    End Sub
```

```
' Implement the SwitchOn method from ITimeable
Public Sub SwitchOnAt(ByVal HourOn As Integer) _
              Implements ITimeable.SwitchOn
    mHourOn = HourOn
    Console.WriteLine("Device comes on at {0}.00 hours", mHourOn)
End Sub


' Implement the SwitchOff method from ITimeable
Public Sub SwitchOffAt(ByVal HourOff As Integer) _
              Implements ITimeable.SwitchOff
    mHourOff = HourOff
    Console.WriteLine("Device goes off at {0}.00 hours", mHourOff)
End Sub


' Implement the IsOn property from ISwitchable and ITimeable
Public ReadOnly Property IsOn() As Boolean _
    Implements ISwitchable.IsOn, ITimeable.IsOn

    Get
        Dim Now As Integer = DateTime.Now.Hour
        If (mAlwaysOn) Or (Now >= mHourOn And Now < mHourOff) Then
            Return True
        Else
            Return False
        End If
    End Get

End Property

End Class
```

Note the following points in the `TimerSwitch` class:

❑   `TimerSwitch` implements `ISwitchable` and `ITimeable`.

❑   The `SwitchOnConstant` and `SwitchOffConstant` methods implement the `SwitchOn` and `SwitchOff` methods from `ISwitchable`. We've chosen these method names deliberately, to make it clear they pertain to the `ISwitchable` interface (rather than the `ITimeable` interface).

❑   The `SwitchOnAt` and `SwitchOffAt` methods implement the `SwitchOn` and `SwitchOff` methods from `ITimeable`. We've chosen these method names deliberately too, to make it clear they pertain to the `ITimeable` interface (rather than the `ISwitchable` interface).

❑   The `IsOn` property in our class implements the `IsOn` property from the `ISwitchable` and `ITimeable` interface. We could have provided separate implementations for `ISwitchable.IsOn` and `ITimeable.IsOn`, but the rules for determining whether a timer switch is on or off depend on a combination of its manual switched status (defined by `mAlwaysOn`) and the time of day (relative to `mHourOn` and `mHourOff`).

298

Now that we've implemented the `ISwitchable` and `ITimeable` interfaces, let's see some client code that uses these interfaces. We'll write three different methods in the client code, as follows:

❑ `UseTimerSwitch`

This method takes a `TimerSwitch` parameter, and therefore has access to all the members defined in the `TimerSwitch` class (using the member names defined in `TimerSwitch`).

❑ `UseSwitchable`

This method takes an `ISwitchable` parameter, and therefore only has access to the members defined in the `ISwitchable` interface (using the member names defined in `ISwitchable`).

❑ `UseTimeable`

This method takes an `ITimeable` parameter, and therefore only has access to the members defined in the `ITimeable` interface (using the member names defined in `ITimeable`).

We call these three methods from `Main`, passing a `TimerSwitch` object in each case:

```
Public Class MyApp

    ' Entry point for this application
    Shared Sub Main()

        ' Create a TimerSwitch, and pass it to UseTimerSwitch
        Dim timerSwitch1 As New TimerSwitch()
        UseTimerSwitch(timerSwitch1)

        ' Create a TimerSwitch, and pass it to UseSwitchable
        Dim timerSwitch2 As New TimerSwitch()
        UseSwitchable(timerSwitch2)

        ' Create a TimerSwitch, and pass it to UseTimeable
        Dim timerSwitch3 As New TimerSwitch()
        UseTimeable(timerSwitch3)

    End Sub

    ' This method specifically takes a TimerSwitch object
    Shared Sub UseTimerSwitch(ByVal aTimerSwitch As TimerSwitch)

        Console.WriteLine("Using a TimerSwitch object")

        ' Use TimerSwitch methods that implement ISwitchable
        aTimerSwitch.SwitchOnConstant()
        aTimerSwitch.SwitchOffConstant()
```

```
                  ' Use TimerSwitch methods that implement ITimeable
                  aTimerSwitch.SwitchOnAt(6)
                  aTimerSwitch.SwitchOffAt(22)

                  ' Use the IsOn property, which is defined in both interfaces
                  Console.WriteLine("IsOn property: {0}" & vbCrLf, _
                                    aTimerSwitch.IsOn)

      End Sub

      ' This method takes any kind of object that implements ISwitchable
      Shared Sub UseSwitchable(ByVal aSwitchable As ISwitchable)

            ' We must use the member names defined in ISwitchable
            Console.WriteLine("Using an object that implements _
                              ISwitchable")
            aSwitchable.SwitchOn()
            aSwitchable.SwitchOff()
            Console.WriteLine("IsOn property: {0}" & vbCrLf, _
                              aSwitchable.IsOn)

      End Sub

      ' This method takes any kind of object that implements ITimeable
      Shared Sub UseTimeable(ByVal aTimeable As ITimeable)

            ' We must use the member names defined in ITimeable
            Console.WriteLine("Using an object that implements ITimeable")
            aTimeable.SwitchOn(9)
            aTimeable.SwitchOn(11)
            Console.WriteLine("IsOn property: {0}" & vbCrLf, _
                              aTimeable.IsOn)

      End Sub

End Class
```

To compile this application, open a .NET Framework command prompt window, move to the folder that contains the example, and type the following command:

```
> vbc MultipleInterfaces.vb
```

To run the application, type the following command:

```
> MultipleInterfaces.exe
```

The application displays the following output on the console window. This screen shot was captured at 7:43 in the morning - an early start today! Therefore, the first timer switch is 'on' (7:43 is between 6:00 and 22:00); the second timer switch is off (we didn't set an 'on' time for this timer switch, and we haven't turned it on constantly either); and the third timer switch is off (7:43 is not between 9:00 and 11:00):

```
Using a TimerSwitch object
Device is always on
Device is not always on
Device comes on at 6.00 hours
Device goes off at 22.00 hours
IsOn property: True

Using an object that implements ISwitchable
Device is always on
Device is not always on
IsOn property: False

Using an object that implements ITimeable
Device comes on at 9.00 hours
Device comes on at 11.00 hours
IsOn property: False
```

Summary

In this chapter, we've seen how to use inheritance and polymorphism to represent an 'is a kind of' relationship between classes in Visual Basic NET. Inheritance is unavoidable in the .NET Framework, because all types inherit (either directly or indirectly) from System.Object in a unified inheritance hierarchy. But that's just the beginning; we can design our own sub-hierarchy containing superclasses and subclasses to address the needs of our business model.

When we define a superclass in Visual Basic .NET, there are several design issues we need to consider to ensure the class can be inherited easily and meaningfully by subclasses:

❑ We must decide whether to declare the superclass as an abstract class (MustInherit) or a concrete class. Generally, superclasses contain only partial implementation and rely on subclasses to complete the implementation. Therefore, most superclasses tend to be abstract classes.

❑ We must determine which members can be overridden in subclasses (Overridable), which members must be overridden in subclasses (MustOverride), and which members cannot be overridden in subclasses (this is the default case if we do not specify Overridable or MustOverride).

❑ We must choose appropriate accessibility for members in the superclass. As a general rule of thumb, all fields should be declared Private; if we want to expose fields to the subclass, the preferred way is to provide Protected methods or properties to achieve this accessibility.

When we define subclasses in Visual Basic .NET, we are influenced to a very large extent by the existing definitions in the superclass. There are a number of specific issues to bear in mind in the subclass:

❑ We must decide which superclass we want to inherit from. The .NET Framework only allows single inheritance of implementation, which means we cannot inherit directly from multiple superclasses.

- ❑ The subclass inherits everything from the superclass, except for its constructors. The subclass defines its own constructors, and calls the superclass constructors to initialize the base part of the object.

- ❑ The subclass must override all of the `MustOverride` members from the superclass; otherwise, the subclass must itself be defined `MustInherit` because it is missing some of the required implementation functionality.

- ❑ The subclass can choose to override `Overridable` members from the superclass, if it needs to provide customized behavior for these members. Typically, the subclass member invokes the superclass member (using `MyBase`) to leverage the existing functionality in the superclass, and performs additional tasks as required.

- ❑ The subclass can prevent `Overridable` members from being further overridden by subsequent subclasses (using `NotInheritable`). This is appropriate if we need to ensure important business rules are not redefined (and potentially broken) in subsequent subclasses.

- ❑ The subclass can introduce its own members, to address the specific needs of this particular class.

- ❑ The subclass can shadow members defined in the superclass (using `Shadows`).

The distinction between superclasses and subclasses is convenient for the purposes of our discussions, but it's important to remember inheritance hierarchies can be several levels deep. For example, class C might inherit from class B, which inherits from class A. In this scenario, class B is a subclass of class A, but B is also a superclass for class C. When we design class B, we need to wear two different hats: we need to consider how B inherits from A, but we also need to ensure B acts as an appropriate superclass for C.

As well as inheritance of implementation, the .NET Framework supports inheritance of interface. Using the `Interface` keyword, we can define a set of related methods, properties and events that must be implemented by other classes or structures in our application. Interfaces do not contain any implementation code; they simply define a contract that must be fulfilled by the implementing classes and structures. Interfaces enable us to decouple the 'what' from the 'how'; we define interfaces to specify the requirements for types in our application, without limiting ourselves to a particular implementation strategy. Most applications in the .NET Framework define, implement, or consume interfaces in one way or another.

That concludes our investigation of inheritance and polymorphism in Visual Basic .NET. In the next chapter, we change gears and see how to organize applications logically into namespaces, and how to organize applications physically into assemblies. We also investigate the meaning and role of metadata in the .NET Framework. This will help you understand how applications and types fit together, and will enable you to make important decisions about the logical and physical organization of your code.

VB.NET

Class Design

Handbook

8

8

Code Organization and Metadata

This is the last chapter in the book, and it gives us a good opportunity to consider the larger issues that affect the logical and physical organization of our Visual Basic .NET applications.

In this chapter, we'll discuss how to use **namespaces** to partition an application into groups of related types. Namespaces emphasize the logical structure of the application, and avoid name clashes between types with the same name in different namespaces. The .NET Framework class library highlights the importance of namespaces; the class library has been designed in a modular fashion, and namespaces reinforce the organization of the class library. We'll see how to define namespaces in Visual Basic .NET, and provide design guidelines that will help you use namespaces effectively. As an overview, in this chapter we:

❑   Discuss the definition of namespaces and how to create nested namespaces, reinforced with code

❑   Investigate MSIL metadata, which contains, among other things, versioning information, the assemblies necessary to run an application, and the various types defined

❑   Discover how to deploy applications in multi-assembly format

❑   Learn how to create shared assemblies and place them in the Global Assembly Cache for easy discovery by the runtime

❑   See how to furnish an assembly with information such as our company name, a copyright notice, and a description of the assembly

Parts of this chapter make use of Visual Studio .NET, rather than just the Framework SDK. We start this chapter with a discussion of namespaces.

Structuring Applications with Namespaces

All the types in a .NET application are logically defined in namespaces. The .NET Framework class library is itself logically organized into a hierarchical namespace structure. The following table describes some of the namespaces defined in the .NET Framework class library:

Namespace	Description
System	Contains fundamental classes, structures, interfaces, delegate types, and events that are used extensively in .NET applications. For example, the System namespace contains the Object class, from which all other classes inherit. Object provides basic methods such as Equals(), ToString(), and Finalize().
System.Windows	Contains classes and other types for creating Windows-based GUIs.
System.Web	Contains classes and other types for creating ASP.NET pages and server controls.
System.Data	Contains basic ADO.NET classes and types for querying, updating, and managing databases.
System.Xml	Contains classes and types for creating and processing XML documents.

If we create a new Visual Basic .NET project, Visual Studio .NET implicitly assigns a root namespace for the project. To illustrate this, open Visual Studio .NET and create a new project (for example, a Windows application). Now, if you right-click on the project name in Solution Explorer, and select **Properties** from the Shortcut menu, then the Property Pages dialog box appears as follows:

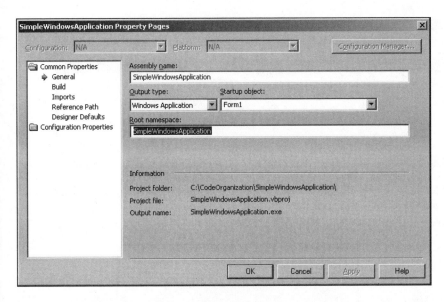

Our project has the default root namespace `SimpleWindowsApplication`. This is just the default namespace for our project, assigned by Visual Studio .NET. By default, the root namespace is the same as the project name, but we can change this namespace if we want a different one. For example, if we create several different projects and we want them all to inhabit the same namespace, we can change the root namespace in each project to what is required.

It's also possible to write `Namespace` statements explicitly into our code. For example, we can edit `Form1.vb` in our simple application as follows:

```
Namespace MyNamespace

        Public Class Form1
            Inherits System.Windows.Forms.Form

        #Region " Windows Form Designer generated code "
        ...
        #End Region

        End Class

End Namespace
```

However, when we try to build the application, we get the following compiler error:

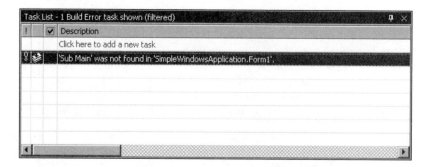

Double-click on this error message. A dialog box appears, and indicates the reason for the compiler error – the application's main form is now `SimpleWindowsApplication.MyNamespace.Form1`:

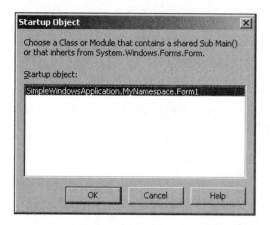

`SimpleWindowsApplication.MyNamespace` is a dotted (or nested) namespace, where the namespace name is derived from concatenating the root namespace (in this case `SampleWindowsApplication`) with the explicit namespace specification above using the `Namespace` directive (in this case `MyNamespace`).

Click **OK** to set `SimpleWindowsApplication.MyNamespace.Form1` as the startup object for the Windows application. This enables us to build and run the application without any errors. If you want to compile this application on the command line, then the code to create a simple form is shown below, and is in `form.vb`:

```
Imports System
Imports System.Windows.Forms

Namespace SimpleWindowsApplication
    Public Class Form1
        Inherits System.Windows.Forms.Form

        Private Components As System.ComponentModel.IContainer
```

```
Public Sub New()
    MyBase.New()
    InitializeComponent()
End Sub

Protected Overloads Overrides Sub Dispose( _
                            ByVal Disposing As Boolean)
    If Disposing Then
        If Not (Components Is Nothing) Then
            Components.Dispose()
        End If
    End If
    MyBase.Dispose(Disposing)
End Sub

Private Sub InitializeComponent()
    Components = New System.ComponentModel.Container()
    Me.Text = "Form1"
End Sub

Shared Public Sub Main()
    Application.Run(New Form1())
End Sub
    End Class
End Namespace
```

To compile this at the command line, you need to reference System.dll, and System.Windows.Forms.dll using the /r switch.

> *What is useful to note is that if you need to specify the location of the Main()
> method in a file (if there are a number of classes, say) with the /m switch, you
> need to specify the full namespace of the class in which it is located.*

If you look at the resulting IL in the MSIL Disassembler window, it appears as follows. The window confirms that the Form1 class is defined in the namespace SimpleWindowsApplication.MyNamespace:

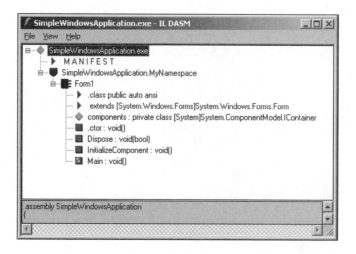

If you don't want to use a default namespace in your project, you can set the root namespace to an empty string. In Visual Studio .NET, right-click the project name in Solution Explorer, select Properties, and delete the namespace in the Root namespace field in the Properties dialog box. However, we would strongly discourage you from defining classes and other types outside a namespace, because it dramatically increases the likelihood of name clashes between your types and other types in the system.

Setting Namespaces using the Command-Line Compiler

In this section, we are using a simple console application as shown below:

```
Imports System
Imports System.DateTime

Class Person
  Private MName As String
  Private MDOB As Date

  Sub New(Name As String, DOB As Date)
    MName = Name
    MDOB = DOB
  End Sub
```

```
Private Sub New()
End Sub

Public ReadOnly Property Age As Integer
  Get
    Dim ReturnValue As Integer = 0
    ReturnValue=Now.Year-MDOB.Year
    If Now.Month < MDOB.Month Or _
      (Now.Month = MDOB.Month And Now.Day < MDOB.Day) Then _
      ReturnValue -= 1
    Return ReturnValue
  End Get
End Property

Public Property Name As String
  Get
    Return MName
  End Get

  Set(Value As String)
    MName = Value
  End Set
End Property

Public Overrides Overloads Function ToString() As String
  Return "Name: " & Me.Name & " - Age: " & Me.Age
End Function

Public Shared Sub Main()
  Dim Employee As Person = New Person("Andrew", "07/07/1975")
  Console.WriteLine(Employee.ToString())
End Sub
End Class
```

The easiest way to define a namespace for your types is by using the
/rootnamespace: compiler switch as follows:

```
> vbc /rootnamespace:MyNamespace simple_console_application.vb
```

This sets the namespace to MyNamespace for all types defined in the Visual Basic .NET
source file, simple_console_application.vb. We can open the executable file in
the MSIL Disassembler, to confirm that the Person class is now defined in the
MyNamespace namespace:

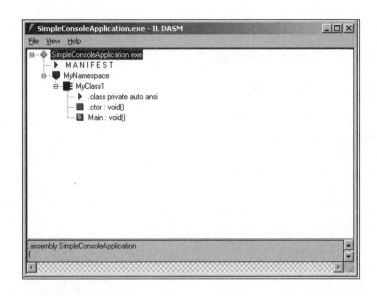

Designing and Implementing Namespaces

We can learn a lot about namespaces by looking at the .NET Framework. There are thousands of classes and other types in the .NET Framework class library, and Microsoft has organized these classes and types into a hierarchical namespace structure as follows:

❑ Namespaces that start with the word System contain classes and types that are common to all .NET languages. For example: System.Data contains ADO.NET types; System.Drawing contains graphical types; System.Security contains security-related types; and so on.

❑ Namespaces that start with the word Microsoft contain classes and types that are specific to a particular .NET language. For example, Microsoft.VisualBasic contains the Visual Basic .NET runtime, plus classes and other types that support compilation and code generation for Visual Basic .NET. Similarly, Microsoft.CSharp contains classes that support compilation and code generation for C#.

You should start thinking about namespaces during the design phase of the project, because they provide an excellent way of partitioning a large system into discrete sub-systems.

Many organizations use the Unified Modeling Language (UML) to model their object-oriented systems. For more information about UML, see *Instant UML* 1-86100-0-87-1 published by Wrox Press. UML includes graphical notation for *packages*, which contain groups of related classes and types in the system being modeled. During object-oriented design, we identify which classes are dependent on each other, and put these classes into the same package. Packages are a means to compartmentalize dependent classes into a cohesive unit of logic and functionality – this has an ancillary benefit of presenting a system that is easier to understand.

Example of Designing Namespaces

Imagine a system that allows people to borrow books from a library. The system might have classes such as Member, Book, and so on. The following diagram shows a simplified UML-like object model for this system:

Figure 1

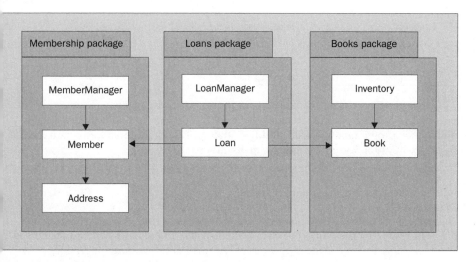

There are three packages in this model:

❑   The Membership package contains all the classes and types to implement the membership rules for the library. The MemberManager object has a collection of Member objects, and each Member has an Address.

❑   The Loans package contains all the classes and types to implement the rules for loaning and returning books. The LoanManager object has a collection of Loan objects. Each Loan object has a reference to a Member object and a Book object, to indicate which member has borrowed which book.

❑   The Books package contains all the classes and types to implement the rules for maintaining the library's inventory. Each Book object holds information about a book, such as its title and author.

Clearly, this is a simplified object model, and we've ignored many details that would be present in a real library system. Nevertheless, we can already see how packages help us to view the system as a collection of loosely coupled sub-systems.

In object-oriented design, we aim to minimize the dependencies between the classes in different packages. This makes it easier to change the implementation details within a package, without adversely affecting the other packages in the system.

Example of Implementing Namespaces

When we start writing code for our system, each package should be represented with a separate namespace. The Visual Basic .NET application for our library system will therefore comprise three namespaces:

Namespace	Classes in this namespace
Membership	MemberManager, Member, and Address
Loans	LoanManager and Loan
Books	Inventory and Book

By mapping UML packages to namespaces in our code, we achieve continuity between the design phase and the construction phase of the project. In addition, it will help maintenance programmers understand how the application is structured when they have to fix bugs, or add new features, in six months time.

Namespaces define the logical grouping of types in our system. They do not specify where we should write these namespaces in Visual Basic .NET source files. Here are two options:

❑   Write all the namespaces in a single Visual Basic .NET source file. This is only feasible if the namespaces are small and few in number. Otherwise, the size of the source file will grow unacceptably large. This will make the code difficult to understand (because there is so much of it), and could lead to some seriously unpleasant build times (every time we change any code in the source file, we'll have to rebuild all the code in that file).

❑   Write each namespace in a separate Visual Basic .NET source file. In each source file, we use Imports statements to import the namespaces accessed in that file.

We'll take the latter approach, and create a Visual Basic .NET application that comprises four files:

Filename	Description
membership.vb	Implements all the types in the Membership namespace
books.vb	Implements all the types in the Books namespace
loans.vb	Implements all the types in the Loans namespace
library_app.vb	Contains the Main() method for our application

Writing the Membership Namespace

Here is the full source code for the Membership namespace. The code is defined in membership.vb. We'll discuss the salient design issues after the code listing; the point we'd like to make at the outset is that the Membership namespace has no dependencies on any of the other namespaces in our application. All the source code is defined within the Membership namespace:

```
Imports System.Collections

Namespace Membership
  Public Class MemberManager
    Private Shared MInstance As MemberManager
    Private MLibraryMembers As Hashtable

    Private Sub New()
      MLibraryMembers = New Hashtable()
    End Sub

    Public Shared ReadOnly Property Instance() As MemberManager
      Get
        If MInstance Is Nothing
          MInstance = New MemberManager()
        End If
        Return MInstance
      End Get
    End Property

    Public Default Property LibraryMember(ByVal MemberID As Integer) _
                            As Member
      Get
        Return MLibraryMembers(MemberID)
      End Get

      Set(ByVal Value As Member)
        MLibraryMembers(MemberID) = Value
      End Set
    End Property
  End Class
End Class
```

The MemberManager class is a singleton class, which means there will only ever be a single instance of this class. To achieve this effect, we define the constructor as Private. We also provide a Shared property named Instance, which returns the single instance of MemberManager. This property uses lazy initialization; it only creates the MemberManager instance when it is first requested.

The MemberManager class uses a Hashtable to keep a collection of Member objects. There is an indexed property named LibraryMember, which inserts and retrieves Member objects in this collection. Members are identified by an integer member ID.

```
Public Class Member
  Private MName As String
  Private MAddress As Address

  Public Sub New(ByVal Name As String, _
                 ByVal Street As String, _
                 ByVal City As String)
    MName = Name
    MAddress = New Address(Street, City)
  End Sub

  Public Overrides Function ToString() As String
    Return MName & ", address: " & MAddress.ToString()
  End Function
End Class
```

The Member class holds the name and address of a member. The address is encapsulated in the Address class. We have provided ToString methods in each class, to retrieve the information in text format. The Address class is shown below:

```
Public Class Address
  Private MStreet As String
  Private MCity As String

  Public Sub New(ByVal Street As String, ByVal City As String)
    MStreet = Street
    MCity = City
  End Sub

  Public Overrides Function ToString() As String
    Return MStreet & ", " & MCity
  End Function
End Class
End Namespace
```

This source code illustrates several important issues that we have discussed in this chapter and in earlier chapters. Most importantly, it represents a generic membership framework that could be used in another member-based application.

Writing the Books Namespace

Now let's look at the source code for the Books namespace. The code is defined in books.vb:

```
Imports System.Collections

Namespace Books
  Public Class Inventory
    Shared Private MInstance As Inventory
```

```
      Private MLibraryBooks As Hashtable

      Private Sub New()
        MLibraryBooks = New Hashtable()
      End Sub

      Public Shared ReadOnly Property Instance() As Inventory
        Get
          If MInstance Is Nothing
            MInstance = New Inventory()
          End If
          Return MInstance
        End Get
      End Property

      Public Default Property LibraryBook(ByVal BookID As Integer) _
                                 As Book
        Get
          Return MLibraryBooks(BookID)
        End Get

        Set (ByVal Value As Book)
          MLibraryBooks(BookID) = Value
        End Set
      End Property
    End Class

    Public Class Book
      Private MTitle As String
      Private MAuthor As String

      Public Sub New(ByVal Title As String, ByVal Author As String)
        MTitle = Title
        MAuthor = Author
      End Sub

      Public Overrides Function ToString() As String
        Return MTitle & ", written by: " & MAuthor
      End Function
    End Class
End Namespace
```

There are many noticeable similarities between the Inventory class and the MemberManager class. Both classes are singleton classes, and both use a Hashtable to hold a collection of other objects (Inventory holds a list of Book objects, and MemberManager holds a collection of Member objects).

Another similarity is the way Inventory and MemberManager provide access to the objects in their collections. Both classes provide a property to insert and retrieve the items (Inventory has a property named LibraryBook, and MemberManager has a property named LibraryMember).

Notice again that the Books namespace has no dependency whatsoever on any of the other namespaces in our application. This illustrates the design goal of loose coupling between namespaces.

Writing the Loans Namespace

The Loans namespace contains the LoanManager and Loan classes. Every time a member borrows a book, the LoanManager creates a new Loan object to identify the book and the borrower. The LoanManager also allows books to be returned, which is an important business rule for the library.

The code for the Loans namespace is defined in loans.vb. We'll discuss the design issues after the code listing:

```vb
Imports System.Collections
Imports Microsoft.VisualBasic    ' For vbCrLf constant

Imports Membership
Imports Books

Namespace Loans
  Public Class LoanManager
    Shared Private MInstance As LoanManager

    Private MLoans As Hashtable

    Private Sub New()
      MLoans = New Hashtable()
    End Sub

    Public Shared ReadOnly Property Instance() As LoanManager
      Get
        If MInstance Is Nothing
          MInstance = New LoanManager()
        End If
        Return MInstance
      End Get
    End Property

    Public Sub BorrowBook(ByVal BookID As Integer, _
                          ByVal MemberID As Integer)
      Dim Inv As Inventory = Inventory.Instance
      Dim Mem As MemberManager = MemberManager.Instance

      Dim TheBook As Book = Inv(BookID)
      Dim TheMember As Member = Mem(MemberID)

      If (Not TheBook Is Nothing) And (Not TheMember is Nothing)
        Dim TheLoan As New Loan(TheBook, TheMember)
        MLoans(BookID) = TheLoan
        Console.WriteLine("{0}", TheLoan)
      Else
```

```
            Console.WriteLine("Cannot borrow book")
         End If
      End Sub

      Public Sub ReturnBook(ByVal BookID As Integer)
         If MLoans.ContainsKey(BookID)
            MLoans.Remove(BookID)
            Console.WriteLine("Book {0} has been returned", BookID)
         Else
            Console.WriteLine("Cannot return book")
         End If
      End Sub
   End Class

   Public Class Loan
      Private MTheBook As Book
      Private MTheMember As Member

      Public Sub New(ByVal TheBook As Book, ByVal TheMember As Member)
         MTheBook = TheBook
         MTheMember = TheMember
      End Sub

      Public Overrides Function ToString() As String
         Return "Book: " & MTheBook.ToString() & vbCrLf & _
                "Borrowed by: " & MTheMember.ToString() & vbCrLf
      End Function
   End Class
End Namespace
```

Note the following points in this source file:

❑   We import the Membership and Books namespaces. This enables us to
    access the classes defined in these namespaces, without needing to use
    fully qualified class names such as Membership.Manager.

    This is the one occasion where dependencies with other namespaces cannot
    be avoided. Some degree of coupling is inevitable; the important thing is to
    identify where this coupling occurs, and to minimize it as much as possible.

❑   LoanManager is a singleton class, because there is only one LoanManager
    in our library system.

❑   The BorrowBook() method enables books to be borrowed by members.
    The book and member are identified by integer IDs. We use the book ID
    as a lookup key in Inventory, to get a reference to the Book object with
    this ID. Likewise, we use the member ID as a lookup key in
    MemberManager, to get a reference to the Member object with this ID.

    If the Book and Member objects can be located, we create a new Loan
    object to remember which book was borrowed by which member. We
    store the Loan object in a Hashtable, using the book ID as the lookup
    key. This is a good choice for a lookup key, because each book can only
    be on loan to one member at a time; therefore, we can use the book ID to
    identify uniquely a specific Loan object.

❑ The `ReturnBook()` method enables books to be returned to the library. The only information we need when a book is returned is the book ID (it doesn't matter who returns the book – not in our model, anyway).

If the book ID can be located in the loans `Hashtable`, it means the book is indeed on loan. In this case, we remove the `Loan` from the `Hashtable` to indicate that the book is no longer on loan.

❑ The `Loan` class has a reference to a `Book` object, and a reference to a `Member` object. In UML terms, `Loan` is an *association object*; it defines an association between a `Book` and a `Member`.

Writing the Main() Method for the Application

Now that we've seen how to implement the core namespaces in our application, all that remains is to write a `Main()` method to use these namespaces. The code for the `Main()` method is shown below, and is located in the file `library_app.vb`:

```vb
Imports System.Collections

Imports Membership
Imports Books
Imports Loans

Module LibraryApp
  Sub Main()
    Dim Inv As Inventory = Inventory.Instance
    Inv(7167) = New Book("Professional VB.NET", _
                         "Rocky Lhotka et al.")
    Inv(5318) = New Book("Professional XML for .NET Developers", _
                         "Dinar Dalvi et al.")

    Dim Mem As MemberManager = MemberManager.Instance
    Mem(100) = New Member("Emily", "5th Avenue", "New York")
    Mem(101) = New Member("Thomas", "Park Lane", "London")

    Dim LoanMgr As LoanManager = LoanManager.Instance
    LoanMgr.BorrowBook(7167, 100)
    LoanMgr.BorrowBook(5318, 101)

    LoanMgr.ReturnBook(7167)
    LoanMgr.ReturnBook(5318)
  End Sub
End Module
```

Note the following, regarding this code:

❑ We import the `Membership`, `Books`, and `Loans` namespaces. We use classes from all these namespaces in this application.

❑ In `Main()`, we get a reference to the `Inventory` object, and add two books to the inventory. We also get a reference to the `MemberManager` object, and add two members.

❑ We get a reference to the `LoanManager` object, and call `BorrowBook` twice to borrow two books from the library. Then we call `ReturnBook` twice, to return these books to the library. In all these cases, we identify the books and members by their integer IDs.

Building and Running the Application

One way to build this application is to open a .NET Framework Command Prompt window and type the following command:

```
> vbc library_app.vb membership.vb books.vb loans.vb
```

This command compiles the four Visual Basic .NET source files in this application, and creates a single assembly named `library_app.exe`. The assembly is named after the first source file in the list of files to be compiled; to create a different name for the assembly, use the `/out:filename` compiler switch. Another option would be to compile each of the namespaces into a separate DLL. Then we could just use the `/r` switch as necessary to link to these DLLs. Visual Studio .NET can also provide a number of different options for compilation, and you can choose whichever method is most appropriate.

When we run the application, it displays the following output on the console window:

```
Book: Professional VB.NET, written by Rocky Lhotka et al.
Borrowed by: Emily, address: 5th Avenue, New York

Book: Professional XML for .NET Developers, written by: Dinar Dalvi et al.
Borrowed by: Thomas, address: Park Lane, London

Book 7167 has been returned
Book 5318 has been returned
```

Nested Namespaces

Nested namespaces allow us to define a layered architecture, which offers different levels of abstraction in our application. This helps us grasp the overall shape of the system, while at the same time offering enough detail to model extremely large or complex systems in an organized and comprehensible manner.

The .NET Framework class library is a good example of a layered namespace design:

❑ The top-level namespaces `System` and `Microsoft` differentiate system-wide classes (in the `System` namespace) from language-specific classes (in the `Microsoft` namespace).

❑ Nested namespaces, such as `System.Data` and `System.Drawing`, partition the system-wide classes into logical groups. Each namespace exhibits the desirable characteristics of high cohesion (everything that belongs together, *is* together), and low coupling (there are very few dependencies between classes in different namespaces).

❑   A further level of nesting provides still more granularity. For example, the
     following table describes the nested namespaces beneath `System.Data`.

Namespace	Description
System.Data.SqlClient	Contains ADO.NET classes and types for accessing SQL Server 7.0 (and later) databases.
System.Data.OleDb	Contains ADO.NET classes and types for accessing SQL Server 6.5 (and earlier) databases, and other databases such as Oracle and Microsoft Access.
System.Data.Common	Contains common ADO.NET classes and types that are used to access any kind of database. For example, this namespace includes the `DataSet` class, which represents an in-memory cache of data in a disconnected application.
System.Data.SqlTypes	Contains classes to represent common data types in SQL Server.

Defining Nested Namespaces

There are two different ways to define nested namespaces in our code. The following
example illustrates both techniques. The source code for this example is located in the
download folder; the following file is named `nested_namespaces.vb`:

```
Namespace MyNamespace1
    Public Class MyClassA
        ' Members ...
    End Class

    Namespace MyNestedNamespace1
        Public Class MyClassB
            ' Members ...
        End Class
    End Namespace
End Namespace

Namespace MyNamespace2.MyNestedNamespace2
    Public Class MyClassC
        ' Members ...
    End Class
End Namespace
```

Note the following points:

❑   `MyNamespace1` is an outer namespace, and contains a class called
     `MyClassA`. The fully qualified name of this class is
     `MyNamespace1.MyClassA`.

❑   MyNestedNamespace1 is defined inside MyNamespace1. This creates a nested namespace called MyNamespace1.MyNestedNamespace1. This namespace contains a class called MyClassB; the fully qualified name of this class is MyNamespace1.MyNestedNamespace1.MyClassB.

❑   MyNamespace2.MyNestedNamespace2 is a nested namespace. This again illustrates how to use the 'dot' syntax in a Namespace statement, to create a nested namespace. This namespace contains a class called MyClassC; the fully qualified name of this class is MyNamespace2.MyNestedNamespace2.MyClassC.

Using Nested Namespaces

If we want to use the classes defined in nested namespaces, we can use fully qualified class names as follows. The source code below is located in the file named use_fully_qualified.vb.

```
Public Class UseFullyQualified
   Public Shared Sub Main()
      Dim A As New MyNamespace1.MyClassA()
      Dim B As New MyNamespace1.MyNestedNamespace1.MyClassB()
      Dim C As New MyNamespace2.MyNestedNamespace2.MyClassC()
   End Sub
End Class
```

Compile these files into an assembly and open this assembly in the MSIL Disassembler to see what the compiler has made of our namespaces and classes. The MSIL Disassembler window displays the following information:

The MSIL Disassembler shows there are three namespaces in our assembly.

Using fully qualified class names can be tiresome if we use the same classes several times in our code. To save some keystrokes, as you already know, we can import the required namespaces as follows. The source code below is located in the file named use_imports.vb:

```
Imports MyNamespace1
Imports MyNamespace1.MyNestedNamespace1
Imports MyNamespace2.MyNestedNamespace2

Public Class UseImports
   Public Shared Sub Main()
      Dim A As New MyClassA()
      Dim B As New MyClassB()
      Dim C As New MyClassC()
   End Sub
End Class
```

Compile this code with nested_namespaces.vb, and if you open this assembly in the MSIL Disassembler, you will we see the same classes and namespaces as in the previous example.

Understanding Metadata

Whenever we compile Visual Basic .NET code (or any other .NET language), the compiler generates metadata to describe the data types and members in our code. The metadata also lists the types and members that we reference in our code, but that are defined in other assemblies.

Metadata gives the common language runtime all the information it needs to load classes and invoke methods at run time. Metadata replaces older technologies such as Interface Definition Language (IDL) and type libraries, which have kept COM developers occupied for a decade. The CLR also uses metadata to help it enforce security. The security system uses permissions to deny code from accessing resources that it does not have authority to access.

In this section, we'll see how to view all the available metadata for a single-file assembly. Then we'll see how to create an assembly that contains several separate files, and discuss why this might be a useful thing to do.

Viewing Metadata in a Single-File Assembly

The easiest way to view metadata is by using the MSIL Disassembler tool, ildasm.exe. We've used this tool a lot already, and we'll use it much more throughout this chapter.

et's look at the metadata for a simple assembly, for a simple console application. The
ource code for this example is located in `simple_console.vb`:

```
Imports System

Module SimpleConsole
    Sub Main()
        Console.WriteLine("Wrox Rocks!")
    End Sub
End Module
```

uild this application, giving it a namespace of `MetadataSimpleApp`, and open the
SIL Disassembler tool. The following is shown:

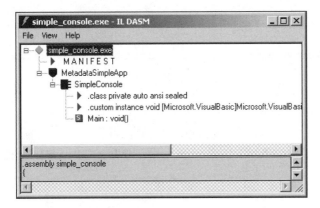

he MSIL Disassembler tells us the following:

- ❑ The **MANIFEST** entry provides manifest information. As we'll see later in
  this chapter, the manifest lists the files and types in our assembly, plus the
  types used from other assemblies.

- ❑ Our assembly has a namespace called `MetadataSimpleApp`.

- ❑ The `MetadataSimpleApp` namespace has a module called
  `SimpleConsole`.

- ❑ `SimpleConsole` has a compiler-generated constructor, plus a `Main()`
  method that we wrote ourselves.

his is just a small part of the information available in the MSIL Disassembler tool.
ecause we used the `/adv` switch when we ran the MSIL Disassembler, we have
ccess to advanced information including full metadata for our assembly. To view this
metadata, click on **View**, select **MetaInfo**, and then select **Show!**. A window appears,
howing comprehensive metadata for our assembly:

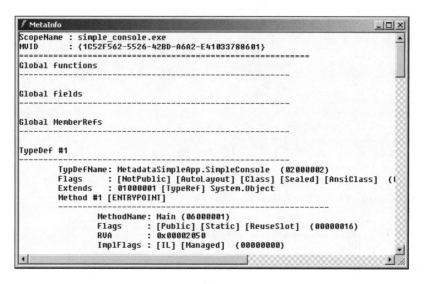

Let's look at the important parts of this metadata:

❑ Metadata about this .NET module.

❑ Metadata about this assembly. At this moment, the assembly only contains one .NET module. We'll explain the distinction between modules and assemblies shortly.

❑ Metadata about the types defined in this assembly.

❑ Metadata about referenced types that reside in other assemblies.

❑ Metadata about other referenced assemblies.

Metadata about this .NET Module

The first two lines in the metadata listing give us information about this *.NET module*. A .NET module is a **Portable Executable** (**PE**) format file, such as a .exe or .dll file. All the Visual Basic .NET examples we've seen so far have been single-module assemblies, which means the assembly only comprises a single file. Later in this chapter we'll see how to create an assembly that comprises multiple .NET modules; we'll also discuss why this might be a useful thing to do, which is perhaps more to the point.

Getting back to our discussion on .NET module metadata, the following module metadata is available:

```
ScopeName : simple_console.exe
MVID      : {4B468EBD-4935-4FB9-A443-38E0658CD1EF}
```

Note the following points in the .NET module metadata:

❏   ScopeName is the name of the .NET module, excluding the path.

❏   MVID is the module version ID, which is a Globally Unique ID (GUID) for the .NET module generated by the compiler. The compiler generates a different MVID every time we build the module.

etadata about this Assembly

ear the end of the metadata listing, we find the following metadata about this
sembly (we've abbreviated this information slightly, by removing metadata about
istom attributes):

```
Assembly
---------------------------------------------------------
          Token: 0x20000001
          Name : simple_console
          Public Key    :
          Hash Algorithm : 0x00008004
          Major Version: 0x00000000
          Minor Version: 0x00000000
          Build Number: 0x00000000
          Revision Number: 0x00000000
          Locale: <null>
          Flags : [SideBySideCompatible]    (00000000)
```

ere is a selective description of some of the assembly metadata:

❏   Token is a 4-byte metadata token. Each item of metadata is uniquely identified by a different token. The top byte of the token indicates what kind of metadata this is: for example, 0x20 denotes an assembly definition, 0x23 denotes an assembly reference, 0x02 denotes a type definition, and so on. For a full list of token types, open the C++ header file CorHdr.h (located in the FrameworkSDK\include sub-folder) and find the CorTokenType enumerated type.

❏   Name is the name of the assembly, excluding the path and extension.

❏   PublicKey indicates the public key that was used to sign the assembly. It's blank here because we haven't signed the assembly. We'll see how to sign an assembly later in the chapter, when we discuss how to install shared assemblies into the *Global Assembly Cache* (*GAC*) on the computer.

❏   Major Version, Minor Version, Build Number, and Revision Number identify the precise version of this assembly. This four-part version number differentiates this assembly from other versions of the assembly, and enables other .NET applications to specify precisely which version of the assembly they want to use.

Each piece of the four-part version number has a particular meaning to the CLR, so that it can decide which version of an assembly to load. Imagine an assembly A references a particular version number of another assembly B. The runtime uses the following rules to load an appropriate version of assembly B:

- If there is a version of B with exactly the same version number as requested by A, the runtime will load this version of B.

- If there is a version of B with a different Build Number, this indicates a compatible change to the assembly (such as a security fix). The runtime will load this version of B, in the absence of an exact match.

- If there is a version of B with a different Revision Number, this indicates an incremental change to the assembly (such as a Service Pack). The runtime considers this assembly is probably compatible with the version requested by A, so the runtime will load this version of B in the absence of a better match.

- If there is a version of B with a different Major Version or Minor Version, this indicates a major difference to previous versions of the assembly (such as major new product release). The runtime will not load this version of B.

Metadata about the Types Defined in this Assembly

We can define types (such as modules, classes, and structures) in an assembly. The assembly contains metadata for each of these types. Our simple Visual Basic .NET application defines a single type, which is a Module called SimpleConsole. Therefore, the assembly's metadata contains a single type definition as follows:

```
TypeDef #1
-------------------------------------------------------------
        TypDefName: MetadataSimpleApp.SimpleConsole  (02000002)
        Flags     : [NotPublic] [AutoLayout] [Class] [Sealed]
[AnsiClass]  (00000100)
        Extends   : 01000001 [TypeRef] System.Object
        Method #1 [ENTRYPOINT]
        -----------------------------------------------------
                MethodName: Main (06000001)
                Flags    : [Public] [Static] [ReuseSlot]  (00000016)
                RVA      : 0x00002050
                ImplFlags : [IL] [Managed]  (00000000)
                CallCnvntn: [DEFAULT]
                ReturnType: Void
                No arguments.
```

Note the following points in this metadata:

- ❑ TypeDefName is the name of the type. The name of this type is MetadataSimpleApp.SimpleConsole. The value in parentheses is the metadata token for this piece of metadata (remember, the value 0x02 in the top byte indicates this is a *type definition*).

❏ `Flags` provides more information about `MetadataSimpleApp.MyModule`. Here's a brief synopsis: `[NotPublic]` indicates `MyModule` is not a public type; `[AutoLayout]` indicates the layout of its members is handled automatically by the CLR; `[Class] [Sealed]` indicates this is a non-inheritable class; and `[AnsiClass]` indicates `LPTSTR` string types will be treated as ANSI strings (rather than Unicode strings).

❏ `Extends` indicates that our type inherits from `System.Object`.

❏ `Method #1` provides metadata about the first (and only) method in our type. This metadata indicates the name of the method (`Main`), its arguments (none), its return type (`Void`), and other information such as the fact it's a `Public` and `Static` method.

Metadata about Other Referenced Assemblies

Our assembly contains metadata about all the other assemblies referenced by our assembly. This information is clearly needed by the CLR, so that it can load these assemblies when needed. Our assembly references several assemblies, for example:

```
AssemblyRef #1
-------------------------------------------------------------
        Token: 0x23000001
        Public Key or Token: b7 7a 5c 56 19 34 e0 89
        Name: mscorlib
        Major Version: 0x00000001
        Minor Version: 0x00000000
        Build Number: 0x00000ce4
        Revision Number: 0x00000000
        Locale: <null>
        HashValue Blob:
        Flags: [none] (00000000)
```

Note the following points in the metadata for the referenced assembly:

❏ `Public Key or Token` indicates the public key that was used to sign the referenced assembly.

❏ `Name` indicates that the name of the referenced assembly is `mscorlib`.

❏ `Major Version`, `Minor Version`, `Build Number`, and `Revision Number` identify precisely which version of the assembly we want to reference. This ensures we always reference the correct version of the assembly, even if later versions of the assembly are subsequently installed on the computer.

❏ `Locale` facilitates localization of assemblies. It's possible to have several assemblies that contain copies of the same data in different languages (such as English and French). We can assign a different locale to each assembly. The `Locale` metadata in our assembly indicates which locale-specific assembly we want to reference.

Creating Multi-File Assemblies

All the examples we have presented in this book so far have used single-file assemblies. A single-file assembly comprises a single PE file (or *.NET module*). The PE file is typically a .dll or .exe file, with a manifest that describes the types in the assembly.

It is also possible to create an assembly that comprises multiple .NET modules (hence the name, 'assembly'). When we compile each .NET module, we get a separate PE file that contains MSIL code and metadata for the .NET module. One of the .NET modules in the assembly must be identified as the 'main' module. This .NET module will have a manifest that identifies all the other .NET modules in the assembly.

There are several reasons for implementing an assembly as a collection of separate .NET modules:

❑   We can write each module in a different .NET programming language. This might be useful for companies that use a variety of languages and/or people to implement different parts of the system.

❑   We can organize our types into separate modules, to optimize how our code is loaded into the common language runtime. We can place related types into the same module, so that they are loaded together when the module is loaded into the runtime. Seldom-used types can be placed in a separate module; the runtime will only load this module when these types are required in the application. This way, we can minimize the footprint of our application and reduce load time too.

❑   We can include data-only modules that contain resources such as images, XML documents, music clips, and so on. The .NET Framework SDK includes a tool called the *Assembly Linker* (AL.exe) to link these non-MSIL modules into our assembly.

Example of a Multi-File Assembly

In this section, we'll see how to create an assembly containing three separate modules. The modules will be written in different .NET programming languages, and will then be linked together to create a single logical assembly. This is a typical reason for creating an assembly out of separate modules (rather than creating an assembly from just one module).

Here's a description of the three modules in this example:

❑   The first module will be called VBMod, and will be written in Visual Basic .NET. This module will have a class named TempConverter, to convert temperatures between Celsius and Fahrenheit.

❑   The second module will be called CSMod, and will be written in Visual C#. This module will have a class named DistanceConverter, to convert distances between miles and kilometers.

❑ The third module will be called `MainMod`, and will be written in Visual Basic .NET. We're going to make this the main module in the assembly, which means the file will contain a manifest that identifies all the other modules in the assembly.

This is how the modules will work together to form a multi-file assembly:

Figure 2

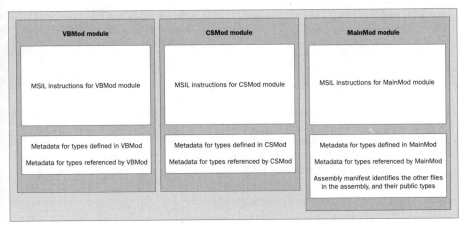

Each module in the assembly contains MSIL instructions and metadata; the metadata describes the types defined and referenced by the module. The main module in the assembly is `MainMod`; this module will contain the manifest for the assembly. The manifest identifies all the other modules in the assembly (`VBMod` and `CSMod`), and the public types defined in these modules. We'll see what this metadata looks like as we work through the example.

This manifest information is required by the CLR, so that it can load the appropriate module when one of these types is used in the application.

Let's see how to implement what we've just described. There are three steps:

❑ Write the source code for `VBMod.vb`, and compile it into a .NET module.

❑ Write the source code for `CSMod.cs`, and compile it into another .NET module.

❑ Write the source code for `MainMod.vb`, and compile it into the main .NET module in the assembly. At this stage, we'll need to specify which other modules we want in the assembly (that is, `VBMod` and `CSMod`).

Creating the VBMod Module

Here is the Visual Basic .NET source code for VBMod.vb. The source code for this module (and all the other modules we're going to see in this example) is located in the download folder ch08\MultiFileAssembly.

```
Public Class TempConverter
    Public Shared Function CelsiusToFahr(ByVal C As Double) As Double
        Return (C * 9.0 / 5.0) + 32
    End Function

    Public Shared Function FahrToCelsius(ByVal F As Double) As Double
        Return (F - 32) * 5.0 / 9.0
    End Function
End Class
```

To compile this file into a module (as opposed to a standalone assembly), we must use the Visual Basic .NET command-line compiler. We can't use Visual Studio .NET to create a .NET module; Visual Studio .NET always creates a standalone assembly for our project (the exception to this rule is for Managed Extensions for C++ projects, where we can set the /NOASSEMBLY option to create a module rather than an assembly).

Open a .NET Framework command prompt window and compile the code as follows:

```
> vbc /target:module VBMod.vb
```

The /target:module compiler switch tells the compiler to generate a module rather than an assembly. The module contains the compiled MSIL instructions for our code, and contains metadata to describe the types defined and referenced in our code. Later, we'll link this module to other modules to create a multi-file assembly.

The /target compiler switch can be abbreviated to /t.

Creating the CSMod Module

Here is the Visual C# source code for CSMod.cs:

```
public class DistanceConverter
{
    public static double MileToKm(double miles)
    {
        return (miles * 1.6093);
    }

    public static double KmToMile(double km)
    {
        return (km / 1.6093);
    }
}
```

'o compile this file into a separate module, run the Visual C# compiler as follows:

```
> csc /target:module CSMod.cs
```

his generates a .NET module named CSMod.netmodule. Note that at this stage, there s no linkage whatsoever between this module and the one we created earlier VBMod.netmodule).

reating the Main Module in the Assembly

Here is the source code for MainMod.vb. Notice that this source code uses the types lefined in the other two modules:

```
Imports System

Public Module MyModule
  Sub Main()
    Console.WriteLine("Select an option: ")
    Console.WriteLine("  1   C to F")
    Console.WriteLine("  2   F to C")
    Console.WriteLine("  3   Miles to Km")
    Console.WriteLine("  4   Km to Miles")
    Console.Write("=>")

    Dim Input As String = Console.ReadLine()
    Dim Opt As Integer = Integer.Parse(Input)

    Console.Write("Value to convert: ")
    Input = Console.ReadLine()
    Dim Value As Double = Double.Parse(Input)

    Dim Res As Double
    If Opt = 1 Then
       Res = TempConverter.CelsiusToFahr(Value)
    ElseIf opt = 2 Then
       Res = TempConverter.FahrToCelsius(Value)
    ElseIf opt = 3 Then
       Res = DistanceConverter.MileToKm(Value)
    ElseIf opt = 4 Then
       Res = DistanceConverter.KmToMile(Value)
    Else
       Console.WriteLine("Invalid option")
       Exit Sub
    End If
    Console.WriteLine("{0}", Math.Round(Res, 2))
  End Sub
End Module
```

This is how we compile this source file:

```
> vbc /addmodule:VBMod.netmodule /addmodule:CSMod.netmodule MainMod.vb
```

This command compiles `MainMod.vb` into `MainMod.exe`. `MainMod.exe` is the main module in the assembly. The `/addmodule` compiler switch adds entries to the assembly's manifest, to indicate `VBMod.netmodule` and `CSMod.netmodule` are part of this assembly.

> *If we forget the `/addmodule` switch, we'll get a compiler error every time we try to access a type defined in one of the other (unspecified) modules. This is because the compiler doesn't know it's meant to look in these other modules to resolve the type definitions.*

Open `MainMod.exe` in the MSIL Disassembler, and view the manifest information in the assembly. Here are the important parts of the manifest information:

```
.module extern VBMod.netmodule
.module extern CSMod.netmodule
...
.assembly MainMod
{
  .hash algorithm 0x00008004
  .ver 0:0:0:0
}

.file VBMod.netmodule
     .hash = (21 FD 53 47 5C C1 3D 53 54 A5 ·18 F5 48
              30 C3 E7 02 73 EF 01 )

.file CSMod.netmodule
     .hash = (F8 FF 71 75 6A CF 6D AD DE D8 12 2E 14
              5C 8F EC 9B A4 E3 9F )

.class extern public TempConverter
{
  .file VBMod.netmodule
  .class 0x02000002
}

.class extern public DistanceConverter
{
  .file CSMod.netmodule
  .class 0x02000002
}

.module MainMod.exe
// MVID: {35B746CD-5057-4332-8B7B-4C9887FD5E4E}
.imagebase 0x00400000
.subsystem 0x00000003
.file alignment 512
.corflags 0x00000001
// Image base: 0x030f0000
```

Notice the following points in this manifest:

☐ The manifest references the other modules in the assembly (VBMod.netmodule and CSMod.netmodule).

☐ The manifest also lists the public types defined in these modules. This information tells the common language runtime which module to load when a user of the assembly uses one of our classes.

> *When we create a multi-file assembly, we must remember to deploy all the modules in the assembly. In the example we've just considered, we must deploy* VBMod.netmodule *and* CSMod.netmodule *along with the main module in the assembly,* MainMod.exe.

Deploying Applications as Assemblies

In the previous section, we discussed how to create an assembly that comprises one or more modules. If we create a multi-file assembly, the main module in the assembly contains manifest information that identifies all the other modules in the assembly.

In this section, we're going to broaden our outlook and consider the physical organization of an entire application. Our discussions will lead us to consider three possible deployment scenarios for our application:

☐ For simple applications, we can deploy our application as a simple assembly.

☐ For larger applications, we can split some of the functionality into separate assemblies. We can group related functionality into the same assembly, so that the CLR can load all the information it needs from a single assembly. We can relegate seldom-used functionality to a separate assembly, so that it is only loaded when required. We can put resources (such as bitmaps) into another assembly, to make internationalization easier to achieve.

To emphasize the logical organization of our application, we can organize our assemblies along namespace boundaries and implement each namespace as a separate assembly.

Typically, we deploy all the assemblies into the same folder on the target computer. It's also possible to provide a configuration file that specifies a different subfolder destination for our private assemblies.

❑   If we want to deploy several applications that share a lot of common code, we can create common assemblies that are shared by all the applications. We can install the common assemblies into the Global Assembly Cache (**GAC**) on the target computer, so that the assemblies are accessible by multiple applications. We'll discuss the GAC later in this section.

Deploying Single-Assembly Applications

This is the simplest of our three scenarios, where we want to deploy an application that comprises a single assembly. To deploy such an application, all we need to do is copy the assembly onto the target computer. This is commonly known as ***xcopy deployment***. There is no need to register anything in the system registry, which means there is no danger of breaking how existing applications work on the computer. This eliminates 'DLL hell', which can happen when traditional Windows applications are installed on a computer. Such applications nearly always update the registry in some way, which may prevent existing applications from functioning correctly.

Uninstalling .NET simple Framework applications is also straightforward. All we need to do is delete the files that were copied during installation, such as the `.exe` and `.dll` files for the assembly, plus any configuration files we installed (we'll discuss configuration files later in this chapter). Compare this situation with the way we uninstall traditional Windows applications; we need to ensure all the registry entries are cleaned up, without breaking how all the other applications work. Uninstalling traditional Windows applications always gives us that nasty suspicion that part of the application lingers on in the dark recesses of the hard disk.

> *There are still some situations where we might want to package our .NET applications ready for distribution. For example, if we want our application to be downloaded over the Internet, we will typically place our application into a* `.CAB` *file so that it can be downloaded more easily. Alternatively, we can package our application into an* `.MSI` *file so that it can be installed by the Microsoft Windows Installer. This will enable users to install the application using Microsoft Systems Management Server (SMS), for example.*

Deploying Applications using Private Assemblies

In this scenario, we describe how to deploy an application that contains several assemblies. For now, we'll assume these assemblies are only needed by this application, so that all the assemblies can be installed in the same folder (or sub-folder) as the main application assembly. Because these assemblies are just used by our application, they are called ***private assemblies***.

*Later, we'll describe how to create **shared assemblies**, which can be deployed in the central Global Assembly Cache so that they can be used by all applications.*

Deploying Private Assemblies in the Same Folder

Imagine we have a large application that provides several distinct services. It makes sense to organize this application into separate assemblies, so that the common language runtime can load just the assemblies that are actually required when the user runs the application. Typically, one of the assemblies will be an .exe file, and the others will be .dll files.

Example of Deploying Assemblies in the Same Folder

Let's consider a simple example, where we have a single .exe assembly file and a single .dll assembly file. The DLL file contains useful functions that are used by the .exe file. We'll perform the following tasks:

❑   Write the source code for the DLL.

❑   Compile this source code into a .dll assembly file.

❑   Write the source code for the executable. Use the functionality offered by the DLL, as required.

❑   Compile this source code into a .exe assembly file. Tell the compiler which other assemblies we reference, so that it can resolve references to these assemblies.

❑   Deploy the .exe file and .dll file. The easiest deployment scenario is to install the .exe file and .dll file in the same folder.

Here's the source code for our DLL file. The source file is named my_useful_library.vb:

```
Imports System

Public Class MyUsefulClass
  Public Shared Sub MyUsefulMethod()
    Console.WriteLine("Hello world")
  End Sub
End Class
```

To compile this source file into a .DLL assembly file, run the Visual Basic .NET compiler as follows from the command prompt:

```
> vbc /target:library MyUsefulLibrary.vb
```

The /target:library compiler switch instructs the compiler to create a library (.dll) file.

337

Now let's look at the source code for our executable file. The source code file is named `hello_world.vb`.

```
Module HelloWorld
   Sub Main()
      MyUsefulClass.MyUsefulMethod()
   End Sub
End Module
```

To compile this source file into an `.exe` assembly file, run the Visual Basic .NET compiler as follows at the .NET Framework Command Prompt window:

```
> vbc /reference:my_useful_library.dll hello_world.vb
```

The manifest in the executable file will contain a reference to the `my_useful_library.dll` assembly file, because of the `/reference` compiler switch.

The `/reference` compiler switch can be abbreviated to `/r`.

When we deploy our application onto the target computer, the easiest way is to install `hello_world.exe` and `my_useful_library.dll` into the same folder. We say that `my_useful_library.dll` is a ***private assembly*** for our application.

When the user runs `hello_world.exe`, the CLR searches for an assembly called and located as follows:

❑   `my_useful_library.dll`

❑   `my_useful_library\my_useful_library.dll`

If the CLR can't find an assembly with a `.dll` file extension, it repeats the search looking for an assembly with a `.exe` file extension:

❑   `my_useful_library.exe`

❑   `my_useful_library\my_useful_library.exe`

If the assembly still can't be located, the CLR throws a `System.IO.FileNotFoundException`.

Creating and Referencing Culture-Specific Assemblies

The .NET Framework allows us to create several different versions of an assembly, to cater for different locales. For example, we can create an English version of the assembly, a Spanish version, a French version, and so on. Microsoft uses the term ***culture*** to denote the locale of the assembly. Later in this chapter, we'll see how to use attributes to set the culture when we create an assembly.

Applications can specify to which culture of our assembly they want to bind. When the CLR probes for the specified assembly, it looks in a subdirectory with the same name as the culture. For example, if we request the `my_useful_library` assembly and specify the en culture (English), the runtime will probe the following locations for the assembly:

❑   en\my_useful_library.dll

❑   en\my_useful_library\my_useful_library.dll

❑   en\my_useful_library.exe

❑   en\my_useful_library\my_useful_library.exe

Deploying Private Assemblies in a Different Sub-Folder

As you are no doubt already aware, applications can grow to be extremely large. Placing all the assemblies in the same folder might not be the best option; for example, if we have dozens of different assemblies in our application, we might prefer to organize these assemblies into a directory structure that reflects the hierarchical namespace structure in our application.

If we want to deploy a private assembly in a differently named sub-folder, we can create an *application configuration file* to tell the CLR where to look. The configuration file is located in the same folder as the requesting assembly, and has a .config filename suffix. For example, the configuration file for MyModule.exe would be named MyModule.exe.config.

The application configuration file is an XML file that tells the CLR where it can find our private assemblies. We write the configuration file as part of our development activities, and deploy the configuration file along with our application.

> *The .NET Framework makes extensive use of XML as the standard way of expressing configuration information, and for a host of other purposes. For example, XML is used to represent data while an application is disconnected from a database (see the System.Data.DataSet class); to represent tags in ASP.NET; to pass information to and from a Web Service (see System.WebServices.WebService), and so on.*

Let's see an example of how to create and use an application configuration file. Imagine we have an application that has two assemblies, located in the following folders:

Figure 3

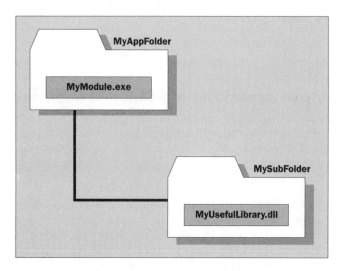

Here is an example of a configuration file named `MyModule.exe.config`. This is the configuration file for our application `MyModule.exe`:

```
<configuration>
  <runtime>
    <assemblyBinding
        xmlns="urn:schemas-microsoft-com:asm.v1">
      <probing privatePath="MySubFolder"/>
    </assemblyBinding>
  </runtime>
</configuration>
```

Note the following points about this configuration file:

❑ The top-level element must be named `configuration`. The `configuration` element can have a variety of child elements, to configure different aspects of run-time execution.

❑ The `runtime` child element specifies how the common language runtime handles assembly loading and garbage collection.

❑ The `assemblyBinding` child element contains information about assembly locations and versions. This element must be qualified with the XML namespace `"urn:schemas-microsoft-com:asm.v1"` for the CLR to identify it properly.

❑ The `assemblyBinding` element has a child element named `probing`.

• The `probing` element has a `privatePath` attribute, which specifies the name of the sub-folder where the CLR should search for private assemblies. To enable users to specify multiple folders (for different assemblies) within the same configuration file, multiple directories can be specified, separated by a semicolon.

340

- Note that you must specify sub-folders here; you cannot specify an absolute folder, or a relative folder such as `..\SomeOtherFolder`. This rule minimizes the chance of conflicts with assemblies installed elsewhere on the computer.

> *Remember that XML is case-sensitive, so you must type in the element names and attribute names exactly as shown in the example above. There are various other pieces of information we can specify in a configuration file, including network settings, cryptography settings, ASP.NET settings, and so on. For more information, see the* `<configuration>` *element in Visual Studio .NET Help.*

When the user runs `MyModule.exe`, the CLR now searches for the `MyUsefulLibrary` assembly in the following locations (in the order shown):

- ❑ `MyUsefulLibrary.dll`
- ❑ `MyUsefulLibrary\MyUsefulLibrary.dll`
- ❑ `MySubFolder\MyUsefulLibrary.dll`
- ❑ `MySubFolder\MyUsefulLibrary\MyUsefulLibrary.dll`

If the CLR can't find an assembly with a .DLL file extension, it repeats the search looking for an assembly with an `.exe` file extension:

- ❑ `MyUsefulLibrary.exe`
- ❑ `MyUsefulLibrary\MyUsefulLibrary.exe`
- ❑ `MySubFolder\MyUsefulLibrary.exe`
- ❑ `MySubFolder\MyUsefulLibrary\MyUsefulLibrary.exe`

One final item to point out is that the application configuration file is just plain XML text, and is deployed onto the user's computer along with the application. If the user wants to organize the private assemblies into a different sub-folder hierarchy from that first envisaged, the user can edit the configuration file at any time to indicate the new location of the private assemblies. There's no need for the user to change any registry settings, so there's less chance than with COM of the user getting it wrong.

Deploying Shared Assemblies

Our previous discussions have shown how to create a private assembly, and deploy it in an application's sub-folder so that the application can access it. It's also possible to create shared assemblies, and add them to the *Global Assembly Cache* (*GAC*). The GAC holds information about all the shared assemblies that are accessible by applications running on our computer. For example, the assemblies essential for the .NET Framework class library reside in the GAC.

This may sound a little like COM. We can create COM components that contain reusable functionality, and install these components to make use of this functionality. However, COM components are registered in the system registry, and this can cause conflicts with other versions of the component in the registry. .NET assemblies are not registered in the system registry, so the possibility of registry conflicts doesn't arise.

You may still wonder if GAC conflicts occur if we install a later version of our .NET shared assembly; they don't. When we add an assembly to the GAC, we must give our assembly a *strong name*. A strongly named assembly has a name, version, public key, and, optionally, culture information; these pieces of information uniquely identify the assembly, and prevent conflicts with any other assemblies.

It is worth noting, however, that Microsoft advises against making your application dependent on installing assemblies into the GAC, and recommends instead that you use private assemblies. Disk space is not regarded as a precious commodity on most platforms, and applications in separate application domains will load code separately even if it is located in the GAC, so you won't end up saving memory. Keeping all your application's files together, and avoiding dependence on GAC registration simplifies everybody's life.

Applications can specify precisely the assembly they want to use by providing a specific assembly name, version, public key, and optionally culture information. There is no way the application can accidentally pick up another assembly that is similar, because that other assembly would have a different name, version, public key, or culture information. This is a major step forward in the world of application deployment and configuration. It signals a possible end to DLL hell, which will be a merciful release for us all.

Note that we can only insert strongly named assemblies into the GAC; assemblies that are not strongly named (that is, assemblies that do not have a public key) cannot be added to it, because they do not contain enough information to prevent possible conflicts.

> *Culture information enables us to create variations of our assembly for different locales. For example, we can create one assembly that contains English text, another assembly that contains French text, and a third assembly that contains Spanish text. Each assembly can have the same name, version, and public key, but a different culture flag.*

Let's summarize what you have learned so far. If we want to create a shared assembly that can be accessed by several applications, then we must perform the following steps:

❏ Create the shared assembly as a strongly-named assembly

❏ Create an application that uses the shared assembly

❏ Install the shared assembly into the Global Assembly Cache

Creating a Shared Assembly as a Strongly Named Assembly

To create a strongly named assembly, we must first generate a ***public-private key pair***. Public-private keys are used extensively in the IT industry for the following security purposes:

❏ A company uses its private key to sign its applications, and then distributes these applications to users.

❏ Users need to verify the application comes from this trusted company. They can do this by using the company's public key to check the digital signature on the application. The only way the signature will be recognized is if it was created with the trusted company's private key (of course, this mechanism relies on the fact the company's private key really is private).

Public-private key pairs enable us to create strong names for our assemblies. The compiler uses the private key during compilation, and writes the corresponding public key into the assembly manifest. For more information about the theory of public-private key pairs, see *Keys, cryptography* in Visual Studio .NET Help.

To create a public-private key, use the ***Strong Name tool*** in the .NET Framework SDK. Open a .NET Framework command prompt window, and type the following command:

```
C:\> sn /k C:\ClassDesign\MyKeyFolder\MyKey.snk
```

This creates a public-private key pair file named MyKey.snk in the folder C:\ClassDesign\MyKeyFolder. We can use this public-private key pair file to create a strongly named assembly. We've provided a simple example in the download folder called signed_assembly.vb, which looks like this:

```
Imports System

Public Class SignedMethod
   Public Shared Sub MyMethod()
      Console.WriteLine("Hi")
   End Sub
End Class
```

The project contains a source file named `AssemblyInfo.vb`. This file defines a set of attributes that will be used by the compiler to generate additional metadata for our assembly, such as its version number and public key:

```
Imports System.Reflection
Imports System.Runtime.InteropServices

' General Information about an assembly is controlled
' through the following set of attributes.
' Change these attribute values to modify the
' information associated with an assembly.

' Review the values of the assembly attributes
<Assembly: AssemblyTitle("")>
<Assembly: AssemblyDescription("")>
<Assembly: AssemblyCompany("")>
<Assembly: AssemblyProduct("")>
<Assembly: AssemblyCopyright("")>
<Assembly: AssemblyTrademark("")>

' The following GUID is for the ID of the typelib if this project
' is exposed to COM
<Assembly: Guid("D887D39A-47B2-41A4-A849-6B04C4804B11")>

' Version information for an assembly consists of the
' following four values:
'
'       Major Version
'       Minor Version
'       Build Number
'       Revision
'
' You can specify all the values or you can default
' the Build and Revision Numbers by using the '*'
' as shown below:
<Assembly: AssemblyVersion("1.0.0.0")>
<Assembly:
AssemblyKeyFile("C:\CodeOrganization\MyKeyFolder\MyKey.snk")>
```

In this example, `<Assembly:AssemblyVersion(...)>` tells the compiler the version number to write to the assembly. `<Assembly:AssemblyKeyFile(...)>` tells the compiler which public-private key file to use. This enables the compiler to generate a strongly named assembly.

Build the assembly as a DLL and you can view the assembly in the MSIL Disassembler. In the MSIL Disassembler window, double-click the **MANIFEST** node to view the assembly's manifest. The manifest now includes a `publickey` property, which means that this is a strongly named assembly. In addition, notice that the `ver` property contains the precise version information we specified:

```
.assembly MyGlobalAssembly
{
    ...

    .publickey = (00 24 00 00 04 ... FB CD B3 86 D2 )
    .hash algorithm 0x00008004
    .ver 1:0:0:0
}
```

The `publickey` property is a very long number. For efficiency, the Strong Name tool also generates an abbreviated version of the public key called the **public key token**. To see the public key token, run the Strong Name tool as follows:

```
C:\> sn /t C:\CodeOrganization\MyKeyFolder\MyKey.snk
```

The public key token is displayed as follows (clearly, the number for the public key token will be different if you try this yourself):

```
Microsoft (R) .NET Framework Strong Name Utility Version 1.0.3705.0
Copyright (C) Microsoft Corporation 1998-2001. All rights reserved.

Public key token is f080656556eddef5
```

Creating an Application that Uses the Shared Assembly

We've provided a simple application to use the strongly named assembly. We'll describe how to view and build this application using Visual Studio .NET first, then we'll see how to do the same from the command line.

The application has a simple source file named `shared_assembly.vb`, which looks like this:

```
Imports MyGlobalAssembly

Class SharedAssembly
  Shared Sub Main()
    SharedGlobalAssembly.MyMethod1()
  End Sub
End Class
```

Notice that `Main` calls `SharedGlobalAssembly.MyMethod1`. `SharedGlobalAssembly` is defined in the `MyGlobalAssembly` namespace, so we've used an `Imports` statement to import this namespace.

345

However, that's only half of the story. The `MyGlobalAssembly` namespace is defined in a different assembly, so we also have to tell the compiler which assembly to use. In Visual Studio .NET, expand the **References** entry in Solution Explorer. The **References** list includes a reference to `MyGlobalAssembly`. Right-click this assembly name, and select **Properties** from the **Shortcut** menu. The **Properties** dialog box appears as follows:

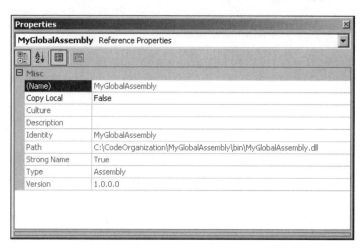

This dialog box indicates the following information about the referenced assembly:

❏ The name of the assembly is `MyGlobalAssembly`.

❏ The `Copy Local` flag is `False`. This tells the compiler not to copy the specified assembly into our application's output folder. This will force the CLR to look in the GAC for the assembly when we run the application.

> *When you add an assembly reference, the `Copy Local` flag is set to `True` by default. This will cause the compiler to copy the specified assembly to the output directory for our application. When you run the application, the CLR will locate and load this copy of the assembly, rather than the one in the GAC. To avoid this behavior, remember to set `Copy Local` to `False` whenever you add an assembly reference to a project.*

❏ The `Path` property tells the compiler where the assembly is currently located, at development time. We set this location when we added this assembly reference to the project.

To add an assembly reference to a project, right-click the project name in Solution Explorer and click Add Reference. In the Add Reference dialog box, click Browse. Browse to the folder that contains the strongly named assembly. Select the assembly, and click Open to add it to the list of selected components. Then click OK to dismiss the Add Reference dialog box.

❑ The `Strong Name` property is `True`, because the assembly was created as a strongly named assembly

❑ The `Version` property indicates the version number of this strongly named assembly

If we build this application in Visual Studio .NET, the assembly reference we've just examined provides all the information required by the compiler to locate the other assembly. Alternatively, we can compile the application from the command line; in this case, we must specify an `/r` compiler switch to tell the compiler about the assembly:

```
> vbc /r:C:\CodeOrganization\MyGlobalAssembly\bin\MyGlobalAssembly.dll
  MyApp.vb
```

Everything seems to be going well, until we try to run the application. The CLR attempts to load the referenced assembly. The runtime looks in our application's folder, on the (incorrect) assumption that the assembly is a private assembly. However, the assembly isn't there, because it's a shared assembly. Therefore, the CLR throws an exception, and our application terminates gracelessly.

To resolve this problem, we must install the shared assembly into the Global Assembly Cache (GAC).

Installing Shared Assemblies into the Global Assembly Cache

The .NET Framework provides a runtime tool named `gacutil.exe`, which enables us to install to and remove assemblies from the GAC. Open a .NET Framework command-prompt window, and move to the folder where the .DLL file resides. Type the following command:

```
C:\ClassDesign\ch08> gacutil -i MyGlobalAssembly.dll
```

> *As a user, you must have Administrator privileges to install assemblies into the GAC.*

The GAC is implemented as a folder named `Assembly` in the Windows folder (for example, `C:\Windows\Assembly`), and when we install an assembly into the GAC, `gacutil` copies the assembly into a special sub-folder beneath the `Assembly` folder. The `gacutil` tool devises a special name for the assembly's sub-folder, based on the name, version, public key, and culture of the assembly. This eliminates any possibility of installing an assembly on top of an existing assembly that happens to have the same filename.

To check that our assembly has been added correctly to the GAC, we can use the *.NET Framework Configuration* tool. Open Control Panel, double-click **Administrative Tools**, and then double-click **Microsoft .NET Framework Configuration**. The following window appears:

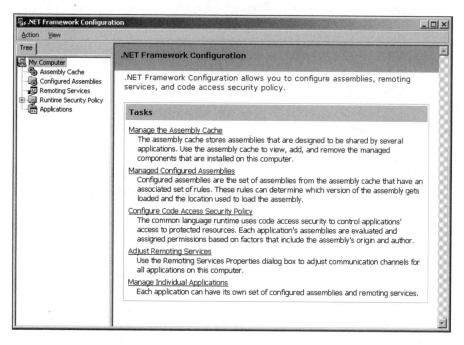

Click the **Manage the Assembly Cache** hyperlink. This takes us to the **Assembly Cache** window, which looks like this:

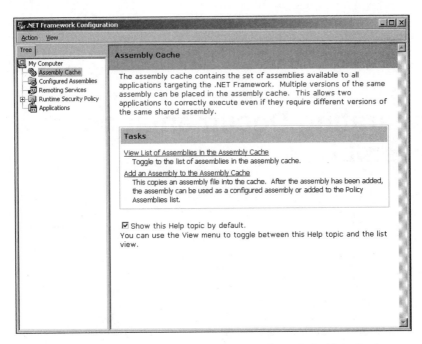

Click the **View List of Assemblies in the Assembly Cache** hyperlink. This displays information about all the assemblies in the GAC. Scroll down the list to find the shared assembly we just inserted.

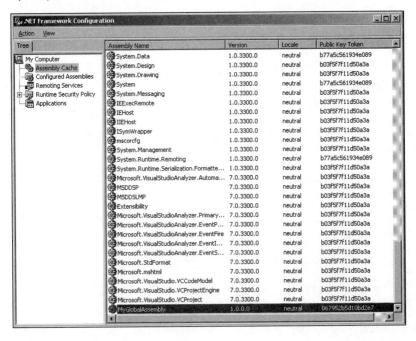

Once you've installed the shared assembly in the GAC, you can run the application. When the application refers to types and members defined in the shared assembly, the CLR inspects the application's metadata to discover which assembly it needs to load. The runtime looks for this assembly in the GAC, finds it, and loads it into memory.

Generating Documentation for an Assembly

In the previous section, we described how to create a shared assembly and install it into the Global Assembly Cache. The GAC insists that the assembly is strongly named, which means the assembly must contain public key information. As we saw earlier, the way to provide this public key is through the `<Assembly: AssemblyKeyFile>` attribute. For example:

```
<Assembly:
    AssemblyKeyFile("C:\CodeOrganization\MyKeyFolder\MyKey.snk")>
```

As well as specifying the name of the public-private key pair file, we can also specify additional information, such as the following:

- ❏ Free-format title of the assembly
- ❏ Description of the assembly
- ❏ Company name
- ❏ Product name information
- ❏ Copyright information
- ❏ A trademark

The following example shows how to define this information. The source code for this example is located in the `Documentation` download folder. The documentation information is defined in the file `AssemblyInfo.vb`:

```
Imports System.Reflection
Imports System.Runtime.InteropServices

' General Information about an assembly is controlled
' through the following set of attributes.
' Change these attribute values to modify the
' information associated with an assembly.

' Review the values of the assembly attributes
<Assembly: AssemblyTitle("My Assembly")>
<Assembly: AssemblyDescription("My cool assembly")>
<Assembly: AssemblyCompany("My Company Inc.")>
```

```
<Assembly: AssemblyProduct("My Product")>
<Assembly: AssemblyCopyright("(c) My Company, 2002")>
<Assembly: AssemblyTrademark("TM My Company")>
<Assembly: CLSCompliant(True)>

'The following GUID is for the ID of the typelib if this project is
'exposed to COM
<Assembly: Guid("575D8341-4935-417E-8BFB-063872A344F9")>

' Version information for an assembly consists of the
' following four values:
'
'       Major Version
'       Minor Version
'       Build Number
'       Revision
'
' You can specify all the values or you can default
' the Build and Revision Numbers by using the '*'
' as shown below:
<Assembly: AssemblyVersion("1.0.*")>
```

When we build this application, we can view the properties for the assembly file in Windows Explorer: select the assembly file in Windows Explorer, and select **Properties** from the **Shortcut** menu. The Properties window shows the following information:

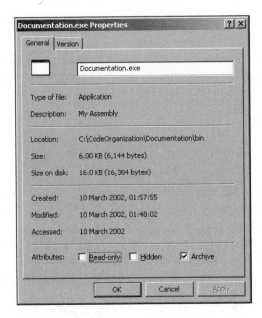

When we click on the **Version** tab, we can see detailed information about the assembly. For example, the **Comments** field appears as follows:

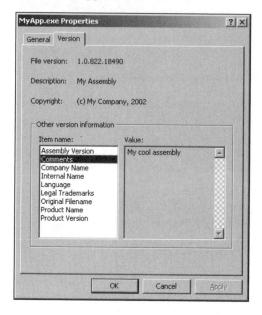

Summary

In this final chapter, we've seen how to control the logical and physical organization of code in a Visual Basic .NET application. In summary, we have covered:

❑ How to use namespaces to partition the application into logical groups of related types, and how these can relate to packages in a UML object model

❑ How to use assemblies and modules to break your applications into workable, and reusable, and uniquely named sections, that could be written in multiple .NET languages

❑ How to compile and deploy your application as separate assemblies, including the use of DLLs, EXEs, and modules

❑ How to use the Global Assembly Cache to create a shared assembly that can easily be located by the CLR, and how the GAC should remove the DLL hell that happened with the Windows Registry

❑ How to build documentation into a compiled assembly

We hope you've found this book interesting, useful, and stimulating. The .NET Framework is an exciting and comprehensive venture from Microsoft, and VB.NET is now a powerful object-oriented language that can be used, without performance overhead, with other .NET languages, to build your applications.

VB.NET

Class Design

Handbook

Appendix

Support, Errata, and Code Download

We always value hearing from our readers, and we want to know what you think about this book and series: what you liked, what you didn't like, and what you think we can do better next time. You can send us your comments, either by returning the reply card in the back of the book, or by e-mailing us at **feedback@wrox.com**. Please be sure to mention the book title in your message.

How to Download the Sample Code for the Book

When you log on to the Wrox site, **http://www.wrox.com/**, simply locate the title through our **Search** facility or by using one of the title lists. Click on **Download Code** on the book's detail page.

The files that are available for download from our site have been archived using WinZip. When you have saved the attachments to a folder on your hard-drive, you will need to extract the files using WinZip, or a compatible tool. Inside the Zip file will be a folder structure and an HTML file that explains the structure and gives you further information – including links to e-mail support, and suggested further reading.

Errata

We've made every effort to ensure that there are no errors in the text or in the code. However, no one is perfect and mistakes can occur. If you find an error in one of our books, like a spelling mistake or a faulty piece of code, we would be very grateful for feedback. By sending in errata, you may save another reader hours of frustration, and of course, you will be helping us to provide even higher quality information. Simply e-mail the information to **support@wrox.com**; your information will be checked and if correct, posted to the errata page for that title.

To find errata on the web site, locate this book on the Wrox web site (http://www.wrox.com/ACON1.asp?ISBN=1861007086), and click on the **Book Errata** link on the book's detail page:

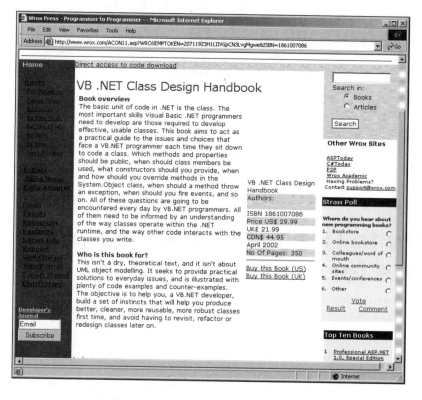

E-Mail Support

If you wish to query a problem in the book with an expert who knows the book in detail then e-mail support@wrox.com, with the title of the book, and the last four numbers of the ISBN in the subject field of the e-mail. A typical e-mail should include the following:

- The name, last four digits of the ISBN (7086), and page number of the problem, in the **Subject** field

- Your name, contact information, and the problem, in the body of the message

We won't send you junk mail. We need the details to save your time and ours. When you send an e-mail message, it will go through the following chain of support:

- ### *Customer Support*

  Your message is delivered to our customer support staff. They have files on most frequently asked questions and will answer anything general about the book or the web site immediately.

- ### *Editorial*

  More in-depth queries are forwarded to the technical editor responsible for that book. They have experience with the programming language or particular product, and are able to answer detailed technical questions on the subject. Once an issue has been resolved, the editor can post the errata to the web site.

- ### *The Authors*

  Finally, in the unlikely event that the editor cannot answer your problem, they will forward the request to the author. We do try to protect the author from any distractions to their writing (or programming); however, we are quite happy to forward specific requests to them. All Wrox authors help with the support on their books. They will e-mail the customer and the editor with their response, and again all readers should benefit.

The Wrox support process can only offer support for issues that are directly pertinent to the content of our published title. Support for questions that fall outside the scope of normal book support, is provided via our P2P community lists – http://p2p.wrox.com/forum.

p2p.wrox.com

For author and peer discussion, join the P2P mailing lists. Our unique system provides Programmer to Programmer™ contact on mailing lists, forums, and newsgroups, all in addition to our one-to-one e-mail support system. Be confident that the many Wrox authors and other industry experts who are present on our mailing lists are examining any queries posted. At http://p2p.wrox.com/, you will find a number of different lists that will help you, not only while you read this book, but also as you develop your own applications.

To subscribe to a mailing list just follow this these steps:

- Go to http://p2p.wrox.com/
- Choose the appropriate category from the left menu bar
- Click on the mailing list you wish to join

❑ Follow the instructions to subscribe and fill in your e-mail address and password

❑ Reply to the confirmation e-mail you receive

❑ Use the subscription manager to join more lists and set your mail preferences

VB.NET
Class Design
Handbook
Index

Index

A Guide to the Index

The index is arranged hierarchically, in alphabetical order, with symbols preceding the letter A. Classes derive from the System namespace unless another namespace is specified. Most second-level entries and many third-level entries also occur as first-level entries. This is to ensure that users will find the information they require however they choose to search for it.

protected fields
superclass, defining, 265
Protected Friend access modifier, 48
protected friend methods, 77
protected methods, 77
Public access modifier, 47
functionality, 48
Public fields, shortcomings, 54
public classes, 30
Public events, 213
public interfaces
interface inheritance, 280
public key token
creating using Strong Name tool, 345
public methods, 76
publickey property
manifest information, 344
public-private key pair
creating shared assemblies as
strongly named assemblies, 343
creating using Strong Name tool, 343
publishing events, 210, 212
Event keyword, 210, 212
firing events, RaiseEvent keyword, 65
Shared events, 222
specifying event signature explicitly, 212
defining several events with
same signature, 216
defining single event using
explicit signature, 212
specifying event signature implicitly
using delegate, 220

R

RaiseEvent keyword, 224
description, 224
events, firing, 65
raising events
RaiseEvent keyword, 224
Read-only fields, 55
ReadOnly properties, 57, 150
scalar properties, 156
compiling into MSIL, 158
defining, example, 156
ReadWrite properties
scalar properties, 156
compiling into MSIL, 158
defining, example, 156
reference data types, 80
arrays, 13
boxed value types, 13, 24
class types, 12, 26, 31
copy-by-reference semantics, 11
delegates, 12, 34
description, 10
managed heap, 18
modules, 29

mutable, always making, 72
null reference, 11
passing, 80
ByRef, 82
ByVal, 82
System.Object root class and, 80
value types and, 10, 72, 80
reference equality
Equals() method, testing for
reference equality, 68
referenced assembly metadata, 329
locale metadata, 329
ReferenceEquals() method,
System.Object, 263
Remove() method, Delegate
class, 201, 208, 215
RemoveHandler keyword
bank account dynamic event handling
example, 243
defining event handlers dynamically, 236
subscribing to events, 224
Return statement
returning values, methods, 101
runtime element
application configuration file, 340

S

scalar properties, 151, 152
as default properties, NOT supported
in Visual Basic .NET, 176
compiling into MSIL, 154
Disassembler, steps using, 154
functionality, 156
Main() method, implementing, 155
members, Person class, 154
Name property, implementing, 155
read-write/read-only/write-only
properties, defining, 158
statements, 156
FootballTeam class example, 166
compiling & running, 169
constructor, 167
Main() method, 168
PlayGame() method, 168
properties, defining, 168
get procedure, writing guidelines, 160
Person class example, 152
Main(), using Name property, 153
private field & public property, 152
read-write/read-only/write-only,
defining, 156
set procedure, writing guidelines, 163
shared, defining, 159
scope & visibility, classes, 29
assembly classes, 31
example, 29
friend classes, 30
private classes, 30